W9-DGP-670

Aircraft Markings
of the Strategic Air Command,
1946–1953

Aircraft Markings of the Strategic Air Command, 1946–1953

RICK RODRIGUES

Foreword by Dana Bell

McFarland & Company, Inc., Publishers
Jefferson, North Carolina, and London

LIBRARY OF CONGRESS CATALOGUING-IN-PUBLICATION DATA

Rodrigues, Rick, 1951–
Aircraft markings of the Strategic Air Command, 1946–1953 /
Rick Rodrigues ; foreword by Dana Bell.
p.   cm.
Includes bibliographical references and index.

ISBN-13: 978-0-7864-2496-6
ISBN-10: 0-7864-2496-6 (illustrated case binding : 50# alkaline paper)

1. Airplanes, Military — Markings — United States.
2. United States. Air Force. Strategic Air Command — Insignia.
3. United States. Air Force. Strategic Air Command — History.
I. Title.
UG1243.R63   2006   358.4'183 — dc22   2006014348

British Library cataloguing data are available

Cover photograph: Tail markings of a Boeing B-29 Superfortress
in the 2nd Bombardment Wing, 1951 (Photograph by E. Van Houten)

Manufactured in the United States of America

*McFarland & Company, Inc., Publishers
Box 611, Jefferson, North Carolina 28640
www.mcfarlandpub.com*

The 93rd Bomb Wing B-50Ds returning to their home station, Castle Air Force Base, after a presidential flyover for President Truman over Springfield, Missouri, 7 June 1952. This photograph captures the essence of service in Strategic Air Command (SAC)— commitment, courage, dedication— and is a tribute to all who served in SAC. I dedicate this book to them.

To those who defend our freedom, secure our liberty,
and preserve our American way of life —
our men and women in uniform — past, present and future.
God bless them all.

Acknowledgments

Over the last 15 years, I have received a tremendous amount of support and encouragement for this book project from many friends, colleagues, veterans, and aviation enthusiasts. My heartfelt thanks to all — but there are several people to whom I'd like to give special mention: Bill Larkins for pointing me in the right direction and helping me understand the expectation for such an endeavor; the incomparable Dave Menard, who was kind enough to review and provide comments on this project and was very generous in supplying photos from his vast collection; Ray Paseka — artist par excellence for his very unselfish support, especially with scanning and photo editing; the wonderful team at the National Personnel Records Center, initially Bill Sibert, the late Carl Paulson, and Mary Parker, and more recently Eric Voelz, John Daly and Wilson D. Sullivan, who made it possible to review numerous boxes of old SAC records; Archie DiFonte and his crew at the Air Force Historical Research Agency at Maxwell AFB, Alabama, for their support during my many research visits that spanned many years; Doug Olson for his advice and generous response to my request for photos; Mark Adamic for his drawing support and enthusiastic encouragement; and Dana Bell for his most generous foreword and for setting the example for all who are interested in aircraft markings. And to the three angels in my life — Lisa, Julie and Katie — without whom the inspiration and motivation to complete this book would not have been there.

My appreciation also to Air Combat Command, Command Records Manager Anita J. Allen-Csaszar, William Banks, Robert Barbour, Earl Berlin, CMSgt Mike Bogna, USAF (Ret), CMSgt Edmond L. Bouton, Jr., USAF (Ret), Jim Brennan of the 91st SRW Association, Richard H. Campbell, Bob Clapton, Russ Clark, Stephen Clugston of the March Field Air Museum, Col. William H. Cox, USAF (Ret), George Cully, Brig. Gen. H.J. Dalton, Jr., USAF (Ret), Col. John Decker, USAF (Ret), Robert Dorr, Gail Dow, George Erkes, Bob Esposito, Gen. Howell M. Estes, Jr., USAF (Ret), Frank Fiorentino, Mel Foley, Ed Galli, CMSgt Elmer V. Gisbert, USAF (Ret), Paul Gladman of Flight International UK, Dale Griffin of the Castle Air Museum, Mark Hague, John Haney, Al Hardy, Herb Harper and Mark Furth of the 98th Bomb Group/Wing Veterans Association, Dick Iler, Col. Russ Ireland, USAF (Ret), Toni Jeske and Dawne Dewey of Wright State University, Maj. Gen. Earl L. Johnson, USAF (Ret), Ed King, Lt. Col. Frank Kleinwechter, USAF (Ret), Ron Kolwak of the *Tampa Tribune*, Maj. Gen. John E. Kulpa, USAF (Ret), Ed Lamboley, Gary Leiser of the Travis Air Museum, Alwyn T. Lloyd, Michael J. Lombardi and Mary E. Kane of Boeing, Tom Long, CMSgt Olav J. Loren, USAF (Ret), Jerry Marshall, Earl Martenson, Lt. Gen. William K. Martin, USAF (Ret), Rick Massimiano, Wayland Mayo, Charles W. Mazurowski, R. G. McCarson, Marv McClain, Dave McLaren, Lt.Col. Jim T. Meredith,

USAF (Ret), Lt.Col. Joseph R. Metivier, USAF (Ret), Maj. William G. Metsopoulos, USAF (Ret), Gerald H. Monson, Col. Earl E. Myers, USAF (Ret), Max Nelson, John Newman, Col. Roy J. Notley, USAF (Ret), David W. Ostrowski, Lt.Col. George Penfield, USAF (Ret), Ralph H. Peterson, Rob Radlein, Alan Renga of the San Diego Aerospace Museum, Bob Rhodes, Danny J. San Romani of the Combat Air Museum in Topeka, SMSgt Herman I. Savely, USAF (Ret), Col. Irving B. Schoenberg, USAF (Ret), Robert T. Schrawger, Marvin Seville, Frank Sheldon, Col. L. Gene Sidwell, USAF (Ret), Joseph M. Slade, C. O. Smith, George Smith, Bill Stenger, Paul D. Stevens, Brett Stolle of the National Museum of the USAF, Chuck Stone, MSgt Calvin L. Stout, USAF (Ret), Brig. Gen. Donald E. Stout, USAF (Ret), Col. Robert H. Stuart, USAF (Ret), Bob Swain , Kevin O. Sullivan of AP/Wide World Photo, Bill Sutton, Warren Thompson, Col. Lyle H. Walker, USAF (Ret), Fred Washek and Katherine Williams of the Museum of Flight.

Table of Contents

Foreword

We are currently blessed with a number of new books and articles on the history of aircraft colors and markings. And it's not unusual for other titles on military units and actions to include a section, or at least a few captions, devoted to the subject. What is unusual is the discovery of a thorough investigation of the topic, one based on research into primary documents. Rick Rodrigues' new work is one of those rare publications. His clear and authoritative presentation of the first seven years of distinctive aircraft markings used by America's Strategic Air Command (SAC) is a book that promises to remain the standard on the subject.

The reader might be surprised to find a community of researchers who follow colors and markings, but such a community exists. Many are modelers, others museum professionals, photographers, collectors, artists, aircraft restorers, historians, or just plain (plane) enthusiasts. After several attempts at locating even a piece of the puzzle most of us in that community had come to the same conclusion: the primary records on Strategic Air Command markings would never be found, either because they remained classified or because they had been destroyed as unworthy of archiving. This seemed all the more frustrating because records of other commands were proving relatively easy to locate.

SAC, almost from the beginning, had a well-defined sense of security and secrecy. In the early days of the cold war, this secrecy was anything but unreasonable: although only a few of SAC's B-29s were capable of delivering an atomic bomb, both the American public and its enemies were led to believe they all could. It was a time when most Americans believed the only defense against an all-out war with the communists was the threat that such a war would be even more horrible than what the Soviet Union had survived in World War II. Everything about SAC would be secretive — its capabilities, its strengths, its order of battle, and its unit identities. SAC aircraft were rarely photographed, and little information was included in captions. In officially released photos of Strategic Air Command bases, unit markings were often cropped out, blocked by a convenient camera angle, or simply censored at the photo lab. Period images commonly showed white-helmeted security police at any air base's front gate; beside them, a sign would state the name of the base and two other things: "Peace Is Our Profession," and "Photography Strictly Prohibited by Order of the Base Commander."

With few secondary sources to guide him, Rick Rodrigues decided to look for the documents that would explain what little material was available on SAC markings. I must admit that, over twenty years ago, I was one of the many who tried to explain how difficult — or impossible — his task would be. But armed with a confidence that comes when one understands how the system works, Rick began his search. There would be no Rosetta Stone, nor did he expect one, but he would slowly gather the pieces of a puzzle that, once organized and analyzed, would yield much of the story; by locating and interviewing veterans, he was eventually able to fill in the rest. His research explained what had been seen in the few commonly available contemporary images, but just as importantly, he uncovered scores of never before seen photos, many of which enrich these pages. He has found a story that reflects the growth and reorganization of SAC as the command developed from a few dozen left-over World War II bombers to an intercontinental sentinel of the jet age.

We often hear that a work is a labor of love, and that is often true. The term is best reserved for those works whose authors invest countless hours on a project because they want answers or results for their own enjoyment. Few, if any, will understand how much work can go into uncovering a fact that, in the end, is explained by little more than a single sentence.

Now, having completed his labor of love, Rick Rodrigues has chosen to share it with us all in the form of this landmark book.

Dana Bell
Arlington, Virginia

Preface

The purpose of this book is to provide a comprehensive, documented record of Strategic Air Command (SAC) tactical aircraft markings from the SAC's inception in 1946 to the end of the tail-marking era in April 1953.

This project has been a pursuit to discover the facts and story surrounding SAC aircraft markings with determination and enthusiasm. To say the project has been a challenge of large magnitude would be an understatement.

My interest in SAC aircraft has been life-long. Born at Castle Air Force Base in the days of B-50s, KB-29s and C-124s, I grew up in an environment dominated by the culture of SAC — deployments, alerts, tight security and the stern beauty of the B-52.

Fast forward to the mid–1980s when I began to notice the paucity of information on SAC aircraft markings after World War II and prior to the introduction of the B-47 Stratojet and B-52 Stratofortress as the primary aircraft in SAC's bomber fleet. In particular, I was curious about the lack of information pertaining to SAC tail markings and the frequent attempts to establish a linkage with the World War II B-29 markings used in the China-Burma-India Theater and the Pacific Theater.

My first contacts with the SAC Historian's Office met with little success and even less encouragement. I was told, "The information is long gone and probably impossible to retrieve." Yet I wasn't ready to accept the idea that the code couldn't be cracked. Given my own experience in the military, I knew very well that nothing happens without approval from the chain of command and that the authority for action was usually found in an official document. That document might be a memorandum, technical order, standard operating procedure, tactical doctrine manual, official letter — something that would provide form and guidance set to an official standard.

I soon discovered that my best chance to ferret out information on SAC aircraft markings would be in examining the old organizational records located at the National Personnel Records Center (NPRC) in St. Louis, Missouri. I was graciously assisted by the Air Force Records Manager at the time, Mrs. Grace Rowe, who added to my understanding of Air Force records and, in particular, the decimal correspondence file system.

Armed with my newly found knowledge of Air Force records as well as permission from the SAC records manager to review noncurrent, unclassified SAC records, I started a time-consuming effort to find primary source materials to document the history of early SAC aircraft markings. Beginning in the early 1990s, I made frequent trips to St. Louis to comb through the old SAC records looking for anything pertaining to aircraft markings. With the able and enthusiastic support of the staff at the NPRC — Bill Sibert, Mary Parker and the late Carl Paulson — I was able to review literally several hundred boxes of SAC records, the results of which ultimately led to the publication of my article on SAC tail markings in the *American Aviation Historical Society Journal* in 1996.

Although much of the story was uncovered in the older SAC records at the NPRC, by no means was it complete. Many of the enclosures showing specific unit aircraft markings had been removed from correspondence, usually by operations personnel. Access to this information has proven to be problematic since many of the operations-type records remain classified or were destroyed as working files and not considered for permanent retention. Also it should be noted that noncurrent Air Force records exist in a somewhat complex, incomplete, and disorganized state. This disorganization has been caused, in part, by the lack of resources to properly retire and review noncurrent records, organizational changes (e.g. deactivation of SAC in 1994), and overlapping jurisdiction and efforts by the Air Force, National Archives and, in the case of nuclear weapons issues, the Department of Energy.

To help fill this void, I conducted an extensive program of contacting former SAC personnel from various SAC units to help verify and complement what I found from the older SAC records. Nearly all I contacted were friendly and encouraging, yet many didn't remember the specifics of aircraft markings and very few could provide any photo coverage of SAC aircraft they had worked with in the late '40s and early '50s. Almost to a man they did remember SAC's very restrictive policy concerning the use of cameras and the prohibition of flight line photography except under very controlled circumstances. For this reason, photos of SAC aircraft displaying their high visibility markings are difficult to find and for some units very rare. The photos used in this book came from the Air Force Collection at the National Archives; the official unit histories located at the Air Force Historical Research Agency at Maxwell AFB, Alabama; long-time collectors and enthusiasts of aviation photography; several large corporate and university photo archives and collections; and finally a few veterans who, notwithstanding SAC's penchant for security, ended up with a few photos.

I would like to think of the book as first and foremost a reference work that documents aircraft markings used by SAC bombardment, strategic reconnaissance, air refueling, fighter and strategic support aircraft from 1946 until 1953. My end point of 1953 coincides with SAC's decision to eliminate tail codes and reduce the visibility of unit identity. Beyond the scope of this work is the subject of base flight aircraft, a subject I hope will someday receive the recognition and coverage it deserves. Another exclusion that readers may question is the 19th Bombardment Group. My rationale for this decision is simple: the very distinguished 19th Bombardment Group did not belong to SAC during the time covered by this book and its story should be told as part of the Far East Air Forces (FEAF) story, the organization to which it was assigned. Finally, this work is not intended to be an operational, technical, or personal history of SAC. Many fine authors have already written on these aspects.

Even after years of research, there is still much information I was unable to find. Over time more documents and photos may become available to provide an even more complete accounting of SAC aircraft from this era. I welcome any corrections and additions to make the story a more complete one.

List of Abbreviations

AAFld   Army Air Field
AB   Air Base — base in territory not administered by the U.S. Government
AD   Air Division
AFB   Air Force Base — base in U.S. territory
AFHRA   Air Force Historical Research Agency
ANG   Air National Guard
ARS   Air Refueling Squadron
BG   Bombardment Group
BW   Bombardment Wing
BS   Bombardment Squadron
ECM   Electronic Countermeasures
FBW   Fighter Bomber Wing
FEAF   Far East Air Forces
FEG   Fighter Escort Group
FES   Fighter Escort Squadron
FEW   Fighter Escort Wing
FW   Fighter Wing
FG   Fighter Group
FS   Fighter Squadron
MATS   Military Air Transport Service
NPRC   National Personnel Records Center
OTU   Operational Training Unit
PCS   Permanent Change of Station
RAF   Royal Air Force
RG   Reconnaissance Group
RS   Reconnaissance Squadron
SAC   Strategic Air Command
SFW   Strategic Fighter Wing
SRG   Strategic Reconnaissance Group
SRS   Strategic Reconnaissance Squadron
SRW   Strategic Reconnaissance Wing
SSS   Strategic Support Squadron
TDY   Temporary Duty
TWX   Teletype message

USAAF   United States Army Air Forces
USAF   United States Air Force

USAF Aircraft Designations

B   Bomber
C   Cargo
F   Photographic (replaced by R in 1948)
F   Fighter (replaced P in 1948)
K   Tanker (prefix)
P   Pursuit (replaced by F in 1948)
R   Reconnaissance prefix (replaced F in 1948)

1

History of Strategic Air Command, 1946–1953

Strategic Air Command (SAC) was created on 21 March 1946 in the aftermath of World War II when the Continental Air Command was redesignated Strategic Air Command. SAC's establishment was part of a post–World War II plan to organize the Army Air Forces around three new organizations, based on strategic, tactical and air defense missions.

SAC's initial mission was provided by General Carl Spaatz, Commanding General, Army Air Forces, who directed that SAC prepare to conduct long-range offensive missions anywhere in the world and become proficient in combat operations, reconnaissance operations, training of units and personnel in strategic air operations and any other duties assigned by Army Air Forces.[1] Later in 1946 this mission statement was modified to include the requirement to develop, test and improve strategic bombardment tactics.

SAC's early resources left a lot to be desired. A collection of units, aircraft and bases were all characterized by limited personnel and materiel resources and an almost nonexistent combat capability. Of the initial B-29 groups assigned to SAC in March 1946, several were "paper" units and minimally manned, most active groups had limited aircraft resources and no combat capability to speak of, and the only atomic capable group, the 509th Composite Group at Roswell AAB, New Mexico, was designated high priority and was scrambling to put together enough trained personnel and aircraft assets to support the AAF mission as part of Operation Crossroads—the project to detonate two atomic bombs—an air burst and a surface burst—in the vicinity of Bikini Atoll in the Pacific.

SAC's initial major subordinate commands were the Fifteenth Air Force (replaced the deactivated Second Air Force on 31 March 1946) with headquarters at Colorado Springs, Colorado; the 311th Reconnaissance Wing (later Air Division) responsible for photographic and mapping missions with headquarters at MacDill AAFld; and the Eighth Air Force (created from the assets of the 58th Bombardment Wing) with headquarters at Fort Worth Army Air Field, Texas.[2]

SAC's initial headquarters was at Bolling Field but later moved (15 Oct 1946) to Andrews Field, Maryland. SAC's first commander was General George C. Kenney who had served as General Douglas MacArthur's air component commander in the Pacific during World War II. General Kenney also served as the Senior U.S. Representative on the Military Staff Committee of the United Nations. For most of General Kenney's tenure as Commanding General, the Deputy Commanding General, (initially Major General St. Clair Street and later major General Clements McMullen) SAC directed the command's day-to-day operations.

The year 1946 brought a great challenge for SAC. Short of nearly everything, SAC's growing pains were acute and exacerbated by the result of demobilization and reduced government spending on defense. General Kenney later described SAC as an organization that "was largely a name on a piece of paper."[3]

B-29 aircraft assignments in SAC during 1946 were driven by the requirement to replace training type B-29s with flyaway aircraft or those modified to move overseas with B-29

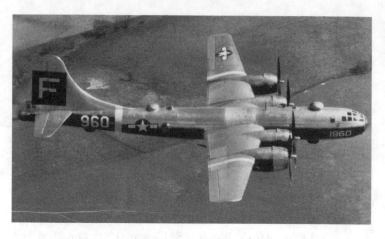

Yet to deploy to Kwajalein, F-13A-55-BN (44-61960) on a flight over Chicago in April 1946 has white identification numbers on the nose and aft fuselage, yellow bands on the wings and fuselage, and a Square F tail marking with the F in silver (National Museum of the USAF).

bombardment groups. This situation was caused, in part, by SAC's plans to rotate both bomber and fighter groups to a network of perimeter and overseas bases located in the North Pacific (Alaska and the Aleutian Islands), Far East (Philippines, Okinawa and Guam), and the North Atlantic (Greenland, Iceland, Newfoundland and Labrador). The following delivery schedule shows the sizeable turnover of aircraft (B-29 and F-13) to SAC units in the fall of 1946:

Organization	Quantity	Type of Radar	Delivery Date
46th Recon Squadron	9	F-13	As soon as possible
28th Bomb Group	16	AN/APQ-13	15 Sep. to 1 Oct.
" " "	6	AN/APQ-23	" " "
" " "	11	AN/APQ-7	" " "
97th Bomb Group	24	AN/APQ-13	15 Dec. to 31 Dec.
" " "	9	AN/APQ-23	" " "
307th Bomb Group	24	AN/APQ-13	15 Oct. to 1 Nov.
" " "	9	AN/APQ-23	" " "
58th Wing	28*	"Silver Plate"	September

*Already assigned to the 58th Wing; will be delivered to depot for winterization, and returned to the 58th Wing.[4]

By the end of 1946, the strategic striking arm of the Army Air Forces had six bombardment groups equipped, to some degree, with B-29 aircraft, one fighter group equipped with P-47 and P-51 aircraft, and one reconnaissance group equipped with F-2, F-9 and F-13 aircraft. SAC's order of battle as of 31 December 1946 is listed below[5]:

STATION	TOTAL(includes Cargo & Others)	BOMBER	FIGHTER	RECON
CG SAC	54	18	0	0
ANDREWS	52	16	0	0
PETERSON	2	2	0	0
8TH AF	169	106	7	5
ALMOGORDO	15	3	7	1
DAVIS-MONTHAN	40	26	0	1

STATION	TOTAL(*includes Cargo & Others*)	BOMBER	FIGHTER	RECON
FT WORTH	60	49	0	1
ROSWELL	54	28	0	2
15TH AF	370	112	109	48
CLOVIS	1	0	0	0
GOWEN	2	0	0	0
GRAND ISLAND	16	9	0	2
GRENIER	2	1	0	1
MACDILL	89	25	0	40
PETERSON	41	19	0	2
RAPID CITY	10	2	6	0
SELFRIDGE	133	4	99	2
SMOKY HILL	76	52	4	2
TOTAL	593	236	116	53

As one can see, not a very impressive picture of U.S. military might. SAC's operational efforts in 1946 were limited and modest. The major effort for SAC was Operation Crossroads covered in Chapter 8. In October 1946 SAC deployed the 28th Bomb Group to Alaska for six months of cold weather training. In addition to the 28th BG, a separate squadron, the 46th Reconnaissance Squadron, was deployed to Ladd Field, Alaska, on a permanent change of station. In mid–November 1946, after Soviet fighters shot down an American C-47 over Yugoslavia, SAC sent a flight of six B-29s from the 43rd Bomb Group at Davis-Monthan Army Air Field to Rhein-Main, Germany, on a show of force mission. The B-29s were supported by C-54s from SAC's 1st Air Transport Unit.[6]

1947 and 1948 would bring major changes in organization and operational efficiency, and would help sow the seeds of an attitude of SAC as an elite force. Perhaps the major organizational change implemented by SAC in 1947 was the adoption of the Hobson Plan for base and unit organization. The Hobson Plan superseded the old system where a base commander exercised authority over every unit at his station. This arrangement permitted non-flying base commanders to control the activities of rated wing and group commanders to the detriment of flying operations. The Hobson Plan created a wing headquarters that bore the same numerical designation as the combat flying organization on the base and supervised all base units, flying and non-flying. Flying operations continued to be conducted by a combat group, normally of three squadrons, with support functions divided among a maintenance group, an airdrome group, and a medical group. The Hobson Plan specified channels of command, eliminated split jurisdiction, and promoted unit mobility and organizational flexibility. By the end of 1947, both of SAC's numbered air forces had implemented the new plan and judged it to be an immediate success.[7]

Another important

The 56th FG flew borrowed P-47Ns in mid–1946. Notice the large aircraft buzz numbers on the fuselage (photograph by W. Bodie, courtesy D. Menard).

date in 1947 was 18 September when the Army Air Forces became the United States Air Force as a result of the National Security Act of 1947. Although it would take several years to truly establish its identity as a separate service, an immediate change occurred with the naming of airfields. The Army Air part of Army Air Field was dropped and only the word "Field" was used. However in January 1948 the term Air Force Base was created and put into immediate effect.

1947 would be a period of growth for SAC and would see the command expand from 279 aircraft to more than 700! These aircraft would be divided among eleven very heavy bomb groups, five fighter groups, one reconnaissance group, one reconnaissance squadron, and one air transport unit.[8]

SAC undertook an ambitious operational schedule built around "maximum effort missions" flown throughout the United States (with very disappointing mission performance) and short-term squadron rotations to Europe and Japan. In addition to providing valuable training for crew members, these flights demonstrated America's long distance combat capability at a time when Communism was threatening much of the world.

1947 brought marked improvement to SAC in the areas of training, personnel and equipment — yet there were still serious doubts about the command's level of operational efficiency to meet the demands of a postwar world especially in light of the ever increasing tension in the world brought on by the competition between the Western powers and the Soviet Union.[9]

1948 would bring several important changes to the command that would have a lasting impact for many years. SAC's bomber force would continue to expand and see the introduction of two new bombers— the B-50 and the B-36. General Curtis E. LeMay would assume command of SAC in October 1948 replacing General Kenney — and in November SAC headquarters would move from Andrews AFB, Maryland to Offutt AFB, Nebraska.[10]

The first B-50 was assigned to the 43rd Bomb Wing at Davis-Monthan AFB on 20 February 1948. The B-50 was an improved version of the B-29 and incorporated the ability to refuel in flight using the British-developed hose and hook system. B-50As followed by the more capable B-50D model would be flown by five SAC bomb wings: 43rd, 2nd, 93rd, 97th and 509th; the 55th SRW would operate reconnaissance versions of the B-50, specifically, RB-50E for photo reconnaissance, RB-50F for aerial mapping and geographical survey, and RB-50G for electronic reconnaissance, surveillance and signal intelligence. The 306th BW would also operate B-50s for a short time as part of its combat crew training mission at MacDill AFB, Florida.

The first B-36, the world's largest bomber, joined the 7th Bomb Group, Carswell AFB, on 26 June 1948. An "A" model, serial number 44-92004 was nicknamed the *City of Ft Worth* and assigned to the 492nd Bomb Squadron.[11] Introduction of the B-36 into SAC as an operational aircraft brought about a major change in the designation of bombardment aircraft. All B-29 and B-50 bombers, which had been designated as Very Heavy, were now designated Medium. Only the B-36 retained the Very Heavy designation.

In 1948 the Soviet blockade of Berlin provided the first test of SAC's deployment readiness and ability to fly missions in response to events far from the shores of the Continental United States. In response to the Soviet threat to Berlin, SAC sent two squadrons from the B-29-equipped 301st Bomb Group to Goose Bay, Labrador, as a show of force. The third squadron of the 301st was already on rotational duty at Furstenfeldbruck, Germany. In mid July, SAC sent two additional B-29 units, the 307th from MacDill AFB, and the 28th from Rapid City AFB, to bases in England. These group rotations to the United Kingdom in the

A formation of yellow-tailed 436th BS B-29As of the 7th BG during Operation Big Town in May 1947. The buzz numbers on the black camouflage aircraft are insignia red (USAF-33128A.C.).

summer of 1948 would start a program of group and later wing deployments to the British Islands that would last through the mid–1950s.[12]

SAC continued operations in other parts of the world to include bomber and fighter unit deployments to Alaska; several group deployments to the Far East, mostly to Kadena Field in Okinawa; and fighter deployments to bases in the Caribbean and Europe. The first Atlantic Ocean crossing by a SAC fighter unit was nicknamed Fox Able One (Fighter, Atlantic) conducted by 16 F-80s of the 56th FW from Selfridge AFB, Michigan, and led by Lt. Col Dave C. Schilling, World War II fighter ace. They departed Selfridge AFB on 14 July 1948 and arrived at Furstenfeldbruck, Germany, on 25 July. The flight was accomplished according to plan and represented the first deployment of jet fighters to overseas bases under their own power.

Other notable events from 1948 would include: SAC's first annual bombing competition held at Castle AFB, California, in June 1948 which was won by the 43rd Bomb Group of the Eighth Air Force; an around-the-world flight completed by two B-29s of the 43rd Bomb Group — *Lucky Lady* and *Gas Gobbler*; the first KB-29M aerial refuelers in SAC assigned to the 43rd ARS and 509th ARS in late 1948; the addition of new bomb groups to the force — the 22nd BG reassigned from the Far East Air Forces in Okinawa to Smoky Hill where it was assigned to SAC's Fifteenth Air Force; and the second B-36 unit, the 11th BG, activated at Carswell AFB in December. SAC's fighter force would see some reductions in 1948 with the F-80-equipped 4th FW and 56th FW transferred to Continental Air Command for air defense purposes in December 1948 as well as the F-84-equipped 33rd FW which had recently moved from Roswell AFB, New Mexico, to Otis AFB, Massachusetts. These transfers would leave SAC with the F-82-equipped 27th FW stationed at Kearney AFB, Nebraska, and the P-51-equipped 82nd FW stationed at Grenier AFB, New Hampshire.[13]

1949 was the first full year in which SAC felt the full force of General LeMay's *strong*

This striking shot of BM-007 B-36A-5-CF (44-92007) was taken at Carswell AFB in 1948. This aircraft was assigned to the 436th BS and has a yellow fin cap and nose gear doors (USAF).

personality and *strict* command style. LeMay would implement measures to make SAC a first class organization—fully trained, manned and equipped to initiate an atomic strike in the event of hostilities.

A 523rd FS F-82E (46-299) clearly shows the PQ-299 buzz number on the aft fuselage. Photograph taken during Air Force Day celebration 18 September 1948 at Fairfield-Suisun (later Travis) Air Force Base (courtesy W. Larkins).

Gas Gobbler and Lucky Lady prepare to leave for Alaska on their round-the-world flight that started on 22 July 1948. These two aircraft would return to Davis-Monthan on 6 August 1948 after completing their 20,000-mile trip with eight en route stops and 103 hours and 50 minutes of actual flight time (USA Signal Corps SC 304905).

Several key organizational changes took place in 1949. The Second Air Force was acquired in November and took control of SAC's strategic reconnaissance assets: the 5th and 9th SRWs at Fairfield-Suisun AFB (later Travis), California, and the 55th SRW at Topeka AFB, Kansas. SAC lost the 82nd FW to Continental Air Command in August 1949, but gained the F-86A-equipped 1st FW at March AFB when the 22nd BW as well as Headquarters, Fifteenth Air Force were transferred there in May 1949.

The 43rd BW made another epic flight in 1949. The first nonstop, round-the-world flight took place on 2 March 1949 by a 63rd BS B-50A-5-BO (46-010) named *Lucky Lady II*. Starting and ending at the same

The first birthday of the USAF was celebrated on 18 September 1948 to great fanfare. The USAF took this opportunity to give the American public its first look at the world's largest bomber. B-36A-CF-1 (44-92024) belonged to the 492nd BS of the 7th BW and is shown flying over Smoky Hill AFB. The B-29 in the foreground is assigned to the 22nd BG (USAF, courtesy Travis Air Museum).

location—Carswell AFB, Texas—*Lucky Lady II* completed the record flight in just over 94 hours and required refueling four times. Aerial refueling support came from KB-29M tankers assigned to the 43rd ARS.[14]

The beginning of the 1950s would bring far-reaching change to SAC. SAC would participate in its first shooting war — Korea — and see an unprecedented expansion of the force in the early 1950s. The transition to jet-powered aircraft would gain momentum with the introduction of the B-47 Stratojet and by 1952 all SAC fighter wings would be flying the F-84G Thunderjet. SAC's organization would continue to change to handle the command and control challenges of an ever expanding, more complex strategic defense force.

SAC was involved in the Korean War almost from the start. The 31st SRS stationed at Kadena Air Base, Okinawa, and equipped with RB-29s was

B-50A (46-010) Lucky Lady II arriving at Carswell AFB after completing its non-stop around-the-world flight in 1949. Like all 43rd BW aircraft, Lucky Lady carries the Wing insignia on its nose. The nose gear doors are painted yellow with black diagonal stripes representing assignment to the 63rd BS (USAF).

assigned to the 5th SRW at Travis AFB and attached to the Far East Air Forces. In November 1950 the 31st SRS, now at Johnson Air Base, Japan, became the 91st SRS and was assigned to the Fifteenth Air Force as a separate squadron and further attached to FEAF for combat operations. This was a "paper" change and did not involve the movement of personnel and equipment. Contrary to commonly held opinion; the 91st SRS from 16 November 1950 forward had no command relationship with the 91st SRW at Barksdale AFB. The 91st SRS would act as a host squadron to detachments of US-based reconnaissance units sent TDY to FEAF. These detachments would include RB-45Cs from the 91st SRW at Barksdale AFB, RB-50Gs from the 55th SRW at Ramey AFB, and RB-29s from both the 5th SRW at Travis AFB and the 111th SRW at Fairchild AFB.

SAC would respond quickly to augment FEAF bomber assets (19th BG) by sending the 22nd BG from March AFB to Kadena, Okinawa, and the 92nd BG from Spokane AFB to Yokota, Japan. Together with the 19th BG, these units formed the FEAF Bomber Command (Provisional) which was organized on 8 July 1950. The 31st SRS was also attached to the FEAF Bomber Command. Three B-29 groups would be deemed insufficient to carry out both strategic bombing and tactical support to ground forces. In August 1950, SAC would respond by sending two more B-29 groups to FEAF, the 98th BG from Spokane AFB and the 307th BG from MacDill AFB. Shortly after their arrival in early August, both bomb groups would fly combat missions one week after leaving their home stations. By late September 1950, the strategic bombing offensive had destroyed all significant targets in North Korea, and General MacArthur released the 22nd BG and the 92nd BG to return home. For the rest of the Korean War SAC would maintain the 98th BG and the 307th BG in the Far East to support FEAF operations.[15]

The only SAC fighter group to see combat in Korea was the 27th Fighter-Escort Group. Equipped with F-84Es, the 27th FEG would deploy on 8 November 1950 to the Far East on two aircraft carriers. Two weeks later, the 27th FEG arrived in the Far East and established a forward operating base at Taegu Air Field in South Korea and a rear echelon detachment at Itazuke, Japan. The 27th FEG would fly its first combat mission on 6 December 1950.[16]

Other SAC accomplishments for 1950 would include a large ferry mission of 180 F-84Es by the 27th FEW from Bergstrom AFB to Furstenfeldbruck, Germany, in September and October for which the Wing received the MacKay Trophy for 1950; the delivery of the first KB-29P flying boom tanker on 1 September to the 97th Air Refueling Squadron at Biggs AFB, Texas; and the delivery on 26 August of the first RB-45C jet reconnaissance aircraft to the 91st SRW at Barksdale AFB, Louisiana.[17]

In January 1951, USAF Headquarters approved a reorganization plan for SAC to change the organization of combat forces at the base level. Prior to this organization, each SAC combat wing consisted of a wing headquarters, a combat group of tactical squadrons, a maintenance and supply group, a medical group and an air base group.

The new organization which went into effect in February 1951 reorganized each wing to consist of a wing headquarters; a combat group of tactical squadrons and, where applicable, air refueling and strategic support squadrons; three maintenance squadrons; and an air base group for base housekeeping. The combat group headquarters was not discontinued, but continued to exist in name only. The wing commander served as the combat group commander. The combat groups would be formally deactivated on 16 June 1952.[18]

As part of this reorganization, SAC received approval to create an air division headquarters on double-wing bases. This new headquarters served as an intermediate echelon of command between the combat wings and the numbered air force headquarters. Under

The crew of Nifty 50 stands at attention prepared for inspection by British prime minister Clement Attlee at Marham on 4 October 1949 during the Battle of Britain Commemoration. Nifty 50 was assigned to the 64th BS and its squadron color was green (USAF-AFHRA).

this plan, the air division commander exercised direct control over the two wing commanders and the air base group commander. The first five air divisions were organized, effective 10 February 1951, at the following bases: 4th at Barksdale AFB, 6th at MacDill AFB, 12th at March AFB, 14th at Travis AFB, and 47th at Walker AFB.[19]

Operational highlights for SAC in 1951 would include: continued combat operations in Korea by the 98th and 307th Bombardment Wings, the 91st Strategic Reconnaissance Squadron, and the 27th Fighter-Escort Wing. The 27th FEW, however, would return to its home station, Bergstrom AFB, in August 1951 and start receiving new F-84G Thunderjets, having left their F-84Es with FEAF; the introduction of the B-47 medium bomber into SAC with the first aircraft delivered on 23 October to the 306th BW at MacDill AFB; also going to the 306th BW was the first KC-97 tanker which was delivered to the 306th Air Refueling Squadron on 14 July; and the first B-36 flights to both England

22nd BW B-29 flying a combat mission over Korea. The 22nd BW would fly missions from Okinawa during July to October 1950 in support of FEAF operations (USAF).

Arriving in Japan in late November 1950, these red-trimmed F-84Es of the 522nd FES are preparing to go to Korea. The 27th FEG would fly their first combat mission from Taegu AB (K-2) on 6 December 1950 (USAF, courtesy D. Menard).

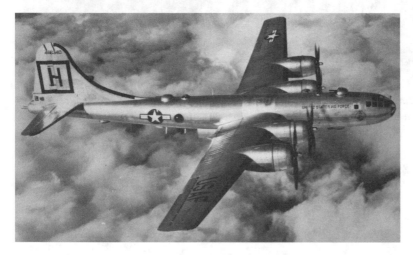

Photographed in October 1951 over Korea, B-29-50-MO (44-86340) is named Wolf Pack and carries the 345th BS colors on the fin cap — white with black diagonal stripes (USAF, courtesy Col. R. Ireland).

on 16 January and to French Morocco on 3 December. SAC would also continue a heavy rotation of its units around the world, mostly to England, but also to Japan, Guam and French North Africa.[20]

The year 1952 would bring organizational changes, record flights, continued participation in the Korean War, and a new insignia for Strategic Air Command.

On 16 June all bombardment, fighter and

The 307th Air Refueling Squadron (attached to the 6th BW until 16 June 1952) provided support for atomic bomb tests in the Pacific during Operation Ivy in the summer of 1952. As part of Task Group 132.4 the 307th ARS used he specialized insignia of the task group on the dorsal fin of its KB-29P tankers (USAF, National Archives).

RB-45C No Sweat, piloted by Major Louis Carrington, made the first nonstop Pacific crossing by a jet bomber on 29 July 1952, flying from Elmendorf AFB, Alaska, to Yokota Air Base, Japan, in nine hours and 50 minutes. For this flight the crew was awarded the MacKay Trophy for 1952 (USAF).

reconnaissance groups were inactivated and the combat squadrons were assigned directly to the wings. This move recognized officially what had been put into practice beginning in 1951 when the combat groups were left unmanned.[21]

SAC continued to support combat operations in Korea with B-29s of the 98th BW at Yokota and the 307th BW on Okinawa. SAC also provided strategic reconnaissance assets with RB-29s from the 91st SRS at Yokota and rotating detachments of RB-50s from the 55th SRW and RB-45Cs from the 91st SRW.

Three major flights took place in 1952. Fox Peter One was the movement of the 31st FEW from Turner Air Force Base, Georgia, to Misawa and Chitose Air Bases, Japan. This flight, conducted in early July 1952, was the first mass fighter deployment to be supported by inflight refueling. Fox Peter Two was the deployment of the 27th FEW to replace the 31st FEW in Japan. Departing from Bergstrom AFB, Texas, on 3 October, the 27th FEW used both inflight refueling and enroute stops at Travis AFB, Hickam AFB and Midway on the 7,800-mile flight to Misawa Air Base, Japan. Finally, a RB-45C (named *No Sweat*) flight from Alaska to Japan by the 91st SRW was the first nonstop, transpacific flight from Elmendorf AFB, Alaska, to Yokota Air Base, Japan. This flight earned the MacKay Trophy for 1952.[22]

On 4 January 1952, Headquarters, USAF approved an insignia for Strategic Air Command and the new insignia started to appear on all SAC aircraft beginning in 1953.

1953 would see continued growth in SAC, but at a slower pace. The year would see an end to fighting in Korea with an armistice signed on 27 July. During the three-year conflict FEAF Bomber Command, composed mostly of SAC units and personnel — with the notable exception of the 19th BG — flew 21,328 combat sorties and dropped 167,100 tons of bombs on various strategic and tactical targets. 1953 would also see more long-distance flights with

With a C-74 Globemaster I in the background, 31st SFW F-84Gs undergo maintenance in North Africa as part of Operation Longstride (USAF, courtesy D. Menard).

*The 306th BW insignia is worn proudly on this B-47B. Of note are the **Square P** tail markings on KC-97 and T-33 aircraft in the background (USAF-46957 A.C.).*

Many units placed crew shields on their aircraft. This photograph shows a 93rd ARS crew inspection at Castle AFB during Fox Peter One, July 1952. This shield is in the squadron color — green — and the crew names are in white (USAF — National Archives).

Operation Longstride in August, where F-84s from the 31st SFW and 508th SFW flew across the Atlantic to French North Africa and England, respectively. Also SAC initiated the first B-47 wing deployment to the UK in June 1953 with the 306th BW deploying to Mildenhall. After the 90-day rotation, the 306th BW was replaced by another B-47 wing, its sister unit at MacDill AFB, the 305th BW. On the other side of the world, SAC sent the B-36-equipped 92nd BW to the Far East in August and September 1953 as part of Operation Big Stick, intended to demonstrate U.S. resolve to maintain peace in the Far East.[23]

The days of using World War II era aircraft in SAC's combat fleet were nearing an end, and soon it would be B-47s, B-52s and KC-135s that would help SAC live up to its motto—"Peace Is Our Profession."

2

Basic Definitions— USAF Aircraft Markings[1]

Radio Call Numbers

Also referred to as tail number and incorrectly as the aircraft serial number. The first two digits of the aircraft serial number represented the fiscal year the aircraft was funded for construction. This number was separated by a hyphen from the production number of the aircraft. Together these numbers formed the aircraft serial number. For example, a serial number of "45-21749" tells us this aircraft (in this case a B-29) was funded for construction in fiscal year 1945. The radio call number or tail number was created by simply dropping the first digit. So in this case, the tail number for "45-21749" would be 521749. These numbers were applied to both sides of the vertical stabilizer and rudder assembly. The radio call number or tail number was painted in black for metal surfaces, and yellow for camouflage surfaces, except that black camouflage planes were to have insignia red tail numbers.

Identification Markings (Buzz Numbers)

On all aircraft, except helicopters and lighter-than-air, operating solely within the continental limits of the United States, an identification marking was placed on the lower surface of the left wing, and each side of the fuselage. These identification markings consisted of two letters and three numerals with the letters separated from the numerals by a dash. Identification markings would be eliminated for medium and heavy type bombers (B-29, B-50 and B-36) in TO 07-1-1 dated 26 July 1948 and would be replaced by **USAF** on wing surfaces and **United States Air Force** on each side of the forward fuselage. Identification markings were to be yellow on camouflage surfaces and black on metal surfaces. Black camouflaged aircraft were to have insignia red identification markings. The earlier versions of TO 07-1-1 (7 June 1946 and 29 September 1947) did not make this clear, so some units painted identification markings in identification yellow on black camouflage aircraft.

Letter designations for type and model of SAC aircraft included:

	Type	Model	
B-29	B	F	
B-36	B	M	
B-45	B	E	
B-50	B	K	
P/F*-47	P/F	E	
P/F-51	P/F	F	
P/F-80	P/F	N	(New letter assigned
		T	in T0-07-1-1 dated
			26 July 1948)
P/F-82	P/F	Q	
P/F-84	P/F	S	
P/F-86	P/F	U	

*Designation of fighters was changed from "P" to "F" on 11 June 1948 and reflected in the revised TO-07-1-1 dated 26 July 1948.

National Star Insignia

The standard national star insignia was required on all USAF aircraft and was to be applied so that in normal flight attitude of the aircraft, the top star point of the insignia pointed upward on fuselage surfaces and forward on wing surfaces. The standard insignia was to be placed on the top surface of the left wing and on the lower surface of the right wing, and on each side of the fuselage midway between the trailing edge of the wing and the leading edge of the horizontal stabilizer.

The standard insignia was an insignia white five pointed star inside an insignia blue circumscribed circle with an insignia white rectangle, one radius of the blue cir-

Converted to an aerial tanker, KB-29M (45–21788) retains its markings from previous service with the 7th BG. This photograph clearly shows the placement of buzz numbers, numbered air force insignia, tail number and tactical tail marking used by SAC's bomb units during 1947–1948. (USAF)

cle in length and one-half radius of the blue circle in width, on each side of the star and the top edges placed to form a straight line with the top edges of the two star points beneath the top star point; with an insignia red horizontal stripe centered in the white rectangles at each end of the insignia , the width of the red stripe to be one-sixth the radius of the star. The red stripe was added to the standard insignia in Amendment -2 to AN-I-9b issued on 16 January 1947.

Aircraft — Arctic Operated

Aircraft being operated in Arctic Regions, or being prepared for Arctic operation, were required to have a distinguishable marking to permit visible location of any aircraft which may be forced down or may crash land on ice or snow covered terrain.

B-36B-5-CF (44–92039) in insignia red Arctic markings at Orchard Place Airport (today's Chicago O'Hare) July 1949. (Courtesy National Museum of the USAF)

The complete area of the fuselage aft of a mark drawn three feet forward of the leading edge of the horizontal stabilizer and all the surfaces of the tail, except for a boundary of three inches around any authorized insignia or other standard marking appearing on these surfaces, were to be painted insignia red. The boundary, between the red painted areas and insignia or other markings such as radio call numbers, was to remain unpainted on bare metal surfaces, but did not require removal of any paint previously applied on fabric surfaces.

The area of each wing outboard of a mark placed at the inboard end of each aileron, including the wing tip, except a boundary within three inches of any authorized insignia, or other markings appearing within this area, were to be painted insignia red. The boundary between the red painted areas and insignia or other markings, such as the standard USAF insignia, was to remain unpainted on bare metal surfaces, but did not require removal of any paint previously applied on fabric surfaces.

Snow-covered flight line at Rapid City, 1949. Notice the United States Air Force fuselage marking on the nearest B-29 and the older, soon to be removed buzz number on a 718th BS B-29–45-MO (44–86308). (USAF, AFHRA)

KB-29M (44–69710) Homogenized Ethyl *is probably the best known tanker from the 43rd BW. Side view shows all tactical markings in effect in 1952 — tail marking, Fifteenth Air Force marking, and blue and white diagonal squadron identification markings. There is also a small identification number on the aircraft nose — 710. Oakland Airport, October 1952. (W. Larkins)*

USAF Markings

These markings were to consist of vertical block type lettering in the colors of yellow for OD camouflaged surfaces, black on metal surfaces, and insignia red on black camouflage aircraft.

The letters **USAF** were to be placed on the lower surface of the left wing and upper surface of the right wing of all USAF aircraft. The height and location of this marking corresponded with the national insignia presently on the opposite wing of the aircraft concerned.

U.S. AIR FORCE was to be placed on both sides, or each outboard side, as applicable, of the vertical stabilizer and rudder assembly of fighters, trainers, and light bombardment type aircraft except those of the National Guard. The bottom of the lettering was to be located 3 inches above the radio call letters and the size of the letters were to be ½ that of radio call letters.

UNITED STATES AIR FORCE was to be placed on each side of the fuselage of medium, heavy, and very heavy bombers except for search and rescue aircraft. This lettering was to be located ahead of the leading edge of the wing and approximately one-third of the way down from the top of the fuselage. Size of the letters was 9 × 6 inches.

Tactical Aircraft Marking

Usually referred to as tail marking or tail code. Tactical aircraft markings were developed during World War II as a means of unit identification and as a visual aid for the assembly of aircraft formations. Early in SAC's history the tail marking for Eighth Air Force units represented the group, and in the case of Fifteenth Air Force units, the geometric symbol represented the wing and the letter designator the group. In October 1949 SAC established a standard tail marking policy where the geometric symbol represented a numbered air force (**Square**— Second Air Force, **Triangle**— Eighth Air Force, and **Circle**— Fifteenth Air Force) and the letter represented the wing assigned to the numbered air force. Due to changing tactics and security concerns, tail markings were deemed unnecessary in

In addition to the Triangle tail marking and squadron colors on the fin cap and nose gear doors, all 7th BG/BW B-29s displayed the Group/Wing marking on the left side of the aircraft nose. This 7th BG B-29A-50-BN (44–61830) was photographed at Andrews Field in 1947. (Photograph by Bern Ederr, courtesy D. Olson)

early 1953, and SAC would order their removal in April 1953 with most units having completed the removal of their tail marking by early summer 1953.

Organizational Insignia

The placing of organization markings or design was the responsibility of the organization itself. Depots were not required to reproduce this insignia. No specific locations were mandatory, but points between wing and tail surfaces on opposite sides of the fuselage were considered most desirable. In no case was the size of the insignia to exceed 75

*Andrews AFB in February 1949. These aircraft display two of the tail markings used by the Eighth Air Force from 1947 to 1949. The **Square** represented the 2nd BG; the **Triangle** represented the 7th BG. (Photograph by Fahey, courtesy D. Olson)*

percent of height of fuselage at point of application. Similar aircraft in the same organization were to have the same size insignia. In all cases organizational insignia was to be clearly subordinate to the United States Air Force identification.

The numbered air forces insignia was a standard marking for most groups and wings and was placed on the dorsal fin of their bomber aircraft. The Second Air Force, however, did not place, as a general practice, their emblem on assigned aircraft due to a new design being developed to replace their World War II insignia.

In general, SAC's policy on the use of unit insignia was left to the discretion of the wing commander — many units displayed organizational insignia on their aircraft, but many units chose not to display any wing, group or squadron insignia. For those units who did use organizational insignia on their aircraft, the insignia was usually placed on the aircraft nose in various sizes; however, in some instances the insignia was placed on the vertical stabilizer.

Above: *The 303rd BW displayed its insignia on the nose of all assigned B-29s. This crew belonged to the 358th BS and wears ball caps in their squadron color — black. (USAF) Below: The 6th BW at Walker AFB was one of the few SAC bomb wings to place large squadron insignia on all assigned aircraft. Crew photograph shows a large squadron insignia for the 40th BS on one of its B-29s. The nose gear doors appear to be painted in blue and green diagonal stripes. (USAF, AFHRA)*

In 1953 SAC began using its command insignia as a required element to its aircraft marking scheme.

Squadron Identification Markings

These markings were left to the wing commander for approval and implementation. Most SAC bombardment units used the colors red, blue, yellow and occasionally green to identify their bomb

In mid–1949, the 43rd ARS started to apply squadron identification markings on its KB-29M tankers. A blue and white diagonal pattern was painted on fin tips, fuselage band and nose gear doors. Many 43rd ARS KB-29Ms were given nicknames; in this case the aircraft name is Hosin Hosea. *(Boeing P10339. © Boeing. Used under license.)*

The nose gear door section for RB-29 (44–61860) with the position of the aircraft identification number on the checkerboard design. Standing next to his ship is the ubiquitous Air Force crew chief with all the tools of his trade — wrench, clean but worn HBT coveralls, notebook in pocket and flightline badge. (USAF, AFHRA)

Left: *Most SAC B-36 units painted squadron identification markings on the jet intake rims as shown in this photo. This example shows a crew from the 6th Bomb Wing working on a General Electric J47-GE-19 turbojet. Walker AFB, early 1953. (USAF, AFHRA)*

squadrons. In one instance, black was used and some units used an orange-yellow instead of identification yellow. After the introduction of air refueling squadrons in 1949, green became the predominant color associated with these squadrons. Most units used a solid color pattern; however, on those bases with two wings assigned, one wing would usually incorporate diagonal stripes over the solid color to distinguish itself from its sister wing. There is one instance of a SAC wing using a checkerboard pattern as part of its squadron identification system. Placement of these markings, again, varied by wing; some wings placed squadron colors on fine tips and nose gear doors, while others expanded the scheme to include fuselage bands, propeller domes, and, in the case of B-36s, jet intake rims.

Publications

The USAF used a series of publications to communicate policy and procedures on the subject of aircraft markings. The national markings— National Star Insignia, USAF markings, identification numbers, radio call numbers and Arctic markings— were covered by Department of the Air Force Technical Order 07-1-1, "Aircraft Camouflage, Markings, and Insignia."

Tactical markings or tail markings, after approval, were found in the SAC Manual 55-1— Tactical Doctrine Manual — Bombardment. The numbered air forces also listed assigned tail markings in their respective tactical doctrine manuals on bombardment and included the size and dimensions of the tail marking for each type of tactical aircraft assigned.

The implementing directive to place tactical aircraft markings on assigned aircraft at the group and wing level was usually a Maintenance Technical Instruction. This instruction was used to guide the application of tactical markings— tail code, squadron identification markings and unit insignia — by maintenance personnel, usually those assigned to the paint and dope section of the field maintenance squadrons (or 3rd echelon level maintenance).

3

SAC Combat Aircraft, 1946–1953

Boeing B-29 "Superfortress"

B-29s were the only bomber aircraft assigned to SAC when that command was established in 1946. They were used again in the conventional bombing role during the Korean War from 1950 to 1953. They were retired as bomber aircraft in 1954, but continued to serve SAC in specialized roles. The largest number of B-29s assigned to SAC was in 1952 with 417; the largest number of KB-29s was 187 in 1951; and the largest number of RB-29s was 62 in 1949.

MANUFACTURER: Boeing, Bell and Martin
TYPE: Bombardment, Strategic Reconnaissance, and Aerial Refueling
CHARACTERISTICS: (B-29A)

Span	141.2 feet
Length	99 feet
Height	27.8 feet
Weight	133,500 pounds maximum normal takeoff
Crew	11

PERFORMANCE:

Maximum speed	365 mph at 25,000 feet
Cruising speed	220 mph
Service ceiling	31,850 feet
Range	1,561 miles with 20,000 pound bomb load

ARMAMENT: 10 or 12 .50-caliber machine guns; 20,000 pounds maximum bomb payload
ELECTRONICS: APQ-7 or APQ-23A bombing-navigation radar
VARIANTS:

B-29	Production aircraft; 11 crew; 3,659 build; doesn't count those completed as B-29Bs.
B-29A	Production aircraft; modified wing and improved engines; 11 crew; 1,119 built.
RB-29/RB-29A	Conversion to photographic reconnaissance; designated F-13/F-13A until 1948; no guns in most aircraft; fitted with cameras and additional fuel tanks in bomb bays; 118 converted from B-29/B-29A.
KB-29M	Aircraft converted to hose-drogue tankers; armament deleted and additional fuel tanks and hose fitted; 92 converted from B-29 from 1948 onward.

B-29A-70-BN (44–62308) has the streamlined four-gun upper forward turret of very late production B-29As. This aircraft would serve with SAC's 40th BG and 43rd BW at Davis-Monthan AFB. (Museum of Flight — Gordon S. Williams Collection)

B-29MR Standard bomber aircraft fitted for long-range operations capable of refueling in-flight from KB-29Ms; 74 modified.

KB-29P Flying-boom tankers; armament deleted; additional fuel tanks and special radar installed; 116 converted from B-29 from 1949–1951.

Convair B-36 "Peacemaker"

The Convair B-36 "Peacemaker" was the world's largest bomber when, after World War II, the aircraft was pursued as a strategic nuclear bomber for the USAF. Not without controversy, the US Navy opposed a US defense strategy based only on nuclear attack by bombardment aircraft. This opposition was labeled the "Admiral's revolt" and resulted in Congressional hearings on the B-36 program. The first operational B-36 was delivered in June 1948 to the 7th Bombardment Wing at Carswell AFB. The B-36 and RB-36 would ultimately equip ten SAC bombardment and strategic reconnaissance wings from 1948 to 1959.

RB-36E-10-CF (44–92023) at Travis AFB in August 1952. This plane was assigned to the 72nd SRS; the fin tip and nose gear doors are in the squadron color — red. Notice the 72nd SRS squadron insignia on the aircraft nose. (Courtesy National Museum of the USAF)

MANUFACTURER: Consolidated-Vultee (Convair)
TYPE: Bombardment, Strategic Reconnaissance
CHARACTERISTICS: (B-36J)

Span	230 feet
Length	162.1 feet
Height	46.6 feet
Weight	410,000 lbs. gross
Crew	15

PERFORMANCE:

Maximum speed	411 mph at 36,400 feet
Cruising speed	391 mph
Service ceiling	39,900 feet combat; 45,200 maximum
Range	3,990 miles with 10,000-lb. bomb load

ARMAMENT:

Payload   4 gravity nuclear weapons or 2 × 42,000-lb. bombs, or 12 × 4,000-lb. bombs or 28 × 2,000-lb. bombs (maximum 72,000 lbs.)

Guns   16 × 20-mm cannon

ELECTRONICS: K-3A bombing-navigation radar, APG-41A 4 tail gunfire control radar

VARIANTS:

B-36A   Production aircraft; no armament; used primarily for training; first flight 28 August 1947; 22 built.

B-36B   Production aircraft; fully armed; 328,000 lbs. gross; 15 crew; first flight 8 July 1948; 73 built.

B-36D   Production aircraft; fitted with 4 turbojet engines; 357,000 gross; 15 crew; first flight 26 March 1949; 64 converted from B-36B and 22 built.

RB-36D   Reconnaissance variant with two bomb bays modified for 14 cameras; guns retained; 357,000 gross; 22 crew; first flight 18 December 1949; 7 converted from B-36B and 17 built; 12 subsequently modified to carry "parasite" fighter.

RB-36E   Reconnaissance variant similar to RB-36D; 22 converted from B-36A.

B-36F   Production aircraft; similar to B-36D; first flight 18 November 1950; 28 built.

RB-36F   Reconnaissance aircraft; similar to RB-36E; 24 built.

B-36H   Production aircraft; similar to B-36F; first flight 5 April 1952; 81 built.

RB-36H   Reconnaissance variant; improved RB-36F; 73 built.

B-36J   Production aircraft; 410,000 lbs. gross; 15 crew; first flight 3 September 1953; 33 built.

Boeing B-47 "Stratojet"

The Boeing B-47 Stratojet was the first swept-wing, jet-propelled bomber produced in large numbers by any nation. In addition to its high speed and sleek configuration, the B-47 was much more automated than its piston engine predecessors in SAC, permitting a reduction in crew from 11 men in a B-50 to only three in the B-47. The more advanced technology of the B-47 also saw the deletion of all gun armament except for a remotely controlled tail turret. Speed and defensive electronics made the large number of guns found in earlier bombers unnecessary. During the tail marking era, only two SAC wings were equipped with B-47Bs; the 306th BW and the 305th BW, both stationed at MacDill AFB as

*B-47B-40-BW (51–2212) landing at MacDill AFB in early 1953. The **Square P** tail marking was smaller on the B-47, given the size of the vertical stabilizer and the requirement to show aircraft number and squadron identification band on the tail. (USAF, courtesy Boeing J46911 A.C. © Boeing. Used under license.)*

part of the 6th Air Division. The number of B-47s in USAF service peaked in early 1957 with 28 bomb wings flying 1,260 B-47s with some additional 300 reconnaissance variants in service.

MANUFACTURER: Boeing, Douglas, and Lockheed
TYPE: Bombardment, Strategic Reconnaissance
CHARACTERISTICS: (B-47E)

Span	116 feet
Length	107.1 feet
Height	28 feet
Weight	221,000 pounds maximum (refueled in flight)
Crew	3

PERFORMANCE:

Maximum speed	606 mph at 16,300 feet
Cruising speed	557 mph at 38,500 feet
Service ceiling	47,000 feet
Range	2,014 miles with 10,000 pound bomb load

ARMAMENT: Two .50 caliber machine guns (B-47B); two 20-mm cannon; 18,000 pounds maximum bomb payload
ELECTRONICS: K-4A bombing-navigation radar, A-5 or MD-4 tail gunfire control radar, APS-54 warning radar
VARIANTS:

B-47B	Production aircraft; 3 crew; provision for two 1,500-gallon wing tanks and in-flight refueling; first flight 26 April 1951; 399 built.
B-47E	Production aircraft; modified wing and improved engines; 3 crew; first flight 30 January 1953; 1350 built.
YRB/RB-47B	Aircraft fitted with 8-camera reconnaissance pod in bomb bay; used mostly as trainers for RB-47E; 24 B-47B converted in 1953–54.
RB-47E	Reconnaissance aircraft; 11 cameras fitted in bomb bay; 3 crew; first flight 3 July 1953; 240 built.

Boeing B-50 "Superfortress"

The Boeing B-50 Superfortress was basically a B-29 with improved engines and could be easily distinguished from the B-29 by the larger, streamlined engine nacelles, taller tail fin, and 1,500-gallon wing tanks. The B-50 also had improved wing materials, undercarriage, and hydraulic controls. Developed during World War II, a low production rate was continued into the post-war as the B-50 began to replace the B-29 as the primary SAC bomber. The B-50 would serve in a bomber role with SAC's 43rd, 2nd, 93rd, 97th and 509th Bombardment Wings. The RB-50 variants would see service in a strategic reconnaissance role with the 91st SRW (RB-50B) and the 55th SRW (RB-50E/F/G).

MANUFACTURER: Boeing
TYPE: Bombardment, Strategic Reconnaissance
CHARACTERISTICS: (B-50A)

Span	141.2 feet
Length	99 feet
Height	32.75 feet
Weight	168,480 pounds maximum
Crew	12

PERFORMANCE:

Maximum speed	385 mph at 25,000 feet
Cruising speed	235 mph
Service ceiling	37,000 feet
Range	2,325 miles with 10,000 pound bomb load

ARMAMENT: 13 .50 caliber machine guns; 20,000 pounds maximum bomb payload
ELECTRONICS: APQ-24 bombing-navigation radar
VARIANTS:

B-50A   Production aircraft; 11–12 crew; first flight 25 June 1947; 79 built.

B-50B   Production aircraft; modified wing and improved engines; 11–12 crew; first flight 14 January 1949; 45 built.

The 2nd Bombardment Group changed from B-29s to B-50As starting in early 1949. This early example B-50A-25-BO (46–053) belonging to the 20th BS is shown at an air show at Andrews AFB, 12–15 February 1949. There has been a change to one fuselage band. Squadron color is green. (Photograph by Jim Fahey, courtesy D. Olson)

RB-50B	Reconnaissance aircraft; fitted with 9 cameras and weather monitoring equipment; 700-gallon wing tanks; 44 B-50B converted.
B-50D	Production aircraft; 11 crew; fitted with 700-gallon wing tanks; first flight 23 May 1949; 222 built.
RB-50E	Photographic reconnaissance and observation; 14 RB-50B converted.
RB-50F	Mapping, charting and survey missions; 14 RB-50B converted.
RB-50G	Electronic reconnaissance configuration; 15 RB-50B converted.

North American P/F-51D/H "Mustang"

SAC would use the P/F-51 Mustang in four of its fighter groups beginning in 1946 with the 56th Fighter Group, and in 1947 with the 82nd, 27th and 33rd Fighter Groups. The 56th FG would convert to P-80s in 1947, and in 1948 the 27th FG would transition to the F-82E while the 33rd FG would receive SAC's first F-84s, leaving the 82nd FG as the only Mustang-equipped fighter unit in SAC. In August 1949 the 82nd FG would be reassigned to the Continental Air Command taking with them their F-51D Mustangs. The F-51s would return to duty with SAC for a very brief time in 1951 when four Air National Guard units — the 108th FBW, 131st FBW, 132nd FBW and 146th FBW — were assigned to SAC, three of which were equipped with the F-51Ds. These units, however, would all be transferred to Tactical Air Command in November 1951. The number of P/F-51s assigned to SAC by year was: 85 in 1946, 230 in 1947, 131 in 1948, 97 in 1949, and 107 in 1951.

MANUFACTURER: North American Aviation, Inc., Inglewood, California and Dallas, Texas
TYPE: Single-Seat Fighter, Ground Attack, and Long-Range Escort
CHARACTERISTICS: (F-51H)

Span	37 feet
Length	33 feet 4 inches
Height	13 feet 8 inches
Weight	11,054 pounds gross

PERFORMANCE: (F-51H)

Maximum speed	487 mph at 25,000 feet
Cruising speed	380 mph
Service ceiling	41,600 feet
Range	850 miles

ARMAMENT: Six .50 caliber machine guns or ten 5-inch rockets

F-51 (44–73825) was taken out of storage at Kelly AFB, Texas, in June 1951 and assigned to the 131st F-B Wing at Bergstrom AFB, Texas, in July 1951. The 131st FBW aircraft served in SAC for only six months; the marking scheme remains undocumented. (Museum of Flight)

Lockheed P/F-80A "Shooting Star"

On 23 April 1947 SAC received its first P-80A fighter aircraft and started to equip two of its fighter groups, the 4th FG at Andrews Field and the 56th FG at Selfridge Field. The

P/F-80 would be hindered with many maintenance difficulties in its first year of service with SAC and the range limitation issue would ultimately cause the removal of the P/F-80 from SAC's fighter force. However, 16 F-80s of the 56th FG did conduct a pioneer transatlantic jet flight in July 1948. Departing from Selfridge AFB on 20 July 1948, and making refueling stops in Labrador, Greenland and Iceland, the 56th FG would land in Scotland nine hours and 20 minutes after leaving the United States. The F-80s would leave SAC when both the 4th FG and 56th FG were transferred to the Continental Air Command on 1 December 1948.

Left: P-80A (44–85273) was flown by the 56th Fighter Wing Commander, Col. William T. Hudnell, and carried the markings of the 61st Fighter Squadron with the exception of the four fuselage bands that indicated wing commander status. (Courtesy of Special Collections and Archives, Wright State University)

MANUFACTURER: Lockheed Aircraft Corporation
TYPE: Fighter
CHARACTERISTICS:

Span	39 feet 11 inches
Length	34 feet 6 inches
Height	11 feet 4 inches
Weight	14,500 pounds gross

PERFORMANCE:

Maximum speed	558 mph at 7,000 feet
Cruising speed	410 mph
Service ceiling	45,000 feet
Range	540 miles

ARMAMENT: Six .50 caliber machine guns

North American P/F-82E "Twin Mustang"

The P/F-82E served as an interim escort fighter for SAC and was considered the best available fighter to meet SAC's long-range operations requirements at the time. Serving with the 27th Fighter Wing, the first P-82E was assigned on 23 January 1948, and by the end of 1948 SAC would have 81 F-82Es among its tactical fighter aircraft. The 27th Fighter-Escort Wing would begin its conversion to F-84Es in December 1949 and the F-82Es would be transferred to other commands on a staggered basis. All F-82Es would be transferred out of SAC by August 1950

MANUFACTURER: North American Aviation, Inc.
TYPE: Long-Range Escort Fighter

CHARACTERISTICS:

Span 51 feet 3 inches
Length 42 feet 5 inches
Height 13 feet 10 inches
Weight 25,591 pounds gross
Crew 2

PERFORMANCE:

Maximum speed 461 mph at
21,000 feet
Cruising speed 286 mph
Service ceiling 38,900 feet
Range 2,240 miles

ARMAMENT: Six .50 caliber
machine guns in wing center section
Four 1,000-pound bombs external

*The **FQ** prefix and U.S. Air Force lettering now appear on this 523rd FS F-82E (46–275). Concord, California, May 28, 1949. (Courtesy W. Larkins)*

Republic P/F-84E/G "Thunderjet"

The F-84 was probably the most significant fighter assigned to SAC. Several models were assigned and in greater numbers than any other fighter. SAC used F-84s from June to December 1948 and from September 1949 to July 1957. The F-84 became the standard jet fighter for SAC and helped create stability in SAC's fighter program that prior to 1950 had been lacking.

SAC started with F-84Cs with the 33rd Fighter Group in June 1948, but would lose the 33rd FG and its F-84s to Continental Air Command in December 1948. SAC would receive its first F-84Es in September 1949 with the 27th Fighter Wing, who in December 1950 as the 27th Fighter-Escort Wing, would deploy to Korea with the F-84E and be the only SAC fighter unit to fly combat missions during the Korean War. Beginning in August 1951, the 31st FEW would be the first SAC unit to receive the F-84G. The F-84G brought both an atomic capability as well as an air refueling capability to SAC's fighter force. By 1952 all fighter wings in SAC were using the F-84G (the 12th FEW, 27th FEW, 31st FEW, and 508th FEW). 1953 would see an additional F-84G wing assigned to SAC—the 506th SFW. Total number of F-84s assigned to SAC in 1953 was 235.

MANUFACTURER: Republic Aviation Corporation, Long Island, New York and General Motors Corporation, Kansas City, Missouri

TYPE: Fighter, Fighter-Bomber, Fighter-Escort

An F-84E has the red-yellow-blue fuselage bands indicating the aircraft of the 27th FEG commander — in this case, Col. William Bertram. (Photograph by Balogh, courtesy D. Menard)

CHARACTERISTICS:	F-84E	F-84G
Span	36 feet 5 inches	36 feet 5 inches
Length	37 feet 5 inches	38 feet 1 inch
Height	12 feet 10 inches	12 feet 7 inches
Weight	19,689 pounds gross	23,525 pounds gross

PERFORMANCE:

Maximum speed	587 mph at 4,000 feet	622 mph
Cruising speed	436 mph	483 mph
Service ceiling	40,750 feet	40,000 feet
Range	1,282 miles	2,000 miles

ARMAMENT: Four .50 caliber   Six .50 caliber
              machine guns   machine guns
              32 5-inch rockets   32 5-inch rockets
                                 Two 1,000 pound bombs

North American F-86A "Sabre Jet"

SAC's only experience with the F-86A was with the 1st Fighter Wing from 1 May 1949 to 1 July 1950. When SAC assumed command of March AFB, California in May 1949 it inherited the 1st Fighter Wing with the base. The 1st FW was equipped with 82 of the short-ranged F-86A and on 16 April 1950 was redesignated the 1st Fighter-Interceptor Wing. The Wing would be assigned to the Continental Air Command on 1 July 1950 ending its 14 month stint of service with SAC.

MANUFACTURER: North American Aviation, Inc.
TYPE: Fighter and Fighter-Bomber
CHARACTERISTICS:

Span	37 feet 1 inch
Length	37 feet 6 inches

The 94th Fighter Squadron color was blue and would appear on the upper tail band, the stylized flash on the fuselage and the crew nameplate located between the gun port and the forward portion of the flash. (San Diego Aerospace Museum)

Height   14 feet 8 inches
Weight   16,357 pounds gross
PERFORMANCE:
  Maximum speed   672 mph at 2,500 feet
  Cruising speed   527 mph
  Service ceiling   48,300 feet
  Range   785 miles
ARMAMENT: Six .50 caliber machine guns, two 1,000-pound bombs or 16 5-inch rockets

North American Aviation RB-45C "Tornado"

The RB-45C was a photo reconnaissance version of the B-45C; thirty-three aircraft were modified for the photo-reconnaissance role and redesignated RB-45C. The aircraft featured a redesigned nose section which replaced the bombardier's compartment with cameras. Up to five cameras could be carried in the nose; 4 vertical mounted and one forward-facing oblique camera at the tip of the nose. Other cameras could be installed in a compartment aft of the bomb bay. The RB-45C was also equipped with in-flight refueling (IFR) capability. The IFR receptacle was installed behind the cockpit. The pilot used reference lights and markings on the bottom of the refueling aircraft to stay in formation while the refueling boom operator "flew" the probe into the refueling recepticle.

Some RB-45Cs flew combat missions during the Korean Conflict. The RB-45C began flying daylight high-altitude reconnaissance missions in late 1950 in place of the older and slower RB-29s. With the appearance of the MiG-15 in November 1950, the RB-45Cs also became vulnerable during daytime operations. In the spring of 1951, the RB-45Cs were restricted from daylight operations unless fighter escort was available. By the end of the year, the aircraft were restricted from flying any daytime combat missions and only night-time missions were carried out. However, the RB-45C performed poorly as a nighttime reconnaissance platform primarily because of stability problems.

On July 29, 1952, using in-flight refueling, two RB-45Cs of the 91st Strategic Reconnaissance Wing made the first nonstop trans–Pacific flight by multi-engine jet bombers. In

RB-456 (48–033) piloted by Col. Joseph H. Preston, CO of the 91st SRW, lands the first RB-45C at Lockbourne AFB, Columbus, Ohio, having just departed Barksdale AFB, Louisiana, September 1951. (Boeing H81–278–2. © Boeing. Used under license.)

flying the 3,640 miles from Alaska to Japan in 9 hours and 50 minutes, Major Louis H. Carrington's crew won the MacKay Trophy for the most meritorious flight of that year.

All RB-45Cs in SAC service were assigned to the 91st Strategic Reconnaissance Wing at Barksdale AFB, and later Lockbourne AFB, from August 1950 to December 1953.

• Serial numbers: 48-011 to 48-043

MANUFACTURER: North American Aviation, Inc.

TYPE: Jet Reconnaissance Bomber

CHARACTERISTICS:

Span	89 feet
Length	75 feet 11 inches
Height	25 feet 2 inches
Weight	110,000 pounds gross
Crew	4 or 3 when tail gunner position eliminated

PERFORMANCE:

Maximum speed	570 mph at 4,000 feet
Cruising speed	506 mph
Service ceiling	40,250 feet
Range	2,500 miles with tip tanks

ARMAMENT: Two .50-cal. machine guns with 600 rounds each in the tail and 25 photoflash bombs (for aerial photography at night). Many RB-45Cs were modified to eliminate the tail gunner position.

Boeing C-97/KC-97 "Stratofreighter"

The C-97 Stratofreighter was a transport version of the B-50 long-range bomber with a common wing, engine and tail assembly. SAC would use the YC-97A and C-97A in the 1st Strategic Support Squadron with the first deliveries taking place in 1948. The most important development of the Stratofreighter was the KC-97 tanker. The first production version was the KC-97E, 60 of which were built by Boeing. The first deliveries were made to SAC in July 1951 when the 306th Air Refueling Squadron at MacDill AFB received their first KC-97. A newer and more powerful version, the KC-97F, was first delivered to SAC in April 1952. Deployment within SAC was usually 20 tankers to each wing of 45 Boeing B-47 bombers. In all, 890 aircraft were ordered, 74 C-97s and 816 KC-97s. The KC-97 would be replaced by Boeing's KC-135 as SAC primary tanker beginning in the late 1950s.

MANUFACTURER: Boeing

TYPE: Cargo and Aerial Refueling

CHARACTERISTICS:

Span	141 feet 2 inches
Length	117 feet 5 inches
Height	38 feet 4 inches
Weight	153,000 pounds

PERFORMANCE:

Maximum speed	400 mph
Cruising speed	230 mph

The 305th BW received its first KC-97E tankers in 1952. The 305th ARS was one of the few KC-97 units to use tactical tail markings. The squadron color — green — was applied to the fin tip. KC-97E-BN-40 (51–191) is shown in its cargo configuration. (Boeing P12885. © Boeing. Used under license.)

Service ceiling	30,000 feet
Range	2,300 miles

ARMAMENT: None

Douglas C-124 "Globemaster II"

The C-124 Globemaster II heavy cargo transport was based on the earlier C-74 Globemaster I of which only 14 were built. The first operational C-124s went to SAC in July 1950 when C-124A (49–235) was assigned to the 2nd Strategic Support Squadron at Walker AFB. SAC would eventually equip four strategic support squadrons with C-124As and C-124Cs. These squadrons supported SAC's deployment operations and also was used to transport SAC's atomic weapons. The C-124s would continue in SAC service until the early 1960s when the strategic support squadrons were deactivated and the Globemasters transferred to other commands.

MANUFACTURER: Douglas
TYPE: Cargo

Another view of the first C-124A to arrive at Walker AFB being taxied to the ramp by Colonel Avery J. Ladd, Commanding Officer, 2nd Strategic Support Squadron, after landing on 17 July 1950. (USAF, AFHRA)

CHARACTERISTICS:

Span	174 feet
Length	130 feet
Height	48.3 feet
Weight	185,000 pounds max take-off
Crew	6

PERFORMANCE:

Maximum speed	295 mph at 22,600 feet
Cruising speed	191 mph
Service ceiling	23, 500 feet
Range	1,840 miles

ARMAMENT: None

4

Development of SAC
Aircraft Markings Policy

Strategic Air Command (SAC) aircraft markings during its early history have been difficult to trace for several reasons. At the time SAC was formed on 21 March 1946, the Army Air Forces were still trying to demobilize. Many of the B-29s assigned to SAC upon its activation were veterans of the bombing campaigns against Japan and retained markings from their World War II service, or were assigned to stateside units and carried large aircraft identification numbers, usually on the nose or tail. By November 1946, the only fully-manned bomber unit originally assigned to SAC was the 509th Bombardment Group (BG) at Roswell Field, New Mexico. The other bomb groups had either been deactivated or redesignated. During this time, a standardized aircraft marking policy was the least of SAC's worries. The constant transfer of aircraft from one organization to another and the lack of personnel and resources to spend on painting and marking aircraft initially caused SAC to de-emphasize "unnecessary markings" for its aircraft.[1]

The first SAC bomber unit to use an authorized tail marking was the 509th BG. Using its marking from World War II, a **Black Circle,** originally used to identify the 313th Bombardment Wing (BW) to which the 509th Composite Group (CG) was a subordinate group during World War II, with a **Black Arrow** inscribed, the 509th BG employed some variation of this tail marking until SAC issued a new marking policy on 26 October 1949. The 509th CG did use some specialized tail markings during its participation in Operation Crossroads to identify aircraft roles (**B** for bomb carriers, **F** for photo, and **W** for weather).[2] In 1947 the 509th BG started to paint the arrow within the circle in squadron color — yellow for the 393rd Bomb Squadron, green for the 715th Bomb Squadron and red for the 830th Bomb Squadron; the aircraft tail number was located on the dorsal fin. Later, in July 1947, the 509th BG started to place the aircraft tail number in a contrasting color inside the forward pointing arrow.[3]

Other than the 509th BG, no SAC bomber unit used tail markings during 1946 and early 1947 until the Eighth Air Force assigned geometric symbols as tail markings for its bombardment groups: the 7th BG located at Fort Worth Army Air Field (later Carswell Air Force Base) was assigned a **Black Triangle**; the 43rd BG located at Davis-Monthan Army Air Field (later Air Force Base) was assigned a **Black Diamond**; and the 2nd BG, reactivated in September 1947 and also located at Davis-Monthan, was assigned a **Black Square**. All aircraft of bomb groups assigned to the Fifteenth Air Force (28th BG, 92nd BG, 93rd BG, 97th BG, 98th BG and 301st BG) or directly to SAC Headquarters (307th BG), as well

Sandia, New Mexico, in early 1947. B-29-A-75-BN (44–62310) of the 64th Bombardment Squadron clearly shows the newly authorized and recently applied **Black Diamond** *tail marking with the radio call number centered inside the diamond. (San Diego Aerospace Museum)*

Wright-Patterson AAFld, 1946. TB-29–90-BW (45–21728) with a recruiting message painted on the aft fuselage. It was not uncommon to see this enlistment advertisement on AAF aircraft in 1946. What the triangle above the tail number represents is unknown. (National Museum of the USAF)

as the reconnaissance units of the 311th Reconnaissance Wing had plain tails with only the aircraft tail number painted on the vertical stabilizer as required by Technical Order 07–1-1 (Aircraft Camouflage, Markings, and Insignia). Some of the early Fifteenth Air Force bomb groups (the 28th BG and 97th BG) had a small Fifteenth Air Force insignia positioned below the aircraft tail number on the vertical stabilizer. The 307th BG started painting their group insignia on the top of the vertical stabilizer during the summer of 1947. The only other SAC bombardment group to use group insignia on the vertical fin was the 97th BG during the first part of 1947 before switching over to the small Fifteenth Air Force Insignia mentioned above.

In response to a SAC letter dated 26 September 1947 regarding the painting of aircraft, Fifteenth Air Force sent a message to SAC on 29 September 1947 outlining wing and

In the summer of 1947 the 28th Bombardment Group started to place a small Fifteenth Air Force insignia under the radio call number. B-29–60-BA (44–84096) is a 77th BS aircraft displaying the Fifteenth Air Force insignia during its deployment to Germany in the fall of 1947. (Boeing HS 5773. © Boeing. Used under license.)

group distinctive markings which would appear in the Fifteenth Air Force Very Heavy Bombardment (VHB) Tactical Doctrine then in preparation.[4] Aircraft markings outlined in the Fifteenth Air Force Tactical Doctrine were:

- 28th Bomb Group — **Black Triangle** with black letter **R** inscribed.
- 92nd Bomb Group — **Black Diamond** with black letter **W** inscribed.

Approaching Washington, D.C., these three B-29s from the 492nd BS of the 7th BG were part of a flight from Tokyo to Andrews AFB. The 492nd BS left Yokota AB on 2 August and covered 7,086 miles in 31 hours. (USAF B-33460 A.C.)

- 98th Bomb Group —**Black Diamond** with black letter **B** inscribed.
- 93rd Bomb Group —**Black Square** with letter **M** inscribed.
- 97th Bomb Group —**Black Triangle** with black letter **S** inscribed.
- 301st Bomb Group — black letter **C**

Al-Ask-Her, B-29–95-BW (45–21760), coming in for a landing at Castle AFB. Aircraft was assigned to the 328th BS and has a blue fin cap. Early 1949. (USAF, courtesy Castle Air Museum.)

The message further explained that the geometric figures would be the wing designation and the letters would be the group designation. Due to limited geometric figures available to use as aircraft tail markings, it was noted that the markings would be similar to those in use with the Eighth Air Force but a distinction would be made in group letter identification.

This policy still reflected the World War II organization of the wing as a tactical headquarters controlling several groups; however, in August through October 1947 the Hobson Plan went into effect making the wing headquarters, bearing the same numerical designation as the group, the highest level of command over all combat and combat support units on a base. SAC sent another letter on aircraft identification markings to the Fifteenth and Eighth Air Forces, as well as to the 307th Bomb Wing at MacDill AFB, Florida, on 3 November 1947. This letter proposed aircraft identification markings for SAC aircraft and stated the basic policy of SAC on the marking of aircraft:

> VHB aircraft of the air forces or wings will be identified by the geometric figure on the vertical fin, and the group in the air force or wing will be identified by the letter or numeral within the geometric figure.
>
> Because of the small number of suitable geometric figures available for aircraft identification, it will be necessary to use the geometric figures as air force or wing identification instead of group identification...
>
> Each VHB group will assign each aircraft within the group a two-digit numeral, approximately 3'6" high, and positioned approximately 14'6" forward of the leading edge of the horizontal stabilizer. This number will be used for local identification.
>
> Lead crew VHB aircraft for all groups will be identified by a belly band similar to that presently used as group identification in the 43rd Bomb Group.
>
> Squadron identification in all VHB groups will be the colored tail tip as indicated in the attached drawings.
>
> No other identification on VHB aircraft will be used. Group and squadron insignia will be painted on the aircraft at discretion of air force or wing commander.
>
> Fighter groups will be identified by the colored nose and vertical fin. Squadrons, within a group, will be identified by the colored wing tips and horizontal fins.
>
> Fighter group leaders will be identified by 3 stripes around the fuselage; squadron leaders will have 2 stripes and flight leaders will have one stripe.[5]

The staffing of this proposal and the feedback provided by the major subordinate commands ultimately resulted in approved markings which started to appear on Fifteenth Air Force and the 307th BW aircraft in early 1948, while the Eighth Air Force continued to use their earlier geometric symbols. These markings were listed in the Eighth Air Force and Fifteenth Air Force Tactical Doctrines and eventually appeared in SAC Manual 55–300–1 Tactical Doctrine, dated August 1948. (See Figures 1 and 2.)

By the time SAC Manual 55–300–1 was printed in August 1948, some of the information concerning aircraft markings was already out of date. For example, the 301st BW never used a black C as a tail marking but was assigned a **Black Triangle** with a black **V**. This marking started to appear on 301st BW B-29s in March and April 1948. Giving the 301st BW a **Black Triangle** as a tail marking and the letter **V** to the 301st BG brought the 301st BW in line with the Fifteenth Air Force aircraft marking policy of assigning bomb wings an appropriate geometric symbol and their bomb groups a letter. Following this policy the 22nd BW, which was assigned to SAC in May 1948 and shared a common wing commander with the 301st at Smoky Hill AFB, Kansas, used a **Black Triangle** with a black letter **I** inscribed as its tail marking.

There was one error on the 307th BW aircraft marking plate in SAC Manual 55–300–1. An Eighth Air Force patch appears on the dorsal fin of a 307th B-29. In fact, the 307th BW was assigned to the Fifteenth Air Force on 16 December 1948 ending nearly two years of being under the direct command of SAC Headquarters.

SAC's 1948 Tactical Doctrine Manual did not show tail insignia for two of its bomber wings: the 22nd BW which had recently transferred to SAC from the Far East Air Forces, and the 97th BW which had changed jurisdiction from the Fifteenth Air Force to the Eighth Air Force and still did not have an approved tail marking.

Although SAC had approved the tail markings being used by the Eighth and Fifteenth Air Forces, the actual markings did not reflect a standardized marking policy employed throughout SAC. This lack of standardization was being studied when a newly assigned bomber unit, the 306th BG at MacDill AFB, requested approval of a tail marking in December 1948.[6] Initially disapproved by Fifteenth Air Force as not consistent with command policy in using a geometric design for wings (the 306th BG was assigned to the 307th Bomb

*A 33rd BS B-29A-65-BN (44–62160) on the ramp at March AFB with the 22nd BG's first assigned tail marking — **Triangle I**. The fin tip is in the 33rd BS color — yellow. The 22nd BG transferred to March AFB in May 1949. (USAF)*

Approved SAC Tail Markings
Eighth Air Force 1948
Figure 1

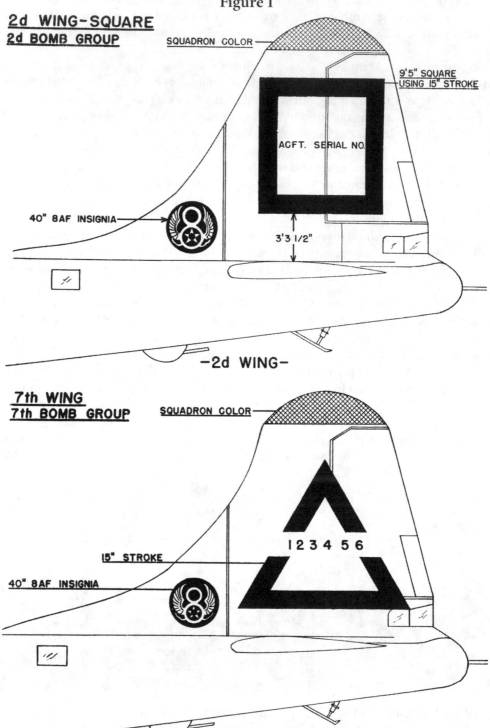

Approved SAC Tail Markings
Eighth Air Force 1948
Figure 1 (cont.)

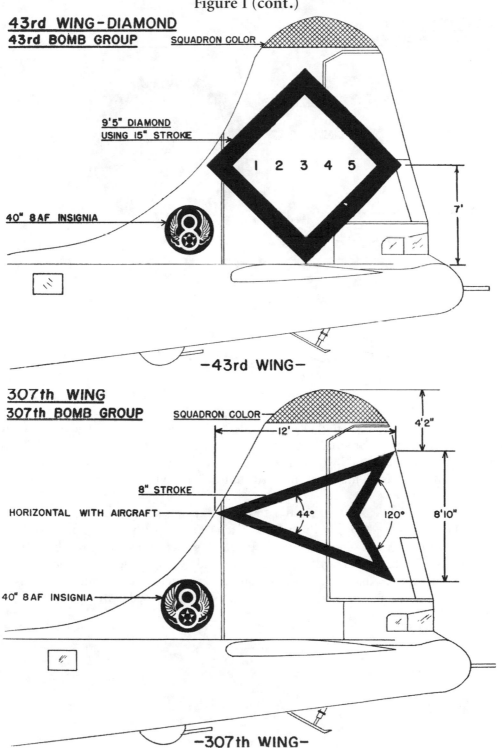

43rd WING - DIAMOND
43rd BOMB GROUP

SQUADRON COLOR

9'5" DIAMOND
USING 15" STROKE

1 2 3 4 5

40" 8AF INSIGNIA

7'

—43rd WING—

307th WING
307th BOMB GROUP

SQUADRON COLOR

12'

4'2"

8" STROKE

HORIZONTAL WITH AIRCRAFT

44°

120°

8'10"

40" 8AF INSIGNIA

—307th WING—

Approved SAC Tail Markings
Eighth Air Force 1948
Figure 1 (cont.)

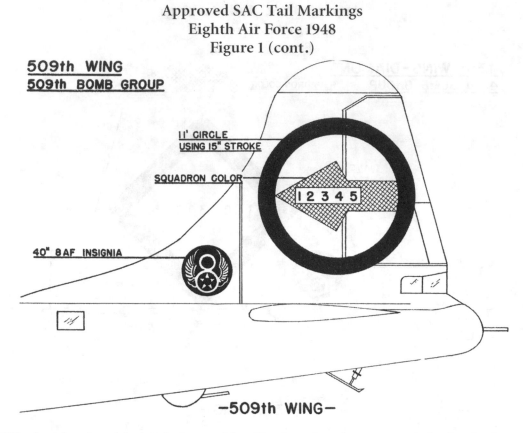

509th WING
509th BOMB GROUP

11' CIRCLE
USING 15" STROKE

SQUADRON COLOR

1 2 3 4 5

40" 8 AF INSIGNIA

—509th WING—

Wing) and assigned letters for group identification, the request was resubmitted using a Fifteenth Air Force proposed design on 14 March 1949. SAC Headquarters answered the 306th BG's request on 2 April 1949 and stated, "All Strategic Air Command aircraft markings and identifications are under consideration. In the near future the new SAC Tactical Doctrine will be published, including all approved aircraft markings."[7] The final result for the 306th BG was no tail marking until SAC finished its review and published its new tactical doctrine.

On 15 June 1949, SAC sent a letter to its three major subordinate commands (these included the 311th Air Division which was created from the 311th Recon Wing) on the subject of aircraft markings. The letter stated that SAC's Tactical Doctrine was being revised and that SAC desired a standard marking be utilized. The letter forwarded proposed aircraft markings for SAC tactical units and requested comments and recommendations from the subordinate commands as soon as possible.[8] SAC's proposed markings were:

Eighth AF—Triangle	*Fifteenth AF—Circle*	*311th Air Div—Square*
43 BW — N	93 BW — M	55 SRW — X
2 BW — Z	92 BW — O	91 SRW — F
509 BW — H	98 BW — P	
9 BW — I	301 BW — A	
7 BW — V	22 BW — E	
11 BG — R	28 BW — K	
	307 BW — T	
	306 BW — S	

Approved SAC Tail Markings
Fifteenth Air Force 1948
Figure 2

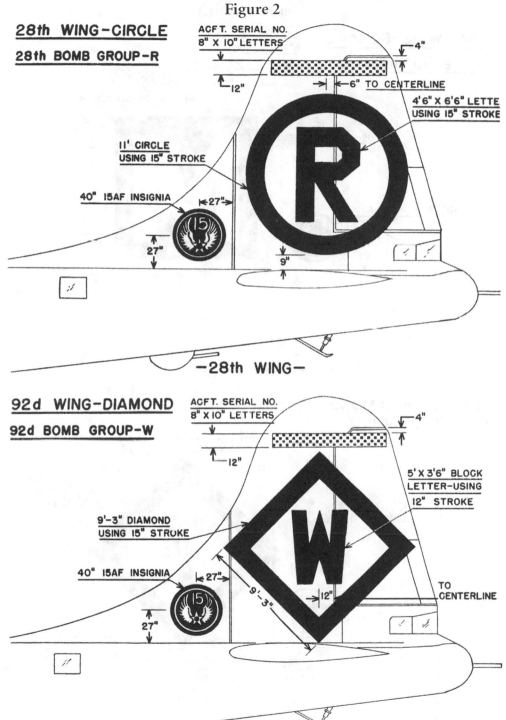

Approved SAC Tail Markings
Fifteenth Air Force 1948
Figure 2 (cont.)

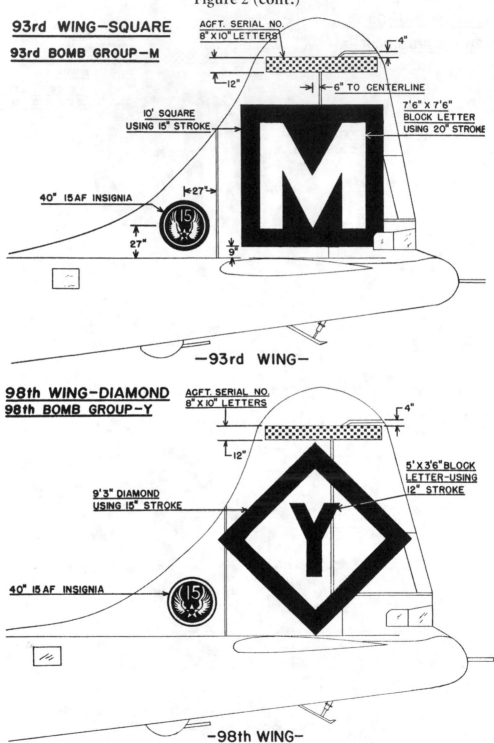

93rd WING—SQUARE

93rd BOMB GROUP—M

ACFT. SERIAL NO.
8" X 10" LETTERS

4"

12"

6" TO CENTERLINE

10' SQUARE
USING 15" STROKE

7'6" X 7'6"
BLOCK LETTER
USING 20" STROKE

40" 15 AF INSIGNIA

27"

27"

9"

—93rd WING—

98th WING—DIAMOND
98th BOMB GROUP—Y

ACFT. SERIAL NO.
8" X 10" LETTERS

4"

12"

9'3" DIAMOND
USING 15" STROKE

5' X 3'6" BLOCK
LETTER—USING
12" STROKE

40" 15 AF INSIGNIA

—98th WING—

Approved SAC Tail Markings
Fifteenth Air Force 1948
Figure 2 (cont.)

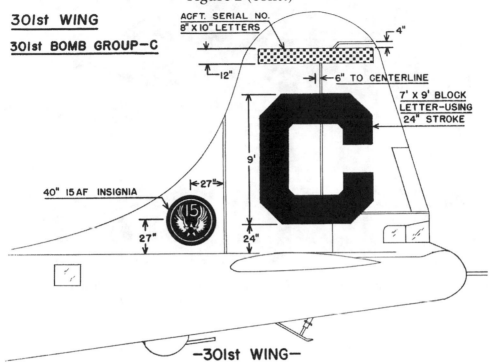

301st WING

301st BOMB GROUP—C

ACFT. SERIAL NO.
8" X 10" LETTERS

4"

12"

6" TO CENTERLINE

7' X 9' BLOCK
LETTER—USING
24" STROKE

9'

40" 15 AF INSIGNIA

27"

27"

24"

—301st WING—

Sometimes markings can be confusing. B-29B-40-BA (42–63577) assigned to Wright-Patterson AFB in 1948 retains markings from previous service with two bombardment groups. The **Circle and Arrow** *tail marking was left over from its service with the 509th BG until Aug 1947 when the aircraft was sent to the 93rd BG at Castle AFB. The red fin cap and small squadron insignia on the nose is from its service with the 329th BS at Castle AFB from August 1947 to April 1948. (Photograph by Krieger, courtesy P. Stevens)*

This "plain tail" 7th BW B-36B-15-CF (44-92078) displays its Wing insignia on the nose and Eighth Air Force emblem on the dorsal fin during a test flight on 19 November 1949 at Carswell AFB. (USAF)

The Fifteenth Air Force provided a response to the SAC letter on 24 June 1949.[9] They concurred with the proposed geometric design for the Fifteenth (**Black Circle**) and recommended that the subordinate commands be assigned a consecutive block of letters to be used for wing identification. Specifically, they recommended the following scheme: Fifteenth Air Force — Letters **A** through **J**; Eighth Air Force — Letters **K** through **T**; 311th Air Division — Letters **U** through **Z**.

The Fifteenth Air Force believed this assignment of letters would provide markings for all units currently assigned, allow a reserve for future changes, and provide a simple and systematic method of identifying unit aircraft.

The Eighth Air Force routed the letter to its assigned wings (2nd BW, 43rd BW, 97th BW, 509th BW and 7th BW) for comment and provided a response to SAC on 14 September 1949.[10] The Eighth Air Force units agreed with assigning a **Black Equilateral Triangle** as an Air Force marking but made a recommendation that angular letters be avoided to ensure harmony of composition and clarity of marking. Consequently, they requested that an **S** be adopted as the designator for the 2nd BW in exchange with the 306th BG of the Fifteenth Air Force giving the 306th the letter **Z**. In addition, Eighth Air Force provided comment on the size and dimensions of proposed markings for different types of aircraft, and in some instances subordinate units requested that old markings be retained until new aircraft were received.

The 311th Air Division responded to SAC's proposal on 24 June 1949.[11] The 311th AD recommended that the division marking be an inverted triangle since this marking would be easily identifiable from markings on other SAC aircraft. They also recommended that reconnaissance aircraft not be marked too distinctively for security reasons. The 311th AD also proposed markings for its subordinate strategic reconnaissance wings (SRW): 5th

*A varied display of SAC aircraft markings to include the **Diamond** for the 43rd BW and two different markings for the 301st BW — the older **Triangle V** and the newly assigned **Circle A**. In the foreground is the Convair XC-99-CO (43–52436). Kelly AFB, 1950. (USAF)*

SRW —**P** (Photography); 9th SRW —**R** (Reconnaissance); 55th SRW —**T** (Triangulation); and the 91st SRW —**M** (Mapping).

On 26 October, SAC announced its new tactical aircraft markings and forwarded advance copies of the markings to the major subordinate commands. Eighth and Fifteenth Air Force markings were approved. Second Air Force (311th Air Division was redesignated Second Air Force on 4 November 1949) markings were still proposed since they hadn't received formal approval yet from SAC Headquarters.[12]

Strategic Air Command appeared to have accepted the Eighth Air Force recommendation on not using angular letters with the equilateral triangle since none of the approved markings match those markings proposed in June 1949. SAC did not accept Fifteenth Air Force's proposal to assign blocks of letters to the major subordinate commands nor did it accept the 311th Air Division's (later Second Air Force) proposal for an inverted triangle tail marking. Although the 55th SRW was recommended for a tail marking in June 1949, it did not appear on SAC's October 1949 list of proposed markings because it was deactivated on 14 October 1949. SAC did accept the 311th Air Division's recommendation for the letter assignment for the 5th SRW and 9th SRW, **P** and **R** respectively.

These markings were significant in

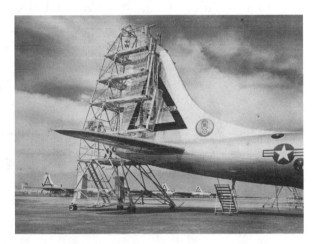

*When SAC established a standard policy for tail markings in October 1949, the 7th BS was assigned a new tail marking — **Triangle J**. This photograph shows several 7th BW B-36s already displaying the new tail marking and B-36B-10-CF (44–92063) of the 436th BS having the new marking applied. Carswell AFB in early 1950. (USAF)*

that they represented a standard marking policy (geometric symbol for the air force; letter designator for the wing) that would last until SAC eliminated tail markings in 1953. These markings also reflected the use of the wing as the primary combat organization in SAC and the decline of the group as a combat unit eventually resulting in all combat groups being deactivated in 1952. Squadron color assignments and the use of wing and squadron insignia on assigned aircraft continued to be left to the discretion of the wing commander. (See Figures 3 and 4.)

Due to SAC's reorganization on 1 April 1950, many of the markings approved by SAC in late 1949 were never fully implemented. This was particularly true of wings that were reassigned to another numbered air force. For example, the 28th BW at Rapid City, South Dakota had 11 of 16 assigned B-29s painted with the **Circle K** marking when SAC transferred the 28th to the Eighth Air Force and a new tail marking, **Triangle S**, was assigned.[13] The 43rd BW never adopted the **Triangle D** marking prior to being assigned to the Fifteenth Air Force, probably due to its temporary duty (TDY) in the UK from August to November 1949. Also there is no documentation or photo evidence that the 306th BW ever used its tail marking—**Circle H**—while assigned to the Fifteenth Air Force. Within the Second Air Force, there is no evidence of the 91st SRW using **Square X** as its tail marking.

Prior to 1 April 1950, each numbered air force had a particular orientation: the Eighth Air Force had medium and heavy bombardment units; the Fifteenth Air Force had only medium bombardment units; and the Second Air Force possessed strategic reconnaissance units. With the reorganization that went into effect, each air force was assigned units by geographical region — the Second Air Force was in the Eastern part of the U.S., the Eighth Air Force covered the Central region, and the Fifteenth Air Force was in the West.[14]

The two air forces most affected by the changes were the Second and Fifteenth. The Second lost two wings to the Fifteenth: the 5th SRW and 9th SRW. It picked up three wings from the Fifteenth: the 301st BW, 306th BW, and 307th BW, as well as one wing from the

*The **Circle K** tail marking was assigned to the 28th BW in late 1949 and was painted on only 11 B-29s before the 28th was notified of its transfer to the Eighth Air Force effective 1 April 1950. Photograph taken at Travis AFB during Armed Forces Day, 20 May 1950, shows a recently transferred 28th BW B-29 with the rare **Circle K** tail marking. The other B-29 shows **Square R** (Arctic marked tail and outer wings), the 9th SRW tail marking from November 1949 to April 1950. (Courtesy W. Larkins)*

Approved SAC Tail Insignia
26 October 1949
Figure 3

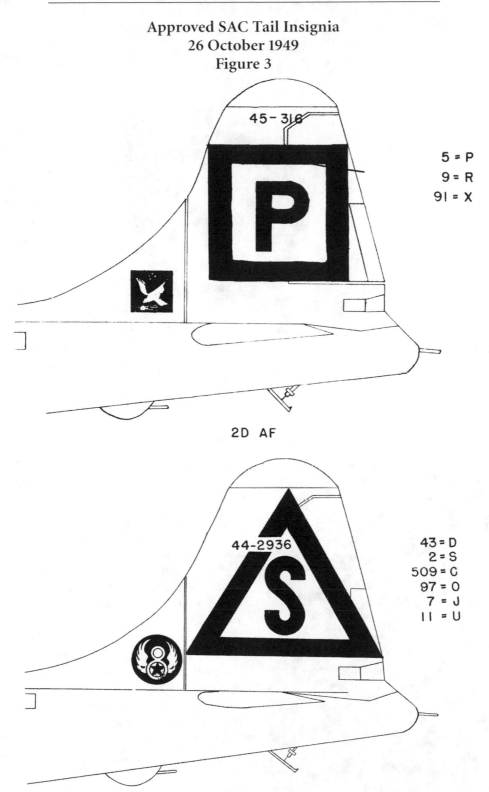

5 = P
9 = R
91 = X

2D AF

43 = D
2 = S
509 = C
97 = O
7 = J
11 = U

8TH AF

**Approved SAC Tail Insignia
26 October 1949
Figure 3 (cont.)**

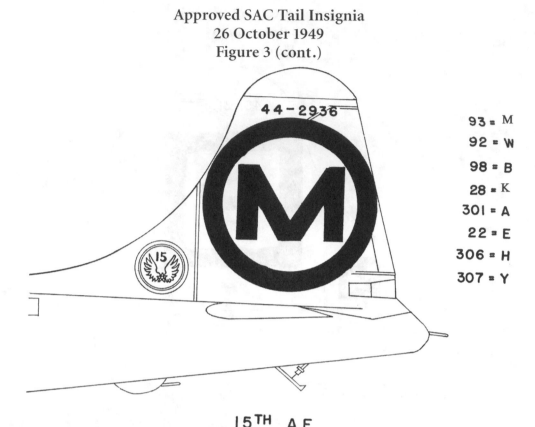

93	M
92	W
98	B
28	K
301	A
22	E
306	H
307	Y

15TH AF

Eighth — the 2nd BW. In addition to the two wings received from the Second, the Fifteenth also received one wing from the Eighth — the 43rd BW. Besides the losses already mentioned, the Eighth received one wing from the Fifteenth — the 28th BW.

SAC published a new Tactical Doctrine Manual, SAC Manual 55–1, dated April 1950, which contained new tactical aircraft markings for the Second, Eighth, and Fifteenth Air Forces.

By the summer of 1950, most of SAC's tactical units were displaying their new tail markings. However, the transition to the new markings had not been trouble free. Shortly after the new markings were announced, the 98th BW sent a letter to Fifteenth Air Force

Approved on 9 November 1951, the squadron insignia for the 342nd Bomb Squadron is proudly displayed on the right side of a B-50D. Biggs AFB, 1952. (USAF, AFHRA)

SAC Tail Insignia in SAC Manual 55-1,
Tactical Doctrine — Bombardment, April 1950
Figure 4

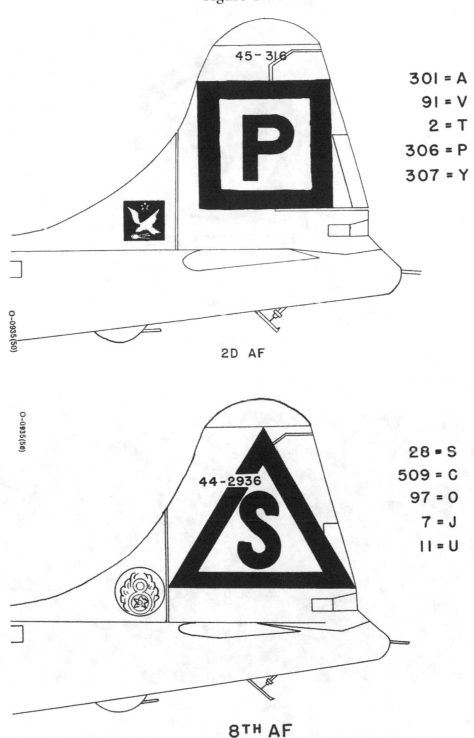

301 = A
91 = V
2 = T
306 = P
307 = Y

2D AF

28 = S
509 = C
97 = O
7 = J
II = U

8TH AF

SAC Tail Insignia in SAC Manual 55-1,
Tactical Doctrine — Bombardment, April 1950
Figure 4 (cont.)

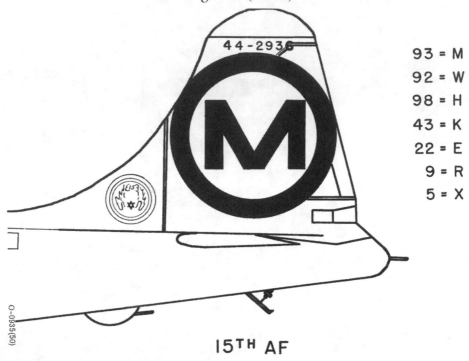

44-2936

93 = M
92 = W
98 = H
43 = K
22 = E
9 = R
5 = X

O-0935(50)

15TH AF

*Spokane AFB. 98th BG markings in transition with one B-29 showing the **Diamond Y** on the tail — first authorized in February 1948 — and the other B-29 with the **Circle B** tail marking used for just a few months in early 1950. (98th BG/BW Association)*

One of the first SAC bomb units called to action for Korea was the 22nd BW at March AFB. Displaying its new **Circle E** *tail marking and 22nd BW insignia, this B-29 taxis to its take off position for the long flight to the Far East, July 1950. (USAF)*

requesting exemption from compliance with Fifteenth Air Force letter dated 3 April 1950 which implemented SAC's new tail markings and, in this case, required the 98th BW to change its tactical markings to **Circle H**. The reasons for requesting the exception to policy were: (1) 80 percent of the 98th BW's B-29s were marked with **Circle B** as required by Fifteenth Air Force letter dated 8 December 1949; (2) the 98th BW anticipated moving to the jurisdiction of the Second Air Force which would require completely new markings on aircraft; (3) to save man-hours and materials. Pending the outcome of their request, the 98th intended to remove the **Diamond Y** marking (this marking had been approved for the 98th in early 1948) on remaining aircraft and leave the vertical stabilizer clear.[15] Interestingly enough, the 98th at this time had aircraft marked with both **Diamond Y** and **Circle B** tail markings, had a tail marking change to **Circle H** required by the newly published SAC Tactical Doctrine, and was facing reassignment to the Second Air Force which would require new tail markings. It is no wonder that this time period is confusing for understanding aircraft markings.

The outbreak of war in Korea in June 1950 would affect SAC in several ways. Responding to an emergency request from the Far Eastern Command (FEC), SAC sent several B-29 units to assist the only Far East Air Forces (FEAF) B-29 group, the 19th BG. The first SAC units to deploy to the Far East were the 22nd BG from March AFB, California, and the 98th BG from Spokane AFB, Washington. The 22nd BG arrived at Kadena Field, Okinawa, in early July and flew its first mission on 12 July 1950. The 98th BG, staging from Yokota AB, Japan, also flew its first mission on 12 July. Two more SAC bomber units were sent to help turn back the North Korean advance into South Korea: the 92nd BG joined its sister group from Spokane at Yokota and the 307th BG from MacDill AFB, joined the 22nd BG at Kadena. Both the 92nd and 307th Bomb Groups started flying bombing missions in August 1950. Another SAC unit, the 31st Strategic Reconnaissance Squadron, assigned to SAC's 5th SRW at Fairfield-Suisun AFB, California, and attached to FEAF for operations, supported the bomb groups and used the **Circle X** tail marking of its parent wing.[16]

Since the SAC units were only attached and not assigned to the Far East Air Forces for operations, the tail markings were unchanged and still reflected air force assignment and letter designator for the wing. However, the 98th BG found itself in an unusual situation with its **Square H** tail marking during its involvement in the early days of the Korean conflict. Some have thought the **Square H** represented a FEAF marking or an individual wing marking. In fact, the 98th BW had been transferred to the jurisdiction of the Second Air Force on 17 May 1950, and was scheduled to deploy to Ramey AFB, Puerto Rico, during the summer of 1950. In anticipation of this move to Ramey and the Second Air Force, the 98th BW applied its new marking, **Square H**, in May and June 1950 and continued to use these markings through 1950 and part of 1951, even though the 98th BW had been transferred back to the Fifteenth Air Force on 28 July 1950. As time and resources permitted, the correct **Circle H** marking was applied to all of the 98th BW Superfortresses.

With increased tensions in the world, SAC's order of battle began to grow and new bomb wings were established. Most of these new units were equipped with B-29s taken from storage. By the middle of 1951, SAC had reactivated five bomb wings: the 6th at Walker AFB, New Mexico; the 44th initially at March AFB, then Lake Charles AFB, Louisiana; the 90th at Forbes AFB, Kansas; the 305th at MacDill AFB; and the 376th at Barksdale AFB, Louisiana. With more units coming into the inventory, SAC decided it was necessary to revise its tac-

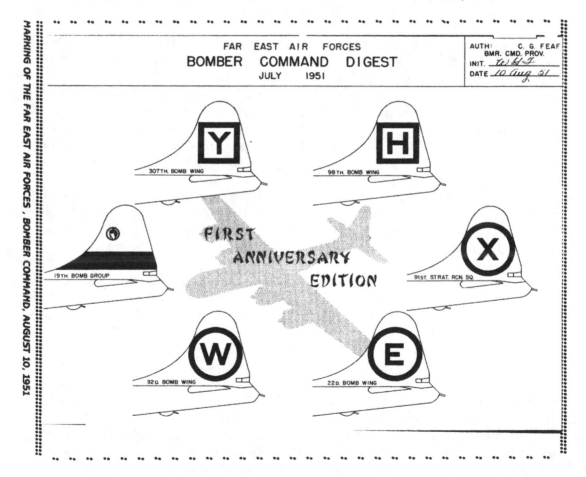

The first anniversary edition of the Far East Air Forces Bomber Command Digest *dated July 1951 shows the tail markings used by various B-29 units during the first year of the Korean War. (USAF, courtesy Travis Air Museum)*

The outbreak of war in Korea caused SAC to send several units to the UK to reinforce United States forces in Europe. Here, B-50D-105-BO (48–116) of the 328th BS, 93rd BW gets ready to depart Castle AFB for duty in the UK. (USAF 39932 A.C.)

tical doctrine manual and update the plates assigning aircraft tail markings. (The revised markings appeared in Plates Q, R, and S to SAC Manual 55–1, dated May 1951, and are displayed in Figure 5.) Before the updates to the tactical doctrine manual were published, the newly activated wings were informed by message or letter on their new tail marking assignment.

In March 1951 SAC announced a change to policy on marking the aircraft serial number on the vertical stabilizer of assigned aircraft. Based on the experience of SAC B-29 combat operations in Korea, it was deemed impractical to have any part of the serial number painted on the rudder control surfaces due to frequent rudder changes. As stated in SAC letter dated 19 March 1951, subject: Tactical Aircraft Markings, SAC directed "...that all future numbering of assigned tactical aircraft be as prescribed by Technical Order Number 07–1–1. Subject Technical Order requires the deletion of the first number of the serial number and the Hyphen (-) with numbers being shown in a group of not less than four numbers. Numbers will not be smaller than 8 inches by 12 inches and evenly placed in the area prescribed.... Future numbering or re-numbering of aircraft will make every attempt to comply with subject Technical Order and prevent placing serial numbers on the rudder control surfaces."[17]

The next set of changes to Plates Q, R, and S would appear in Change 3 to SAC Manual 55–1, May 1951, which was published on 29 January 1952 and included markings for additional units that had been reactivated since the middle of 1951. These units included: the 68th SRW at Lake Charles AFB, the 72nd SRW at Ramey AFB, the 106th BW (later redesignated 320th BW) at March AFB, the 111th SRW (later redesignated 99th SRW) at Fairchild AFB, and the 303rd BW at Davis-Monthan AFB. (See Figures 5 and 6.)

Although most of the changes to these plates represented tail markings for new units, there were some changes from the previous manual for older units such as the 6th BW which was assigned **Triangle R**; the transfer of the 44th BW from the Fifteenth Air Force to the Second Air Force; and the reassignment of **Circle T** to the 303rd BW. The 44th would eventually use **Square K** after its transfer to Lake Charles AFB and eventually to the Second Air Force. Both the 90th BW at Forbes AFB and the 44th at Lake Charles AFB were

SAC Tail Insignia in SAC Manual 55-1,
Tactical Doctrine — Bombardment, May 1951
Figure 5

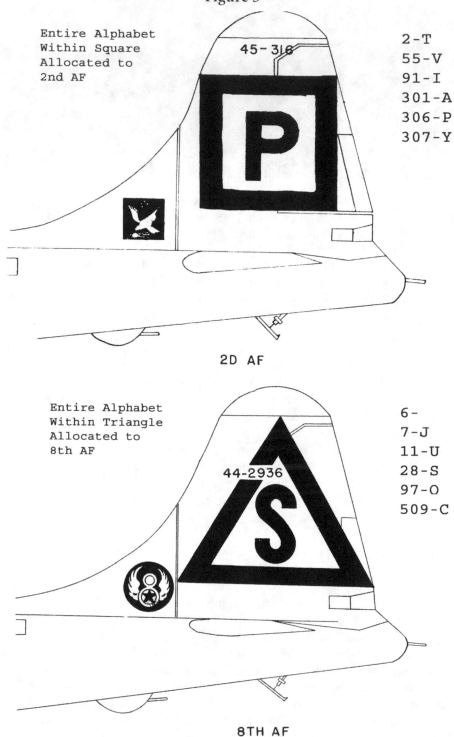

Entire Alphabet
Within Square
Allocated to
2nd AF

2-T
55-V
91-I
301-A
306-P
307-Y

45-316

P

2D AF

Entire Alphabet
Within Triangle
Allocated to
8th AF

6-
7-J
11-U
28-S
97-O
509-C

44-2936

S

8TH AF

SAC Tail Insignia in SAC Manual 55-1, Tactical Doctrine — Bombardment, May 1951
Figure 5 (cont.)

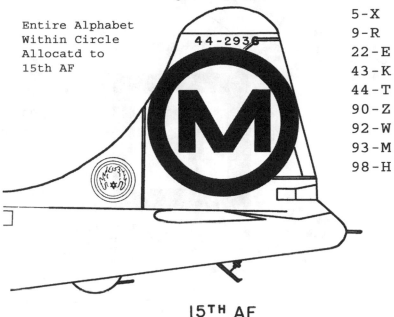

Entire Alphabet
Within Circle
Allocatd to
15th AF

44-2936

5	X
9	R
22	E
43	K
44	T
90	Z
92	W
93	M
98	H

15ᵀᴴ AF

Operational Training Units (OTU) with the mission of providing the final phase of training for combat replacement crews, operational training for newly activated medium bombardment wings, and to supervise the SAC instructor training program. Both wings were assigned to the 21st Air Division which had the status of a major subordinate command and reported directly to Headquarters, SAC. This relationship lasted until 16 July 1952 when the 90th SRW (redesignated from BW) was assigned to the Fifteenth Air Force and the 44th BW was assigned to the Second Air Force.[18] During the OTU phase, the 90th and 44th did not use a tactical tail marking. After their transfer to the Fifteenth and Second Air Forces respectively the 90th used the **Circle Z** marking and the 44th the **Square K**. It should also be pointed out that Plate R in change 3 shows the letter R being assigned to both the 6th BW and the 307th Air Refueling Squadron (ARS). This would seem to be inconsistent, except that the 307th ARS was attached to the 6th BW at Walker AFB and used the same tail marking.

A 23rd SRS RB-36F-1-CF (49–2704) undergoes a tail cleaning. Fin tip is blue. (USAF photograph, courtesy Brig. Gen. Don Stout)

SAC Tail Insignia in SAC Manual 55-1,
Tactical Doctrine — Bombardment, Change 1, 29 Jan 1952
Figure 6

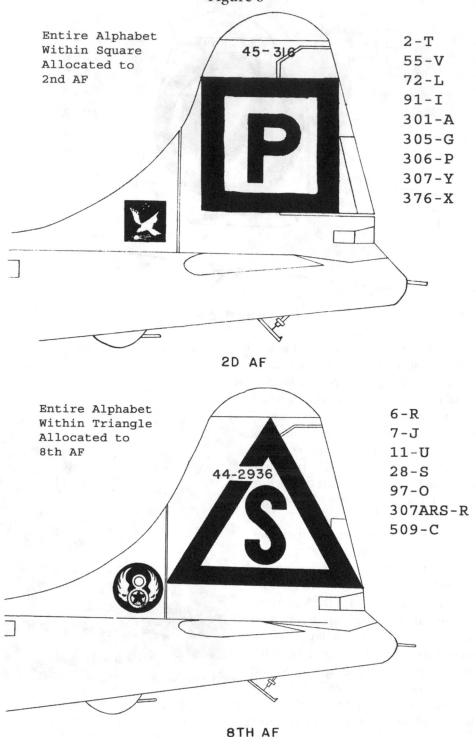

Entire Alphabet
Within Square
Allocated to
2nd AF

45-316

2-T
55-V
72-L
91-I
301-A
305-G
306-P
307-Y
376-X

P

2D AF

Entire Alphabet
Within Triangle
Allocated to
8th AF

44-2936

6-R
7-J
11-U
28-S
97-O
307ARS-R
509-C

S

8TH AF

SAC Tail Insignia in SAC Manual 55-1, Tactical Doctrine — Bombardment, Change 1, 29 Jan 1952 Figure 6 (cont.)

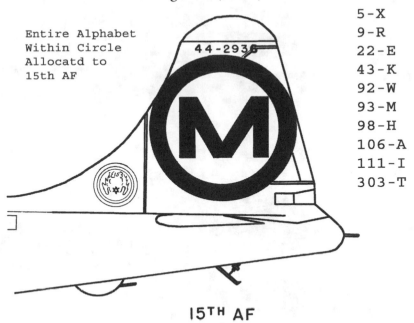

Entire Alphabet
Within Circle
Allocatd to
15th AF

44-2936

5	X
9	R
22	E
43	K
92	W
93	M
98	H
106	A
111	I
303	T

15ᵀᴴ AF

The introduction of the B-47 into SAC's combat fleet by the 306th BW at MacDill AFB in 1951 caused a small problem for the 306th BW with marking their B-47s with its assigned tail marking—**Square P**. The problem was caused by the smaller vertical stabilizer of the B-47 compared to those of B-29s, B-50s and B-36s for which dimensions for the tail marking had been published. As stated in a 6th Air Division letter to Headquarters, Second Air Force dated 4 March 1952, "Considerable difficulty is being experienced in attempting to comply with existing directives.... In addition to the markings shown, a twelve inch strip in Squadron color is usually painted along the top of the horizontal stabilizer, but on B-47 aircraft the antenna is installed in that location, and would necessitate the re-location of aircraft serial number."[19] The Second Air Force would request

*The **Circle A** tail marking was assigned to the 106th BW on 2 June 1951. This photograph of B-29A-60-BN (44-62021) shows its crew preparing for an ORI inspection at March AFB — August 1952. (USAF–AFHRA)*

Lake Charles AFB flightline— Armed Forces Day, May 1952. The two B-29s with insignia on the nose are from the 66th Bombardment Squadron. (USAF)

308th BW B-29 shows the "Box" O on the vertical tail as well as a four-digit tail number on the vertical stabilizer. The red band around the fuselage was a temporary marking for Exercise "Signpost" conducted in July 1952 which was a joint maneuver of USAF and RCAF forces. (USAF, AFHRA)

authority from SAC to reduce the tail marking size to the maximum size the vertical stabilizer surface area would permit and would mention that the 91st SRW had already received permission to reduce the size of the tail marking to conform to the area available on the RB-45C and B-45A aircraft.[20] In an endorsement dated 21 May 1952 to the 6th Air Division original letter, SAC granted approval to the Second Air Force recommended specifications for a

RB-36D-10-CF (49–2690) taking off from Rapid City AFB during the summer of 1951. Nose gear doors and main wheel doors as well as fin cap are in the 77th SRS color — blue. (USAF)

reduced tail marking for B-47 aircraft and stated that the new specifications would be incorporated in the next revision of SAC Manual 55–1.[21]

Several more SAC wings would make their debut in 1952 and receive tail markings: the 40th BW (**Circle S**) at Smoky Hill AFB; the 72nd SRW (**Square L**- later revised to **Square F**) at Ramey AFB, Puerto Rico; the 310th BW (**Circle B**) at Smoky Hill AFB; and the 308th BW (**Square O**) at Hunter AFB, Georgia. Although additional SAC bomber wings were activated during the year, namely the 95th BW at Biggs AFB, Texas, and the 340th BW at Sedalia AFB, Missouri, these units were initially minimally manned "paper units" and were never assigned tail markings.

Some organizational changes within SAC affected tail markings during 1952 and early 1953. In October 1952, the 55th SRW was transferred to the Fifteenth Air Force from the Second Air Force and changed its tail marking from **Square V** to **Circle V**. The replacement of the 106th BW at March AFB with the 320th BW in December 1952 resulted in

The Castle AFB flightline during the Fox Peter Two deployment of the 27th FEW to Misawa AB, Japan, in October 1952. In the background are KB-29Ps of the 93rd and 91st Air Refueling Squadrons. The B-50Ds in the foreground belong to the 330th BS. Squadron color appearing on the fin cap is yellow. October 5, 1952. (Boeing P12908. © Boeing. Used under license.)

Armed Forces Day 1953. Remnants of 305th BW tail markings can be seen on the T-33, KC-97 and B-47s in the background. (USAF, AFHRA)

the 320th receiving the **Circle A** tail marking from the 106th. The same thing happened in January 1953 when the 111th SRW was replaced by the 99th SRW and the **Circle I** tail marking was taken over by the 99th. Also, 1952 marked the first appearance of the SAC command insignia on tactical aircraft. In March 1952, the 55th SRW at Ramey AFB, started to display the SAC emblem on the right side of the nose on its RB-50s.

In November 1952 SAC sent a letter to Second, Eighth and Fifteenth air forces on the subject of a standard SAC insignia aircraft marking. The letter stated, "It is planned to make a standard and uniform installation of the SAC insignia on all aircraft assigned this command. Wherever possible, we propose to locate the insignia as shown on the attached drawings. It is proposed that the SAC insignia be placed on the left side of the aircraft nose section and the organizational insignia be placed on the right side of the nose section. It is intended that both insignia be superimposed on a diagonal blue strip impregnated with stars.... Since the above outlined plan may result in some conflict with the present placement of command, wing and squadron insignia, your comments and recommendations are solicited before a final decision on placement is made."[22]

The Fifteenth Air Force provided feedback to SAC on 26 November 1952 where it stated, "The proposal to make a standard and uniform installation of the SAC insignia on all assigned aircraft is concurred by this headquarters. There are no objections to the proposed locations. It is anticipated, however, that some units may desire to place their squadron insignia on the left side of the aircraft in addition to the SAC insignia. It is suggested that this possibility be considered."[23] The responses from Second and Eighth air forces to SAC on this subject are unknown. (See Figure 7.)

By early 1953, SAC had decided that high-visibility markings, including tail codes, were no longer necessary. A changeover to tactics that emphasized small "cells" to deliver nuclear weapons, together with a much greater emphasis on security, made it undesirable to advertise unit identity. In April 1953, SAC published a new SAC Manual 55–1 which eliminated any reference to tail markings for the Second, Eighth, and Fifteenth air forces. Some markings lingered on in the units through the spring, but by early summer all of the tail

*A 369th BS B-47B-45-BW (51–2277) shown during Armed Forces Day at MacDill AFB in May 1953 with a clean vertical tail showing the remnants of the **Square P** tail marking. (USAF, AFHRA)*

SAC Command Insignia Placement Proposal, 1952
Figure 7

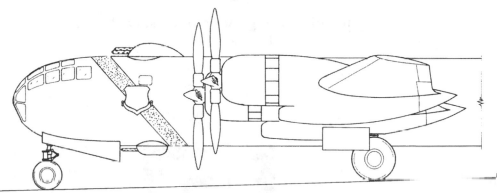

B-50 - B-29

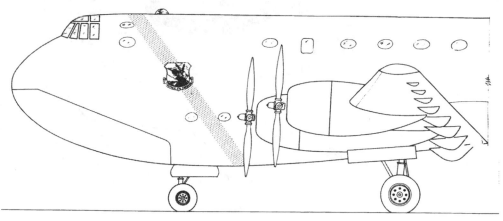

C-124

SAC Command Insignia Placement Proposal, 1952
Figure 7 (cont.)

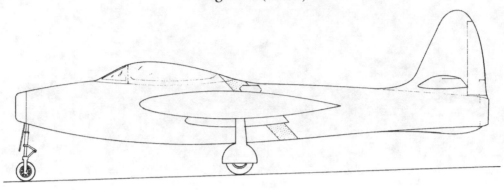

F-84

markings were gone. The only distinguishing marks remaining were squadron color markings and in some cases a wing or squadron badge which would soon give way to the SAC command insignia. (See Figure 8.)

SAC's Final Tail Markings Assignments, 1952–1953
Figure 8

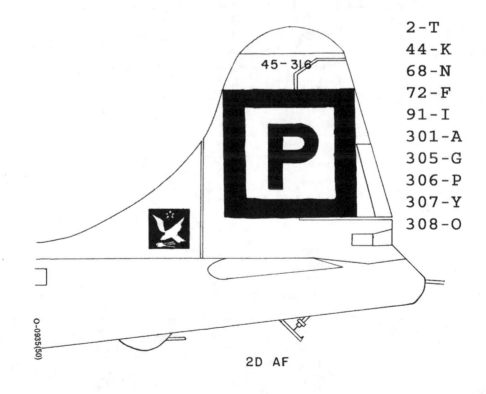

2-T
44-K
68-N
72-F
91-I
301-A
305-G
306-P
307-Y
308-O

2D AF

SAC's Final Tail Markings Assignments, 1952–1953
Figure 8 (cont.)

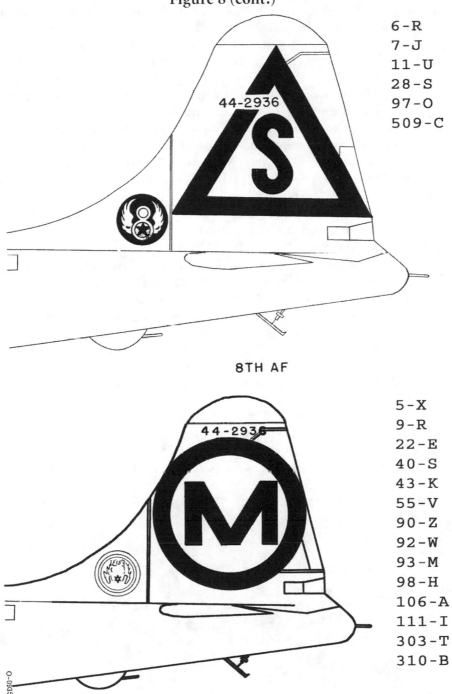

6-R
7-J
11-U
28-S
97-O
509-C

8TH AF

5-X
9-R
22-E
40-S
43-K
55-V
90-Z
92-W
93-M
98-H
106-A
111-I
303-T
310-B

15TH AF

O-0935(50)

Strategic Air Command Fighter Aircraft

From the beginning of Strategic Air Command in 1946, fighter aircraft were part of its force structure. The mission initially assigned to SAC's fighter fleet of veteran World War II–era P-51 Mustangs and P-47N Thunderbolts was fighter escort for its B-29 bombardment groups. However, early on it became evident that technology had passed these stalwarts of World War II and that they were no longer adequate for escort missions. The replacement of the B-29 by more modern B-50 and B-36 bombers combined with the advent of jet propulsion made the propeller-driven aircraft obsolete and would cause SAC to plan for the retirement of all its P-51s by the end of 1948.[24] In 1947, P-80s made their debut in SAC fighter units, and by December 1947 SAC had five fighter wings assigned with five groups and 15 squadrons: the 4th Fighter Wing with P-80s stationed at Andrews Field, Maryland; the 56th Fighter Wing with P-80s stationed at Selfridge Field, Michigan; the 33rd Fighter Wing with P-51s stationed at Roswell Field, New Mexico; the 82nd Fighter Wing with P-51s stationed at Grenier Field, New Hampshire; and 27th Fighter Wing with P-51s and one P-82B stationed at Kearney Field, Nebraska. SAC's fighter aircraft assets totaled 230 P-51Hs, 120 P-80As, and one P-82B.[25]

The year 1948 brought several changes to SAC's fighter program. First, the "Pursuit" designation was changed to "Fighter" effective 11 June 1948. So, for example, P-51s now became F-51s. Second, in June 1948 SAC's first F-84s were assigned to the 33rd Fighter Wing at Roswell Air Force Base. Finally, due to the lack of range with assigned jet fighter aircraft, the 4th, 33rd, and 56th Fighter Wings were assigned to Continental Air Command for air defense purposes effective 1 December 1948, thus leaving SAC with only two fighter units— the F-82E equipped 27th Fighter Wing at Kearney Air Force Base and the F-51H equipped 82nd Fighter Wing at Grenier Air Force Base, a mere 133 aircraft between the two fighter groups![26]

There were several organizational changes to SAC's fighter force in 1949. The U.S. Air Force assigned March Air Force Base to SAC and with it came the 1st Fighter Wing equipped with F-86As. The second change pertained to the 82nd Fighter Wing which had converted to F-51Ds and was transferred from SAC to the Continental Air Command in August 1949.

F-84E (49–2094) continues to display its TAC markings after the 31st FBW was transferred to SAC on 30 July 1950. The 31st Wing badge was carried on both sides of the cockpit. (USAF, AFHRA)

The last change was the transition of the 27th Fighter Wing from F-82Es to F-84Es making SAC's fighter force an all jet one by the summer of 1950.

The year 1950 and the outbreak of war in Korea brought both expansion and many organizational changes to SAC's fighter program. This event brought an end to the first phase of SAC fighter operations which had often followed an erratic course with six separate fighter wings and five different types of fighter aircraft operated by the units. By 1950, most of the instability that characterized SAC's early fighter program was gone and a more stable approach was adopted. Turner AFB, Georgia, and Bergstrom AFB, Texas, became SAC's main fighter bases and these two bases would support the bulk of SAC fighters until 1957 when fighters were transferred out of SAC.[27] SAC's fighter inventory lost the 1st Fighter-Interceptor Wing to the Air Defense Command in July 1950, but gained the 31st Fighter-Bomber Wing from Tactical Air Command and the newly activated 12th Fighter-Escort Wing, both equipped with F-84Es and giving SAC 67 F-84Es. The "Fighter-Escort" designation replaced "Fighter" beginning with the 27th Fighter Wing in April 1950. On 8 November 1950 the 27th Fighter-Escort Wing was deployed to the Far East with 75 F-84Es to augment the Far East Air Forces (FEAF) fighter force and became the first SAC fighter unit to see combat.

There was further expansion of SAC's fighter force in 1951 with the assignment of four Air National Guard fighter groups in March and April: The 131st Fighter-Bomber Wing with F-51Ds; the 108th Fighter-Bomber Wing with two squadrons equipped with F-47Ds and one squadron equipped with F-47Ns; the 132nd Fighter-Bomber Wing with both F-51Ds and F-84s; and the 146th Fighter-Bomber Wing with F-51Ds. The 131st was stationed at Bergstrom Air Force Base, Texas; the 108th was based at Turner Air Force Base, Georgia; the 132nd was stationed at Dow Air Force Base, Maine; and the 146th was stationed at Moody Air Force Base, Georgia. The assignment of the four Air National Guard (ANG) wings to SAC was short-lived, however, as all four wings were relieved from assignment to SAC in November 1951 and assigned to Tactical Air Command (TAC) to support Army ground training. Also, on 11 May 1951 a USAF Reserve Corollary Unit, the 87th Fighter-Escort Wing (FEW), was ordered into active federal service, but on 25 June 1951 it was inactivated and its personnel assigned to other units. For a short time in 1951, from the assignment of the fourth ANG wing until all four ANG wings were transferred to TAC, Strategic Air Command had attained its authorized level of seven fighter wings.[28] In early 1951, Strategic Air Command activated two fighter air divisions, the 40th located at Turner AFB and the 42nd located at Bergstrom AFB. The air divisions served as an intermediate echelon of command providing a link between the combat wings and the numbered air force. 1951 also brought the introduction of the F-84G into SAC service with the 27th FEW receiving its first G model in September 1951, followed by the 31st FEW in October 1951 and the 12th FEW in December 1951.

As part of the USAF expansion program, SAC added one additional fighter wing in 1952 — the 508th Fighter-Escort Wing stationed at Turner Air Force Base, Georgia, and equipped with F-84Gs. It was assigned to the Second Air Force and the 40th Air Division. This increase to four fighter wings in SAC was the beginning of the post–Korean War buildup.[29]

In January 1953, SAC redesignated all fighter-escort units as strategic fighter wings and squadrons due to a change in the primary mission of the SAC fighter force to that of the delivery of nuclear weapons in support of strategic offensive operations. The final unit to be activated through the end of 1953 was the 506th Strategic Fighter Wing equipped with

F-84Gs and stationed at Dow Air Force Base, Maine. This activation raised the total of SAC fighter wings to five, all equipped with F-84Gs.

SAC Fighter Aircraft Markings

In 1946 the only SAC fighter unit equipped with aircraft was the 56th Fighter Group. The issue of aircraft markings for the 56th FG was the subject of a letter dated 12 July 1946 submitted by the 56th Fighter Group Commander, Colonel David C. Schilling, to Headquarters, Army Air Forces (AAF). The letter mentioned that the proposed aircraft markings were desired as squadron identification and as a morale factor for the unit. In addition, the 56th Fighter Group participated in many air shows and demonstrations and it was believed the aircraft markings would aid in the AAF recruiting program.[30] (The specific markings proposed and adopted by the 56th FG are covered in the specific section on the 56th Fighter Group).

No standard policy on fighter aircraft markings existed in SAC in 1946 and for most of 1947; however, in a letter dated 3 November 1947 from Headquarters SAC to all major subordinate commanders, SAC proposed that fighter groups would be identified by a colored nose and vertical fin and squadrons within a group would be identified by colored wing tips and horizontal fins. Also the letter stated that fighter group leaders would be identified by three stripes around the fuselage, squadron leaders with two stripes and flight leaders with one stripe.[31]

On 10 February 1948, SAC sent a letter to Headquarters, USAF requesting approval for proposed markings for fighter aircraft presently assigned and for those fighter aircraft proposed for assignment. The letter mentioned two classifications of aircraft: conventionally propelled, such as the P-51s presently assigned and the P-82s proposed for assignment; and jet propelled, such as P-80s currently assigned and P-84s proposed for assignment.

Early 56th FGP-80 markings included squadron insignia forward of the cockpit and squadron identification markings: a large arrow on the tip tanks and a horizontal band on the vertical fin. P-80A (44–85401) displays the 63rd FS insignia and has a white plane-in-group number inside the tail band. (Photograph by Peter M. Bowers, courtesy D. Menard)

The letter stated that for jet propelled aircraft the group color would be displayed on the nose of the aircraft and on the forward portion of the external tip tanks. Squadron colors would be displayed on the vertical and horizontal stabilizers, the wing tips, and the aft portion of the external tip tanks. For propeller driven aircraft the group color would be displayed on the nose and squadron colors would be displayed on the vertical and horizontal stabilizers as well as the wing tips. The letter also assigned high visibility colors to each of the assigned fighter groups:

> 4th Fighter Group — Black
> 27th Fighter Group — Light Blue
> 33rd Fighter Group — Green
> 56th Fighter Group — Red
> 82nd Fighter Group — Yellow

Within the groups, the high visibility colors of red, white (outlined by ½" strip of black), and blue were proposed for assignment to the squadrons. Finally the letter stated that the group insignia would be displayed forward of the cockpit on the right side and squadron insignia forward of the cockpit on the left side.[32]

In a letter dated 17 February 1948 Headquarters, USAF gave approval for SAC's proposed fighter aircraft markings.[33]

SAC sent a letter to its subordinate commands on 20 February 1948. It directed that action be taken to mark fighter aircraft in accordance with the new policy at the earliest possible date. In addition it requested that aircraft identification numbers be shown on both sides of the fuselage using a block numbering system. The recommended block number assignments were "Red" Squadron —1 through 29; "White" Squadron — 30 through 59; and "Blue" Squadron — 60 through 89.[34]

With minor variations, its assigned fighter groups implemented SAC's new policy on

A ground crew member conducts an inspection of a 62nd FS F-80 shortly after its arrival in the UK. All 56th FG F-80s displayed the group insignia on the right side of the nose. The squadron color — yellow — is on the tail band, fuselage stripe (flight leader), and on the aft portion of the tip tank. (USAF)

33rd FW F-84s displayed green trim on the tip tanks as a group/wing identification and in the case of F-84C-2-RE (47–1460) used red on the nose, tail and exhaust cone for squadron identification. It was assigned to the 58th Fighter Squadron at Walker AFB, 1948. (USAF, AFHRA)

fighter aircraft markings in March and April 1948. Some of the exceptions noted included the 27th Fighter Wing not using the recommended block numbering system; the 33rd Fighter Group delaying marking of its P-51 aircraft due to a shortage of paint and change over to P-84 aircraft, but stating in a letter to Eighth Air Force dated 20 April 1948 that markings on P-84 aircraft would be accomplished with the least practical delay;[35] and the 56th Fighter Group using yellow as one of the squadron colors instead of the recommended white.

As mentioned, by the end of 1948, three fighter wings—the 4th, 33rd and 56th—were transferred from SAC leaving only the 27th Fighter Wing equipped with the F-82E Twin Mustang and the F-51D equipped 82nd Fighter Wing which would leave SAC in August 1949. In exchange for the 82nd Fighter Wing, SAC received the 1st Fighter Wing, an F-86A unit, stationed at March Air Force Base.

In February 1950, the 27th Fighter-Escort Wing started to reequip with F-84Es and the policy of SAC fighter units having a group/wing color painted on aircraft came to an end. From this point forward, color-marking schemes on SAC fighter aircraft represented squadron assignment and in some cases flight assignment. The use of wing and squadron insignia continued to be used at the discretion of the wing commander and would vary from unit to unit. The marking pattern used on the vertical stabilizer and the tip tanks were wing specific and appeared in squadron colors. Specific patterns used were:

- 12th FEW/SFW—Single diagonal band on the vertical and horizontal stabilizer, painted tip tanks; nose tip painted with a slight 45-degree extension rearward
- 27th FEW/SFW—Wide fan on vertical stabilizer, forward pointing arrow on the tip tank (later replaced with thin trim line extending the length of the tank); nose tip painted with a slight 45-degree extension rearward
- 31st FEW/SFW—Three sunbursts on the vertical and horizontal stabilizer; wide band on the tip tank; nose painted at a 45-degree angle
- 506th SFW—Unknown

F-84G (51–1066) displays revised squadron markings on the tip tanks and vertical fin. (USAF, AFHRA)

- 508th SFW — White spear along fuselage and tip tanks; three diagonal stripes on the vertical stabilizer

In mid-to-late 1953, the use of the SAC command insignia on SAC's F-84Gs became a requirement, and by 1954 had been fully implemented by all SAC fighter units.

5

Bombardment and Strategic Reconnaissance Groups/Wings

Early SAC Bombardment Units — 1946

When Strategic Air Command was established on 21 March 1946 the following very heavy (VH) bombardment units were assigned:

40th Bombardment Group (VH) — March Field, California
44th Bombardment Group (VH) — Smoky Hill Army Air Field, Kansas
93rd Bombardment Group (VH) — Clovis Army Air Field, New Mexico
444th Bombardment Group (VH) — Castle Field, California
448th Bombardment Group (VH) — Ft. Worth Army Air Field, Texas
449th Bombardment Group (VH) — Grand Island Army Air Field, Nebraska
462nd Bombardment Group (VH) — MacDill Field, Florida
467th Bombardment Group (VH) — Clovis Army Air Field, New Mexico
468th Bombardment Group (VH) — Roswell Army Air Field, New Mexico
485th Bombardment Group (VH) — Smoky Hill Army Air Field, Kansas
497th Bombardment Group (VH) — MacDill Field, Florida
498th Bombardment Group (VH) — MacDill Field, Florida
509th Composite Group — Roswell Army Air Field, New Mexico[1]

All the bombardment units were initially assigned to the Fifteenth Air Force, however, a few months after being assigned to SAC, several of the bomb groups would be deactivated or redesignated, while some bombardment groups like the 93rd BG would be carried as a "paper unit" and not manned until 1947.

In August 1946, SAC activated another major subordinate command, the Eighth Air Force, with headquarters at Forth Worth Army Air Field, Texas. Several bombardment groups changed unit designations and now became part of the new Eighth Air Force. These specific groups were the 7th Bombardment Group at Fort Worth AAFld, the 43rd Bombardment Group at Davis-Monthan Field, and the 509th Bombardment Group at Roswell AAFld.

In addition to dealing with the challenges of equipment shortages and personnel turbulence caused by demobilization activities, 1946 also presented SAC with the daunting task of trying to create some semblance of an operational bombardment force and, specifically, replacing all training-type B-29s in bombardment units with modified tactical B-29s ready for overseas movement.

B-29A-70-BN (44–62308) was assigned to the 444th BG and displays a system of squadron markings to include painted fin cap, belly band, engine nacelle plates and nose gear doors. Spokane Army Air Field, July 1946. (USAF)

By the end of 1946, SAC's bomber fleet would consist of:

Fifteenth Air Force Units

• 28th Bombardment Group (VH): Grand Island AAFld, then to Alaska in October 1946 — 24 B-29s on hand (Former 449th Bombardment Group)
• 97th Bombardment Group (VH): Smoky Hill AAFld, Kansas — 44 B-29s on hand (Former 485th Bombardment Group)
• 307th Bombardment Group (VH): MacDill Field, Florida — 13 B-29s on hand (Former 498th Bombardment Group)

Eighth Air Force Units

• 7th Bombardment Group (VH): Fort Worth AAFld, Texas — 40 B-29s on hand (Former 448th/92nd Bombardment Group)
• 43rd Bombardment Group (VH): Davis-Monthan Field, Arizona — 22 B-29s on hand (Former 40th/444th Bombardment Group)
• 509th Bombardment Group (VH): Roswell AAFld, New Mexico — 23 B-29s on hand (Former 509th Composite Group)[2]

Other than the use of squadron identification markings by a few units (40th Bombardment Group, 444th Bombardment Group and 449th Bombardment Group), most units flew B-29s with only the required national markings and aircraft identification numbers or buzz numbers. The 509th Composite Group did use some specialized tail markings during Operation Crossroad, and the 58th Bombardment Wing insignia, but there were no tactical tail markings used by SAC in 1946, and the use of squadron or group insignia was still very limited.

B-29–65-BW (44–69818) shows the double fuselage band used by the 2nd BW. B-29–65-BW (44–69880) carries the markings of the 7th BW. Both aircraft have just been transferred to the 97th BW at Biggs AFB. Photograph taken in February 1950. (Boeing P9721. © Boeing. Used under license.)

A 20th BS B-50A-1-BO (46–005) during the 2nd Bombardment Wing's deployment to the UK from February to May 1950. During this deployment the 20th BS was stationed at RAF Marham. (Courtesy Quadrant House)

2nd Bombardment Group/Wing

The 2nd Bombardment Group, Very Heavy, was reactivated on 1 July 1947 at Andrews Field, Maryland. The bombardment squadrons assigned to the 2nd Bombardment Group were the 20th BS, the 49th BS and the 96th BS. Still without personnel and airplanes, the 2nd BG was relocated to Davis-Monthan Field in September 1947 where it was attached to

*B-50D-115-BO (49–309) is newly assigned to the 2nd BW and carries the new 2nd BW tail marking — **Square T** — which became effective in April 1950 when the Wing was transferred from the Eighth Air Force to the Second Air Force. May 1950. (Photograph by Ed Deigan, courtesy D. Olson)*

the 43rd Bombardment Group (VH) for operations and support. With the assignment of personnel and its first B-29 aircraft, the 2nd BG began the process of becoming proficient in its assigned mission which was, "...to man, train and maintain aircrews and aircraft as a powerful, long-range strike force of the Strategic Air Command."[3]

By the end of December 1947, the 2nd BG had a full complement of thirty B-29s; however, during the first quarter of 1948, when the Group was trying to qualify ground crews and aircrews in B-29 operations, the Group was ordered to transfer 26 B-29s to the Far East Air Forces (FEAF). To maintain flight proficiency, B-29s were loaned to the 2nd BG from its neighbor at Davis-Monthan, the 43rd Bombardment Group. It wouldn't be until June 1948 that the 2nd BG would return to full strength, and be declared a fully operationally ready SAC B-29 group.[4]

A 2nd ARS KB-29–50-BA (44–83993) somewhere over the Pacific in support of the Fox Peter One movement of the 31st FEW from Turner AFB, Georgia, to Yokota Air Base, Japan, in early July 1952. Fin cap is in squadron color — green (USAF)

Top: *2nd Bombardment Wing B-50D-105-BO (48–117) in May 1951. It was assigned to the 49th BS and shows the final configuration of squadron markings for 2nd Bombardment Wing aircraft. Notice the painted nose and tapered trim on the fuel tank. The absence of squadron insignia is reflective of SAC's preference for toned-down aircraft markings. (Photograph by E. Van Houten, courtesy D. Menard)* Bottom: Miss Fit *was B-29A-70-BN (44–62307) and assigned to a provisional bomb squadron of the 444th BG with duty station at Spokane AAFld. The permanent station for the 444th BG in July 1946 was Davis-Monthan AAFld. (USAF)*

Flightline shot of Spokane AAFld in July 1946 shows three B-29As assigned to the 444th BG in various stages of squadron markings. Squadron colors were red and blue. These aircraft would eventually be assigned to the 43rd BG at Davis-Monthan on 1 October 1946 with the deactivation of the 444th BG. (USAF)

The Group's first assigned tail marking was an **Open Black Square**, which started appearing on their assigned B-29s in early 1948. In addition to the **Open Black Square** tail marking and required national insignia and aircraft tail numbers, 2nd Bombardment Group B-29s displayed buzz numbers below the left wing and aft of the national insignia on the fuselage. The buzz numbers were black for silver finish B-29s and red for those B-29s with black undersurfaces. All B-29s carried the Eighth Air Force insignia on both sides of the dorsal fin. Much of the squadron identification marking scheme was inherited from the 43rd BG which had transferred many of their B-29s to the 2nd BG while in the process of converting to new B-50A aircraft. In the case of 2nd BG B-29s, squadron identification markings were painted on fin tips, two bellybands around the center of the fuselage (to distinguish itself from the single belly band used by the 43rd BG), outer engine cowling panels and nose gear doors. Beginning in 1948, the 2nd BG assigned squadron colors were: 20th Bombardment Squadron — yellow; 49th Bombardment Squadron — blue; and 96th Bombardment Squadron — red.[5] Some B-29s carried squadron insignia on the left side of the nose and several aircraft had nicknames and nose art on the right side. Examples of named aircraft were: *Ole Faithful, Beetle Baum,* and *Forever Ambling* — 20th BS; *Pride of Tucson* and *Satan's Mate* — 49th BS; and *Piccadilly Tilly* and *Bad Penny* — 96th BS.[6] These markings were in full force during the 2nd Bombardment Group's first overseas deployment to the United Kingdom from August to November 1948.

As part of a U.S. show of force in response to Soviet pressure on Berlin, the 2nd BG, now a medium bombardment group, deployed to RAF Lakenheath in August 1948 following a route that included a stop at Goose Bay, Labrador, Canada, enroute to the U.K. While in England the 2nd BG would conduct joint training exercises with the RAF; send each of its squadrons on mini-deployments to Furstenfeldbruck, West Germany, where 2nd BG B-29s would fly demonstration missions over U.S.–occupied sections of Germany; and participate in several public events to include an aerial review over Oslo, Norway, as part of the celebration of Norwegian Air Force Day on 12 September 1948. The 2nd BG would begin redeploying to its home station, Davis-Monthan AFB, in mid–November and by December 1948 all 2nd BG B-29s had returned from England.[7]

The period from late 1948 to early 1949 was a time of change and challenge for the 2nd Bombardment Group. The Group received orders to transfer from Davis-Monthan AFB to Chatham AFB, Georgia, and this move was completed by March 1949. With the transfer to Chatham AFB came a change in organizational structure as the 2nd Bombardment Wing was activated to control both the tactical and support units. While at Davis-Monthan AFB the 2nd BG had come under the umbrella of the 43rd Bombardment Wing.

In late 1948, the Air Force decided to equip the 2nd Bombardment Group with Boeing B-50A bombers and the 2nd BG received their first B-50s in December 1948. Also, during this time, the 2nd BG swapped its tactical B-29s for atomic capable "Saddletree" B-29s. The other organizational change affecting the 2nd BG was the activation of the 2nd Air Refueling Squadron in 1949 and the assignment of KB-29M tanker aircraft.

With the changeover to B-50s, 2nd BW aircraft markings stayed the same except for a few minor changes. Squadron colors were changed for both the 20th Bombardment Squadron and the 49th Bombardment Squadron. The 20th went from yellow to green while the 49th went from blue to yellow. The 96th Bombardment Squadron retained red as its squadron color. The newly assigned 2nd ARS did not have an assigned squadron color during this time.[8] The squadron identification markings on B-50s were painted on the fin cap, on the fuselage as a single bellyband, and on the nose gear doors. Buzz markings were used and carried the prefix for the B-50 — **BK** — followed by the last three digits of the aircraft serial number; squadron insignia appeared on both sides of the nose for all three bombardment squadrons. These markings remained in effect through the end of 1949 when, as a result of SAC's new policy on tail markings, the 2nd BW received a new tail marking — **Triangle S**. The **Triangle** under the new SAC policy represented the Eighth Air Force and the letter **S** represented the 2nd Bombardment Wing. These were the markings the 2nd Bomb Wing took with them on their second TDY deployment to the United Kingdom from February to May 1950. A few of the B-50s deployed to the UK also had insignia red Arctic markings on the tail and outer wings.

During this overseas deployment to England, the 2nd BW trained extensively with the RAF and other Allied Air Forces; however, only two-thirds of the tactical strength of the Wing deployed. Also the 2nd BW dispersed the tactical squadrons during this deployment — the 20th BS went to RAF Marham, the 49th BS went to RAF Sculthorpe, and the 96th went to RAF Lakenheath. Additionally each bomb squadron location had two KB-29Ms from the 2nd Air Refueling Squadron. The 2nd BW, with B-50As and KB-29Ms, completed its mission in the U.K. and returned to Chatham in late April 1950.[9]

On 1 April 1950, the 2nd Bomb Wing was reassigned from the Eighth Air Force to the Second Air Force in a SAC realignment of wings based on geographical location rather than mission assignment. Again, a new tail marking was assigned — **Square T** and almost immediately started to appear on Wing aircraft. The **Square** represented the Second Air Force and the letter **T** the 2nd BW. After its return from the UK, the 2nd BW replaced its B-50As with B-50Ds and its KB-29Ms were exchanged for boom-type KB-29P tankers. Some squadron colors again were changed: the 20th BS went to blue from green; the 49th BS retained yellow; the 96th BS retained red; and the 2nd ARS was assigned green.[10] Compared to previous 2nd BG/BW marking schemes, 2nd Bombardment Wing B-50D markings were not as elaborate. Squadron identification markings now appeared only on the fin cap, wing fuel tanks and nose gear doors, and squadron insignia no longer appeared on assigned aircraft. Also, buzz markings were removed and replaced by **USAF** and **United States Air Force** on wings and fuselage as required by Technical Order 07–1-1.

Insignia red Arctic marked tail and outer wings on RB-29–95-BW (45–21773) of the 72nd SRS in Bermuda en route to the UK, May 1950. The tail marking and aircraft tail number are yellow. During its service in Alaska this RB-29 was named Leakin Lena. *(Photograph courtesy B. Banks)*

The 2nd Bomb Wing would use these markings while at Chatham AFB and, beginning in September 1950, at Hunter Air Force Base until the spring of 1953 when SAC ordered all tail markings removed from its aircraft. Operationally, the 2nd BW would deploy twice more to the United Kingdom —from May through August 1951 and September through December 1952; conduct B-50 ferry flights to deliver B-50Ds to the 93rd BW in England and to Castle AFB, California; serve as a SAC test bed for the tactical evaluation of electronic counter-measures; support in July 1952, with the 2nd ARS, the deployment of 31st FEW F-84Gs from Turner AFB to Japan as part of the Fox Peter Two deployment; and conduct continuous training with its nuclear delivery mission as part of SAC's War Plan. The 2nd BW would begin the transition to B-47s and KC-97s in mid–1953 with all KB-29s gone by October 1953 and the last B-50D departing the Wing in December 1953.[11]

5th Strategic Reconnaissance Wing

In May 1949, the 5th Reconnaissance Group returned to the United States from Clark Field in the Philippines and ended its assignment to the Thirteenth Air Force, FEAF. Now under the jurisdiction of Strategic Air Command, the 5th SRG was relocated to Mountain Home AFB, Idaho. On 16 July 1949, the 5th Strategic Reconnaissance Wing was activated and assumed control of the 5th SRG and its subordinate squadrons.

The first two squadrons assigned to the 5th SRG were the 23rd SRS which joined the Group at Mountain Home from Forbes AFB in June 1949, and the 72nd SRS which moved from Ladd Field, Alaska, to Mountain Home also in June 1949. A third squadron, the 31st SRS, was assigned to the 5th SRG in November 1949, but remained attached to the Far East Air Forces with duty station at Kadena Air Base, Okinawa.[12] After assignment to SAC and the 5th SRW, the 31st SRS would continue to display its squadron insignia on the tail fin and use green as its squadron color. In early 1950, it is believed that some 31st SRS RB-29s started to display the Second Air Force insignia on the dorsal fin. This would eventually give way to the **Circle X** tail marking and the Fifteenth Air Force insignia beginning in April 1950 when the 5th SRW would transfer from the jurisdiction of the Second Air Force to that of the Fifteenth Air Force.

RB-29-A-45-BN (44-61727) at Yokota in 1949. The 31st SRS insignia shows above the aircraft tail number. (The 31st SRS was assigned to SAC in 1949 while on detached service to FEAF). (USAF photograph, courtesy H. Savely)

The 5th Strategic Reconnaissance Wing transferred again in November 1949 when the Wing moved from Mountain Home AFB to Fairfield-Suisun AFB (later Travis AFB, named for Brig. Gen. Robert F. Travis who was killed in a B-29 crash at Fairfield-Suisun in August 1950), California. Under the double-wing concept, the 5th SRW shared a wing commander with the 9th SRW from 5 November 1949 to 10 February 1951.

Initially equipped with RB-17s and RB-29s, the 5th SRW had no distinctive aircraft markings until November 1949 when the Wing was assigned the tail marking — Square **P**. The **Square** represented the newly-activated Second Air Force and the letter **P** the 5th SRW. This approved tail marking was applied to Wing aircraft at Fairfield-Suisun AFB beginning in December 1949. In addition, according to the December 1949 history for the 9th SRW, a small Second Air Force insignia was placed on the dorsal fin of each aircraft[13]; however, the use of the Second Air Force insignia on 5th SRW B-29s has not been verified.

The 5th SRW assigned squadron colors in early 1950 with blue going to the 23rd SRS, red to the 72nd SRS, and upon relief from attachment to the FEAF in November 1950, yellow to the 31st SRS. The 5th SRW applied squadron colors to the fin cap and to nose gear doors. The last four digits of the aircraft serial number and the ubiquitous **No Smoking Within 100 Feet** warning also appeared on the nose gear doors in a contrasting color.

In April 1950 the 5th SRW was transferred from the Second Air Force to the Fifteenth Air Force and, subsequently, a new tail marking was assigned — **Circle X**. These markings started to appear on Wing RB-29s in May 1950 and the repainting of aircraft was completed by June 1950. Several Superfortresses of the 5th SRW had insignia red Arctic markings, so in this case the **Circle X** tail marking was painted in a contrasting yellow instead of the standard black. The Fifteenth Air Force insignia appeared in the usual dorsal fin position on 5th SRW RB-29s.

Although not a prominent practice within the Wing and SAC in general, several aircraft had nicknames and applied nose art, mostly on 72nd SRS aircraft which had been stationed in Alaska prior to its assignment to the 5th SRW in June 1949. Two examples were: *Leakin Lena* and *Ladies Delight*.[14]

In December 1949, the 5th SRW sent 10 RB-29s of the 23rd SRS to Sculthorpe, England, for an operational deployment that would last until May 1950. The 23rd SRS would be

A blue-trimmed RB-36D-10-CF (49–2693) of the 23rd SRS flying in formation with another RB-36 and a RB-29–95-BW (45–21777) in insignia red Arctic markings. The RB-29 was assigned to the 31st SRS and has a yellow fin tip. Photograph taken in early 1951. (USAF photograph, courtesy Travis Air Museum)

replaced by its sister squadron in the 5th SRW, the 72nd SRS. Arriving in late May 1950, the 72nd SRS would remain in England until November 1950 when — returning home to newly-named Travis AFB — a new challenge awaited the much-traveled 72nd SRS — conversion to the RB-36.

The 5th SRW started to replace its venerable RB-29s with new RB-36s beginning in 1951 with the first B-36 arriving in February 1951. On a one-by-one basis, the RB-29s were replaced by RB-36s. In early November 1951, the 5th SRW participated in its first Operational Readiness Test when 15 fully-loaded RB-36s from the 72nd, 23rd and 31st Strategic Reconnaissance Squadrons took off from Travis AFB and flew a simulated combat mission to Eielson AFB, Alaska (formerly called Mile 26). This exercise required 13 days of planning, eight days of execution, and provided 5,760 miles of photo coverage from flights over the Arctic Circle, the Alaska Range of mountains, and the Brooks Range located in the northern area of Alaska.[15]

The year 1952 would bring the introduction of the H model into the 5th SRW inventory and by September 1952 the total number of RB-36s assigned would be 37. Specific RB-36 models assigned included: one RB-36D, eight RB-36Es, 23 RB-36Fs and eight RB-36Hs.[16]

Markings on RB-36s were little changed from what had appeared on 5th SRW B-29s — **Circle X** tail marking, squadron identification markings on fin tip and nose gear doors, and the **No Smoking Within 100 Feet** warning and the last four digits of the aircraft serial number appearing on the nose gear doors, and the Fifteenth Air Force insignia on the dorsal fin. One change from the B-36 marking scheme to the earlier B-29 era was the use of squadron and wing insignia. The 72nd SRS placed its squadron emblem on both sides of the aircraft nose and the 5th SRW insignia appeared on the left side of the nose on most 5th SRW RB-36s.

It is believed that the 23rd SRS and 31st SRS used squadron insignia on RB-36s as well, but this has not been verified. An additional marking on some RB-36s was a single fuselage band in squadron color which may have been used to indicate lead crew status.

In April 1953, SAC eliminated the use of tail markings and insignia except for the Wing and SAC emblems. As a result, the 5th SRW removed its **Circle X** tail marking, Fifteenth Air Force emblem, and all squadron insignia from its RB-36s in May-June 1953.

The 5th SRW continued to fly RB-36s until September 1958 when the last one departed Travis AFB, California, and the 5th became a heavy bombardment wing equipped with B-52Gs, the first aircraft arriving in February 1959.

6th Bombardment Wing

The 6th Bombardment Wing, Medium, was reactivated at Walker Air Force Base, New Mexico, on 2 January 1951 along with its three bombardment squadrons: the 24th, 39th and 40th. Personnel to man the Wing were transferred from other Eighth Air Force stations. By the end of June 1951, the 6th BW had seven B-29s and 19 crews assigned, 12 of which were combat ready.[17] For the remainder of 1951, the 6th BW put forth a major effort in training maintenance personnel and flight crews to become a combat ready Strategic Air Command B-29 wing. However, the 6th BW experienced heavy personnel turnover due to its low manning priority and its requirement to fill quotas for service in the Far East. By the end of 1951, the 6th BW had 24 B-29s on hand and its crews for the most part were FEAF returnees who had completed their combat tours.[18]

In May 1951, the 6th BW was assigned a **Hollow Black Triangle** as a tail marking. In addition to its tail marking, 6th BW B-29s displayed the customary Eighth Air Force insignia on the dorsal fin and squadron identification markings were painted on fin caps and nose gear doors. The 6th BW assigned squadron colors were: yellow and red for the 24th BS; red and blue for the 39th BS; and blue and green for the 40th BS. The 6th BW used a variation to the usual **No Smoking Within 100 Feet** warning on nose gear doors. Instead, 6th BW aircraft displayed **No Smoking On The Ramp**. Both Wing and Squadron insignia were used; large squadron insignia appearing on the right side of aircraft nose and wing insignia on the left side.

From August 1951 to June 1952, the 307th Air Refueling Squadron was attached to the 6th BW. Equipped with

72nd SRS RB-36 with squadron insignia displayed. Photograph taken in April 1951 on the occasion of Captain Stout becoming qualified in the RB-36. (USAF photograph, courtesy Brig. Gen. Don Stout)

At NAS Glenview in November 1951: a B-29A-75-BN (44–62322) in early 6th BW markings. Wing and squadron insignia would later be applied to both 6th BW B-29s and B-36s. (Photograph by Clay Jansson, courtesy D. Olson)

KB-29Ps and stationed at Walker AFB, the 307th ARS was assigned the **Triangle R** tail marking by a change to the SAC Tactical Doctrine Manual dated January 1952. The squadron color assignment for the 307th ARS is unknown.

In January 1952, the 6th BW received a revised tail marking—**Triangle R**. This marking appeared on 6th BW B-29s and B-36s until the spring of 1953 when all tail codes were removed. In August 1952, the 6th BW received its first B-36 and by early 1953 all B-29s were gone and the 6th BW became a full-fledged B-36 bombardment wing.

6th Bombardment Wing B-36s were marked very similarly to their B-29s with the only difference being the painting of squadron colors on the jet intake lips. Tail marking, squadron identification markings on fin tips and nose gear doors, and the use of squadron and wing insignia remained the same.

The 6th BW continued to operate B-36s until 1957 when it became a B-52 bombardment wing.

During AFROTC training at Roswell AFB. A 24th BS B-29 displays its large World War II–era insignia. The nose gear doors are painted in squadron colors, which are believed to be red and yellow. The "No Smoking On The Ramp" was a variation of the usual no smoking warning used on SAC B-29s. (USAF, AFHRA)

Top: *The 307th ARS was one of several air refueling squadrons used to support the movement of the 31st Fighter Escort Wing during Fox Peter One in August 1952. This 307th KB-29P clearly shows the Task Group 132.4 insignia; it is not known if the 307th ARS ever used squadron identification markings. (USAF, National Archives)* Bottom: *B-36F-1-CF (49–2671) displays the 40th BS insignia as well as the **Triangle R** tail marking. Armed Forces Day 1953 at Walker AFB. (USAF, AFHRA)*

7th Bombardment Group/Wing

The post–WWII history of the 7th Bombardment Group begins with its reactivation on 1 October 1946 at Fort Worth Army Air Field, Texas. Initially assigned to Strategic Air Command's Fifteenth Air Force, personnel and B-29 aircraft for the new group came from the 92nd Bombardment Group. The newly formed group consisted of the 9th, 436th and

492nd BS B-29 arrived at Andrews Field, Maryland, as part of a squadron mass flight from Tokyo to Washington on 1 August 1947. The fin tip is in the 492nd BS color — blue. Buzz markings are insignia red. The members of the crew were all Texans, which explains why the Texas flag is flying while the ship taxis to the parking area. (AP/Wide World Photo)

492nd Bombardment Squadrons. On 19 November 1946, the 7th Bombardment Group was transferred to the jurisdiction of the Eighth Air Force also located at Fort Worth AAFld.[19]

The 7th BG began using distinctive tail markings in the March-April 1947 time frame. A **Hollow Black Triangle** started to appear on assigned B-29s and was used for group identification. The Eighth Air Force insignia was placed on both sides of the dorsal fin. Additionally, the 7th BG placed squadron identification markings on fin caps and nose gear doors. Squadron colors were red for the 9th BS, yellow for the 436th BS, and blue for the 492nd BS. The final component to the 7th Bombardment Group tactical marking scheme was the placement of the 7th Bombardment Group insignia on the left side of the nose. These markings complemented the required markings — national insignia, aircraft tail numbers, and buzz numbers — as outlined in Technical Order 07–1–1.

During 1947 the 7th Bombardment Group added to its reputation as one of SAC's premier B-29 Superfortress units. In addition to participating in SAC maximum effort missions over Los Angeles, New York and Chicago, the 7th BG pioneered B-29 deployments to Japan (492nd BS), and Germany (7th BG). On 3 November 1947, the 7th Bombardment Wing was established under the Hobson Plan and both the 7th Bombardment Group and its three bombardment squadrons were assigned to the Wing.[20]

On 30 January 1948, Fort Worth Air Field was renamed Carswell Air Force Base, in honor of Major Horace S. Carswell, Jr., a Medal of Honor recipient in World War II. Although the 7th BW continued to fly and train with B-29s during the first half of 1948, March 1948 brought an announcement that the Wing would become the first unit in Strategic Air Command to receive the new Consolidated B-36 "Peacemaker" bomber under development at the Consolidated-Vultee plant in Fort Worth. On 26 June 1948, the first B-36 bomber, B-36A (44–92004), was delivered to the 7th BW and named *City of Fort Worth*.[21] The Wing continued to receive B-36s throughout the remainder of 1948 and by December had 36 B-36s (18 A models and 18 B models) and no B-29s.

B-36A-15-CF (44–92018) and (44–92024) display the 7th BW tactical marking, a Hollow Black Triangle. BM-024 also has the blue trim of the 492nd BS on the fin cap and nose gear doors, and the 7th BW insignia on the nose. Carswell AFB, 1948. (USAF)

During the second half of 1948, the Air Force took every opportunity to showcase its newest and largest bomber by having the 7th BW participate in several aerial reviews and air shows. These events included the dedication of New York's Idyllwild Airport on 31 July, the Cleveland Air Races from 5 to 7 September, Air Force Day celebrations on 18 September, the American Legion Convention in Miami in October, and several other air demonstrations and long-distance flights.[22]

Initial B-36 markings were very similar to 7th BW B-29 markings with the **Hollow Black Triangle** tail marking, Eighth Air Force emblem on dorsal fins, squadron identification markings on fin tip, nose gear doors and, occasionally, propeller domes, and the 7th BW insignia on the left side of the aircraft nose. The buzz number prefix for the B-36 was **BM** and

The squadron color for the 9th BS was red and is shown on B-36D-5-CF (49–2652) on the fin cap, jet intake rims and nose gear door. Also above the name Pretty Girl *is a small 9th BS insignia. March AFB. (Courtesy National Museum of the USAF)*

The first 9th SRW B-36B-5-CF (44–92040) with the Second Air Force insignia on the tail. (USAF, AFHRA)

appeared in large block letters on the forward fuselage and under the left wing surface. Many of the B-36Bs carried Arctic markings on the tail and outer wing panels. Most carried no geometric tail marking, but did display the Eighth Air Force insignia on the dorsal fin.

Beginning in 1949 the buzz markings were replaced by **United States Air Force** in small lettering on the forward fuselage and **USAF** in large letters on the upper right and lower left wing surfaces. In October 1949 the 7th BW received a new tail marking assignment when SAC announced their policy on tail markings. The new tail code for the 7th BW was **Triangle J** with the **Triangle** representing the Eighth Air Force and the letter **J** the 7th BW. All other markings remained the same.

B-36B-5-CF (44–92040), the first B-36 assigned to the 9th SRW on 18 November 1949. It bears the Wing insignia on its nose. All three B-36Bs of the 9th SRW were assigned to the 1st Strategic Reconnaissance Squadron. (USAF, AFHRA)

Small changes to 7th BW aircraft markings were implemented in the early 1950s. Squadron identification markings were added to B-36 jet intake rims, a large 3 or 4 digit identification number was placed on the forward fuselage, and in late 1952, the squadron

Top: *B-29–90-BW (44–87765) shows early marking scheme for 9th BW B-29s including a single fuselage band in squadron color — in this case yellow representing the 99th BS. (Boeing 2B2452. © Boeing. Used under license.) Middle: B-29A-75-BN (44–62316) shows all the tactical markings in effect for the 9th BW during 1952–53. Oakland Airport, 7 February 1953. (Courtesy D. Olson) Left: A 99th BS crew undergoes inspection at Travis AFB prior to departure for Guam in June 1952. Squadron color is yellow. (USAF, AFHRA)*

identification on the full fin cap was replaced by a narrow fin stripe in squadron color. Unlike the 11th BW, the 7th BW did not place squadron insignia on most of its aircraft although photographs of B-36D-5-CF (49–2652) *Pretty Girl* of the 9th BS show a small squadron insignia on the right side of the aircraft nose.

The 7th Bombardment Wing continued to operate improved versions of the B-36 (B-36Ds, B-36Fs and B-36Hs) in the early 1950s. Operational activities included many long distant flights to several overseas locations— Alaska, Goose Bay, Labrador, Puerto Rico, United Kingdom and French Morocco. Like the rest of SAC, the high visibility markings were removed in the spring of 1953. The 7th BW would continue to fly B-36s until 1958 when it converted to the B-52.

9th Strategic Reconnaissance/Bombardment Wing

As part of Strategic Air Command's expansion in 1949, Fairfield-Suisun Air Force Base (later Travis AFB) was transferred from the Military Air Transport Service to the jurisdiction of SAC. As part of SAC's plan to station a reconnaissance wing at Fairfield Suisun AFB, the 9th Strategic Reconnaissance Wing was activated on 1 May 1949. The 9th SRW was assigned to the 311th Air Division (later Second Air Force) which controlled SAC's strategic reconnaissance assets. The tactical squadrons initially were the 5th Strategic Reconnaissance Squadron, Photo, and the 99th Strategic Reconnaissance Squadron, Photo. On 1 June 1949 another strategic reconnaissance squadron, Photo, was assigned — the 1st SRS.

During the summer of 1949, the 9th SRW was equipped with a mixture of RB-17s and B-29s with four RB-17s and four B-29s assigned to the 1st Strategic Reconnaissance Squadron, seven RB-17s and four B-29s assigned to the 5th Strategic Reconnaissance Squadron, and nine RB-17s and four B-29s assigned to the 99th Strategic Reconnaissance Squadron as of 31 July 1949. The 9th SRW was earmarked to be an RB-36 wing and was authorized both RB-29 and RB-36 aircraft. By the end of 1949 the 9th SRW would have eight RB-29s, 13 B-29s, 11 RB-17s, and three B-36Bs, having received its first B-36B aircraft on 17 November 1949. Upon receipt of its second B-36B on 22 December 1949, all 9th SRW B-29s and RB-29s were reallocated to the 5th SRS and 99th SRS, leaving the 1st SRS with the B-36Bs. By the end of January 1950, the RB-17s would be gone and the 9th SRW B-29 fleet would be a mixture of RB-29s, B-29As and B-29s.[23]

No tactical markings appeared on 9th SRW aircraft during the first seven months of operations except for those aircraft displaying tactical markings and insignia from previous assignments (The 9th SRW received several of its B-29s from the 93rd Bombardment Wing at Castle AFB and the 28th Bombardment Wing at Rapid City AFB).

In October 1949, the 9th SRW submitted a letter requesting permission to paint squadron insignia on its aircraft and in November 1949 the Wing repainted all serial numbers and started to paint group and squadron insignia on its aircraft.[24]

In December 1949, the 9th SRW was notified that its tail marking was to be a **Square R**. The following quote appeared in the December 1949 history of the 9th SRG: "Authority was received from Headquarters, 9th SRW to begin marking group aircraft with approved insignia consisting of a large square border with the letter "R" on the vertical stabilizer and a smaller Second Air Force insignia located on the dorsal fin of the aircraft."[25] The **Square R** did appear on 9th SRW B-29s. It is not certain that the tail marking was ever placed on the three B-36Bs. What has been verified is the placement of the 9th SRW insignia on the left side of the nose of assigned B-36Bs as well as the use of the Second Air Force insignia on at least one B-36B with Arctic markings.

SAC reorganized the Command in April 1950, and the 9th SRW became part of the Fifteenth Air Force and was redesignated the 9th Bombardment Wing with an authorized increase in B-29 aircraft from 30 to 45. In the next few months, the B-36Bs and RB-29s were transferred out of the 9th BW, many going to the 28th SRW at Rapid City who, in turn, transferred many of their B-29s to the 9th, including several B-29MR (atomic bomb carriers with air refueling capabilities).

The changeover to the Fifteenth Air Force also caused a change in tail marking. The new tactical marking assigned to the 9th BW was the **Circle R**. Also in April 1950, the 9th BW decided upon color assignments for its squadrons— red for the 1st, green for the 5th, and yellow for the 99th.[26] Squadron identification markings were placed on fin caps and nose gear doors. Also appearing on the forward edge of nose gear doors were the last four digits of the aircraft serial number and on the trailing edge the warning **No Smoking Within 100 Feet**, both painted in a contrasting color. 9th Bomb Wing B-29s also displayed the Fifteenth Air Force insignia on the dorsal fin. Several B-29s also wore the 9th BW insignia on the left side of the aircraft nose. Some of the B-29s assigned to the 9th Bombardment Wing showed a single fuselage band and engine cowling panels painted in squadron colors, but these markings were left over from service with the 43rd Bombardment Wing and eventually removed.

In August 1951, the 9th Air Refueling Squadron was activated and equipped with KB-29s. Due to lack of space at Travis AFB, the unit operated from Davis-Monthan AFB and was attached to the 43rd Bombardment Wing. The squadron color assigned to the 9th ARS is unknown.

In May 1953, both the 9th Bombardment Wing and 9th Air Refueling Squadron moved from their respective stations, Travis and Davis-Monthan, to a new home — Mountain Home AFB, Idaho. The 9th BW continued flying B-29s and KB-29s until May 1954 when it converted to B-47s and KC-97s.

11th Bombardment Group/Wing

On 1 December 1948, the 11th Bombardment Group, Heavy, was activated at Carswell AFB, Texas, and assigned to the Eighth Air Force. Also on this date, the 26th, 42nd and 98th Bombardment Squadrons, (H), were activated and assigned to the 11th BG. The 11th BG was further attached to the 7th BW at Carswell AFB and shared a wing commander with the 7th BW. The 11th BG was the second B-36 unit in the Air Force.

The first B-36 aircraft for the 11th BG was B-36A (44–92004) and was transferred from the 7th BW on 17 January 1949, and assigned to the 26th Bombardment Squadron. The 11th BG would take part in its first aerial review on 25 January 1949 when it helped lead a review over Carswell AFB with three B-36As to commemorate the birthdays of both the 7th BW and the Eighth Air Force. The 11th BG would continue to build its aircraft strength with the transfer of B-36s from the 7th BW to include the first B models in March 1949. At the end of April 1949 the 11th BG had a total of 22 B-36s with the 26th and 42nd Bomb Squadrons each possessing eight aircraft and the 98th Bomb Squadron equipped with six B-36s.[27] By the end of 1949, a total of 23 B-36s were assigned (eight-A models and 15-B models) to the 11th BG. The first D model B-36s would reach the 11th BG in August 1950.

Top: *Displaying a small 42nd BS insignia on the nose, B-36B-1-CF (44–92031) was transferred to the 11th BG in 1949. In addition to insignia red Arctic markings this B-36 is marked with its squadron colors of yellow and white on the fin cap and nose gear doors. (USAF)* Bottom: *42nd BS B-36H-25-CF (51–5718) has yellow and white squadron colors on the fin tip and jet air intake rims. Carswell AFB, May 19, 1953. (Jim Fahey, courtesy D. Olson)*

Initial 11th BG aircraft markings included squadron identification markings in the form of striped nose gear doors and fin tips. 11th BG squadron color assignments were: red for the 26th BS; yellow for the 42nd BS; and blue for the 98th BS. The contrasting color on nose gear doors and fin tips was white. The use of a small squadron insignia has been verified for the 42nd BS and appeared on the right side of the aircraft nose. The 11th BG placed its unit emblem on the left side of the aircraft nose and the Eighth Air Force insignia appeared on B-36 dorsal fins. On the forward fuselage appeared **United States Air Force** in small letters and underneath was painted a three-digit identification number in large, black numerals. Since SAC was reviewing its policy on tail markings, no tail marking was assigned to the 11th BG until October 1949 when SAC announced its revised policy on tac-

Above: *B-36H-1-CF (50–1092) was assigned to the 98th BS. In addition to the tail marking, Eighth Air Force and 11th BW insignias, the plane has blue and white squadron identification markings on the nose gear doors and jet intake rims. Detroit-Wayne Major Airport, August 1952. (Courtesy D. Olson)* Right: *The 11th BW insignia is prominently displayed on the nose of this 26th BS B-36. Squadron colors are red and white. (USAF, AFHRA)*

tical markings. The 11th BG's first assigned tail code, **Triangle U**, started to appear on its B-36 fleet in early 1950.

11th BG operational activities paralleled those of the 7th BW to include introducing more **D** models into inventory and participating in the first B-36 training mission to the United Kingdom in January 1951. A major organizational change took place in February 1951 when the 11th BG became the 11th BW and along with the 7th BW was assigned to the newly established 19th Air Division.[28]

Some minor changes to 11th BW aircraft markings took place in 1951 and 1952. Squadron identification markings were expanded to include jet intake rims and the fin cap marking was modified to a narrow band across the fin tips. Local identification numbers were expanded to four digits on the forward fuselage. Large squadron insignia were placed on the right side of the B-36 nose for all three squadrons.

Tail markings started to disappear in May 1953 and were completely gone by June 1953. The squadron markings would give way to the 11th BW insignia on the right side of the aircraft nose and the new SAC command insignia would be located on the left side. The 11th BW would continue to operate B-36s until December 1957 when it moved to Altus AFB, Oklahoma, and began receiving B-52Es.

22nd Bombardment Wing

The 22nd Bombardment Wing, Medium, was assigned to Strategic Air Command in August 1948 when the 22nd Bombardment Group and its three Bombardment Squadrons— the 2nd, 19th, and 33rd—conducted a permanent change of station from Okinawa to Smoky Hill AFB, Kansas. The 22nd BW was assigned to the Fifteenth Air Force and authorized 30 B-29 medium bombers. Many of the B-29s assigned to the 22nd BW at Smoky Hill had either been part of the 22nd Bombardment Group at Kadena Air Base, Okinawa, or the 19th Bombardment Group stationed on Guam.

Upon its arrival in Kansas, the 22nd BW was assigned a **Triangle I** as its tail marking. The 22nd also placed a large 22nd BW insignia on the left side of the aircraft nose.[29] The 22nd BW assigned squadron colors were red for the 2nd, blue for the 19th, and yellow for the 33rd, and appeared only on B-29 fin tips. Completing the marking scheme was the Fifteenth Air Force insignia located on the dorsal fin of assigned B-29s.

These markings were in effect when the 22nd BW was sent to the United Kingdom in November 1948 for a three-month overseas training mission. All three squadrons would operate from Lakenheath and would spend the next three months engaged in fighter affiliation exercises with RAF Fighter Command.[30]

Shortly after its return to the United States, the 22nd BW was notified it would be moving again, this time to March AFB, California. The move to March AFB took place in May 1949 and the 1st Fighter Wing (FW), also in residence at March AFB, was attached to the 22nd BW. Equipped with F-86As, the 1st FW remained a SAC unit until July 1950.

*Several 22nd BW B-29s from the 19th and 33rd BS's. The B-29 with the **Circle A** marking belongs to the 106th BW. (USAF, AFHRA)*

On its way back to Korea, B-29A-65-BN (44-62199) was one of several 22nd BG aircraft with the black underside paint. This particular aircraft was assigned to the 2nd BS as indicated by an insignia red fin cap. (Boeing HS 5577. © Boeing. Used under license.)

With the publication of a new SAC Tactical Doctrine Manual—Bombardment and a reorganization of SAC tail codes, the 22nd BW was assigned a new tail marking—**Circle E**—in October 1949. The 22nd BW delayed implementation of the new tail marking due to its second TDY deployment to the United Kingdom from November 1949 to February 1950. During its second deployment to England, the 22nd BW's squadrons were based according to a dispersal plan where each squadron was stationed at a separate base. The 2nd BS was stationed at Marham, the 19th BS at Sculthorpe, and the 33rd BS would occupy Lakenheath. During this stay in the UK, the 22nd BW would conduct many long-range navigation exercises, long-range bombing runs to North Africa, and live bombing runs on UK ranges. In addition, many practice exercises were flown with the RAF, and the 22nd BW provided familiarization flights to RAF personnel who would fly the B-29s, soon to be provided to the Royal Air Force by the United States under new Lend Lease arrangements.[31]

In the spring of 1950, after the 22nd BW's return to March AFB, the new tail code—**Circle E**—started to make its appearance on 22nd BW B-29s; however, in July 1950, the 22nd BW headed west to Kadena Air Base, Okinawa, to participate in combat operations on the Korean Peninsula. Within nine days after its receipt of orders for combat duty, the 22nd BW was fully operational and flew its first bombing mission against North Korean forces.[32] The 22nd BW would be commended for "its outstanding contributions to the United Nations efforts in Korea" by General Douglas MacArthur and would suffer the loss of only one airplane during its participation in the Korean Conflict (one of its B-29s crashed into the China Sea after take-off on 19 October 1950).[33]

The 22nd BW deployed to Okinawa with a mixture of new tail markings—**Circle E**; old tail markings—**Triangle I**; and a combination of the two on rudders and vertical stabilizers. Eventually all 22nd BW B-29s were painted with the authorized **Circle E** tail marking.

Nose art started to proliferate on 22nd BW B-29s while flying combat missions over Korea. Some notable examples include: *The Riverside Rambler*, *The Mission Inn*, *Spirit of St. Louis*, *Spirit of Freeport*, *Mule Train*, *Peace Maker*, and *Sad Sack*. The nose art was relatively short-lived and was removed soon after the 22nd BW returned to the United States and Strategic Air Command control.

*Mission Inn B-29-35-MO (44-27263) on a bombing run over Korea. Assigned to the 33rd BS, this aircraft still carries the old **Triangle I** tail marking and has a yellow fin cap. (USAF courtesy Travis Air Museum)*

The 22nd BW returned to the United States on 31 October 1950 to resume its long-range bombing training duties at March Air Force Base.

In 1951, the only change to 22nd BW markings was a modification to the Wing insignia on the nose by incorporating a design that had an attached scroll with motto to the emblem shield. The previous Wing insignia had a different shaped shield with a separate scroll painted on its B-29s. Also in August 1951, in preparation for its upcoming TDY to the UK, the 22nd BW painted or repainted all Wing, Fifteenth Air Force, USAF and National insignia on all aircraft. In addition, all B-29s in the 22nd BW painted in black camouflage had their black paint removed.[34]

The 22nd BW would go on a third training mission to the United Kingdom from September 1951 to November 1951 with the aircraft markings noted above. Once again the squadrons would be based at different locations: the 33rd BS at Wyton, then Mildenhall; the 19th BS at Lakenheath; and the 2nd BS at Sculthorpe. The training program was similar to that followed during its 1950 deployment to England — interception exercises with the RAF and USAF, long-range navigation flights to Africa and the Gulf of Aden, live bombing missions and air-to-air refueling flights.[35]

In mid-summer 1952, the 22nd Air Refueling Squadron was organized, manned and equipped with KC-97 tankers. Green was the assigned squadron color and was painted on aircraft fin tips. Both the **Circle E** tail marking and the Fifteenth Air Force insignia appeared on the vertical stabilizer and dorsal fin, respectively. The 22nd BW insignia was displayed on the left side of the KC-97 nose. The 22nd BW was one of the few SAC units to operate KC-97s with tail markings (the other SAC units were the 305th BW, 306th BW, 40th BW, 106th/320th BW and possibly the 310th BW).

In late 1952, the 22nd BW began preparations to receive B-47s and the Wing took delivery of its first B-47 in January 1953; by March 1953 all B-29s were gone. 22nd BW B-47s did not use tactical tail markings and KC-97 tail markings were removed in May-June 1953.

The modified 22nd BW insignia on the nose. Shot taken at March AFB in 1952. (USAF, AFHRA)

28th Bombardment Group/Wing/Strategic Reconnaissance Wing

The 28th Bombardment Group, Very Heavy, was activated at Grand Island Army Air Field, Nebraska, on 4 August 1946 replacing the 449th Bombardment Group (VH) which was deactivated on the same date. The three assigned squadrons for the 28th BG were the 77th, 717th, and the 718th.

Equipped with B-29s, the 28th BG deployed to Elmendorf Army Air Field, Alaska, for six months of training in Arctic operations between October 1946 and April 1947. During this deployment, most 28th BG B-29s had black undersides and buzz numbers in insignia red. Silver finish aircraft had buzz numbers in black. The only unit markings appearing on 28th BG B-29s while in Alaska

*The 22nd ARS was one of the few air refueling units to use tactical markings on its KC-97s. In addition to the **Circle E** tail code and Fifteenth Air Force insignia, these aircraft carry the 22nd BW insignia on the nose and the fin cap is painted in the squadron color — green. (Boeing NNN 1281E. © Boeing. Used under license.)*

Above: *B-29–100-BW (45–21845) in the foreground and B-29–40-MO (44–86253) nicknamed* Snowball *in flight over Alaska.* Snowball *was assigned to the 717th BS and carries its squadron insignia on the nose. (USAF–Castle Air Museum)* Right: *During their stay in Alaska the 28th BG named and painted most of their B-29s.* Early Bird, *B-29–45-MO (44–86303), is one example of the Alaska deployment nose art and also has a cartoon figure on the nose gear door with the crew chief's rank and name. (USAF–Castle Air Museum)*

were squadron insignia placed on both sides of the aircraft nose for the 717th BS, and on both sides of the top of the vertical stabilizer for the 77th BS and 718th BS; and squadron identification markings initially on nose gear doors and later on the fin cap. Squadron color assignments were inherited from the 449th BG squadrons: the 716th BS — blue, went to the 77th BS; the 717th BS retained yellow; and the 718th BS retained red. These squadron color assignments were made by the 449th BG in July 1946 and applied to the nose gear doors of the squadrons.[36] Several B-29s were painted with nose art while in Alaska with names such as *Ramp Queen, Leakin Lena, Al-Ask-Er, Spirit of Anchorage, Early Bird, Eskimo Smoe, Banana Boat, Forever Amber* and *Snowball*.

In April 1947, the 28th BG redeployed to the Continental United States and was assigned to Rapid City Army Air Field, South Dakota, and the Fifteenth Air Force. For the rest of 1947 the 28th BG participated in several major exercises to include Operation Big Town which was SAC's simulated bombing run over New York City on 16 May 1947, and the Cleveland Air Races in September 1947. The 28th BG also began sending squadron-sized elements to overseas locations, specifically, Japan and Germany.

The only change to 28th BG B-29 markings in 1947 was the addition of a small Fifteenth Air Force insignia just below the aircraft tail number on the vertical stabilizer, and

B-36B-10-CF (44–92062) was the first B-36 aircraft assigned to the 28th BW in July 1949 and was assigned to the 77th BS. The 28th BW insignia is prominently displayed on the aircraft. Fall of 1949, Rapid City AFB. Notice the mix of Army and Air Force chevrons on the crew uniforms. (USAF–Castle Air Museum)

expanding the painting of squadron colors to fin tips. Squadron color assignments remained the same from the Alaskan deployment: blue for the 77th, yellow for the 717th, and red for the 718th. The last four digits of the aircraft serial number were painted on the nose gear doors in a contrasting color.

In early 1948, the Fifteenth Air Force assigned the **Circle R** to the 28th Bombardment Wing (activated 15 Aug 1947 and assumed control of the 28th BG and its three tactical squadrons—77th, 717th, and 718th) as its first tail marking. The **Black Circle** with the **Black R** immediately began to appear on Wing B-29s and was prominently displayed on its B-29s when the 28th BG deployed to the United Kingdom (UK) from July 1948 to October 1948 in response to the crisis in Berlin. A considerable number of 28th BG B-29s arrived in the UK carrying names and some nose art. Examples include: *Blackhills Baby* and *Banana Boat*—77th BS; *Percussion Steamboat, Willy's Ice Wagon, Unpredictable,* and *The Red*—717th; and *Hongchow* and *Itywytibad*—718th.

The 28th BG also displayed the Fifteenth Air Force insignia on the dorsal fin of its B-29s. The 717th BS continued the display of squadron insignia but it is believed the other two squadrons did not use squadron insignia on B-29s during their tour of duty in the UK.

The first B-29s of the 28th BG arrived in England on 17 July 1948 via Goose Bay, Labrador. All three squadrons of the 28th BG were stationed at Scampton, also home to

December 1946, Elmendorf Field. B-29–90–BW (45–21733) clearly shows the 717th BS insignia on the right side of the nose. Nose gear door is in 717th squadron color — yellow. (© Boeing. Used under license.)

The 718th BS displayed its squadron insignia on the vertical tail as shown on B-29–95–BW (45–21770) shortly after its arrival at Rapid City AAFld in April–May 1947. (USAF–Castle Air Museum)

Lincoln bombers of the RAF. In addition to being prepared to respond to any Soviet threat as a result of the Berlin crises, the 28th BG participated in many exercises intended to test British air defenses.[37]

The year 1949 brought several changes to the aircraft and aircraft markings of the 28th BW. It was decided to make the 28th BW a heavy bombardment wing and by mid–1949 the

Top: *B-29–60-BA (44–84078)in February 1948 at Rapid City while the de-icer boot is installed. Note the rectangular-shaped 77th BS insignia on the vertical stabilizer, the larger than usual buzz markings, and the AN/APG-15 gun-laying radar system. (USAF, AFHRA)* Middle: *The **Circle R** tail marking started to appear on 28th BW B-29s in early 1948. Early Bird, a 77th BS B-29-45-MO (44–86303), shows its **Circle R** tail marking during its 1948 tour of duty in the UK. (USAF, AFHRA)* Bottom: *RB-36D-10-CF (49–2688) with the lightning bolt in squadron color located on the jet pod — 1952. (USAF, AFHRA)*

Last iteration of aircraft markings for 28th SRW RB-36s during the tail-marking era. The Matthew P. Brady displays a fin stripe in squadron color, 28th BW insignia on the nose and identification numbers on the forward fuselage. (USAF, AFHRA)

28th BW's aircraft inventory was down to seven B-29s and one B-36 (44–92062).[38] The number of B-29 and B-36 aircraft would continue to fluctuate for the rest of 1949 and into early 1950 as many of the B-36s had to be transferred to air depots for fuel tank modifications and additional B-29s were brought in to take care of flying requirements. The only changes to aircraft markings in 1949 were the removal of buzz markings and the addition of **USAF** and **United States Air Force** markings. Also the 28th BW insignia started to appear on the left side of the aircraft nose (both B-29s and B-36s).

A new tactical marking — **Circle K** — was assigned to the 28th BW on 8 December 1949. The December 1949 unit history for the 28th Bombardment Wing stated, "The Maintenance Control Section will start painting the new insignia on all aircraft as they are pulled in for inspection."[39] Such an approach normally took four months to complete the painting of all assigned aircraft with a new tail marking.

The new **Circle K** tail marking was painted on several 28th Bombardment Wing B-29s and B-25s beginning in January 1950, and by early March, eleven B-29s and two B-25s displayed the new tail marking. However, in March 1950 the 28th BW was notified of its transfer to the Eighth Air Force effective 1 April 1950 as part of a major SAC reorganization; consequently, the painting of the **Circle K** tail marking on 28th BW aircraft was halted.[40]

SAC Manual 55–1, Tactical Doctrine — Bombardment dated April 1950 assigned a new tail marking to the 28th BW — **Triangle S**. The 28th BW unit history for April 1950 made the following comments about the new marking, "This station commenced painting the new tactical markings and Eighth Air Force insignias approximately 15 April 1950 during scheduled inspections. As of 30 April, new markings and insignia had been painted on two C-47s and one B-25. It is estimated four months will be required to complete this project."[41] It is interesting to note that in the case of the 28th BW, base flight aircraft like the B-25 and C-47 were also marked with the Wing tactical marking.

In addition to its transfer to the Eighth Air Force on 1 April 1950, the 28th BW was redesignated the 28th Strategic Reconnaissance Wing and its mission was changed to strategic reconnaissance from heavy bombardment.

Aircraft assignments to the 28th SRW during this time (mid–1950) were in a state of flux. At the end of April 1950, the 28th SRW had a mix of aircraft assets—three B-36Bs, sixteen B-29s, seven C-47s and three B-25s. In April and May 1950, ten B-29s were transferred to Travis AFB in exchange for eight RB-29s. For the rest of 1950, the 28th would transfer its B-29s and RB-29s (the last RB-29 would leave Rapid City in November 1950) and would continue to receive RB-36s having twenty RB-36s assigned by the end of the year.

There were no major changes to aircraft marking schemes with the employment of RB-36s by the 28th SRW. All RB-36s displayed the **Triangle S** tail marking; Eighth Air Force insignia; squadron colors on fin tips, nose gear doors, and main wheel doors; plane identification numbers on the forward fuselage; and the 28th BW insignia on the left side of the aircraft nose. Later, in 1952, a lightning bolt would be painted on the outboard portion of the jet engine pod in squadron color. Also, the 28th BW reduced the size of the fin tip marking to a narrow band across the top of the vertical fin.

The 28th SRW would continue to operate RB-36s at Ellsworth AFB (renamed in June 1953 in honor of BG Richard E. Ellsworth, 28th SRW Commander, who was killed in a RB-36 accident on 18 March 1953 in Newfoundland, Canada) until May 1957 when it began to receive B-52Ds.

40th Bombardment Group/Wing

The 40th Bombardment Group, Very Heavy, was one of the original bombardment groups assigned to Strategic Air Command when it was established on 21 March 1946. Assigned to the Fifteenth Air Force, its initial station was March Field, California. The three bombardment squadrons assigned to the 40th BG were the 25th, 44th and 45th. In May 1946, the 40th conducted a permanent change of station from March Field to Davis-Monthan Field, Arizona.

Although equipped with B-29s, the 40th Bombardment Group never possessed a full complement of aircraft prior to its deactivation in October 1946. The 40th BG did use squadron identification markings (blue for the 25th, red for the 44th; it's unknown if the 45th BS had an assigned squadron color in 1946) on its B-29s in the form of painted fin tips, fuselage bands, propeller domes and nose gear doors. Also the 25th Bomb Squadron and 44th Bomb Squadron displayed squadron insignia on the left side of the aircraft nose. 40th Bombardment Group B-29s carried buzz markings on the aft portion of the fuselage and, in some cases, in smaller letters and numbers on the vertical stabilizer above the aircraft tail numbers. All 40th Bombardment Group B-29s were in silver finish with aircraft tail numbers and buzz numbers appearing in black.

When the 40th Bombardment Group was deactivated in October 1946 at Davis-Monthan Field, its personnel and B-29 aircraft became part of the newly activated 43rd Bombardment Group.

On 6 February 1953 the 40th Bombardment Wing, Medium, was activated at Smoky Hill Air Force Base, Kansas. Prior to the activation of the Wing, both the 40th Air Refueling Squadron (on 8 July 1952), and the 40th Tactical and Maintenance Squadron Provisional (on 24 January 1953) were organized. Initially, the 40th ARS was attached to the 310th Bombardment Wing at Smoky Hill Air Force Base. The 40th ARS received its first KC-97 tanker on 18 October 1952 and by late 1952 had a full complement of 20 KC-97s.[42] The 40th Tactical and Maintenance Squadron was located at Davis-Monthan Air Force Base

B-29A-75-BN (44–62322) preparing for flight at Davis-Monthan Field in June 1946. Assigned to the 25th BS, it bears squadron insignia on the nose and blue squadron identification markings placed on the fin cap, propeller domes and on the fuselage in a single belly band. (USAF, AFHRA)

and served as a holding unit for the purpose of operating and maintaining aircraft belonging to the 40th BW until facilities at Smoky Hill could be expanded to accommodate the new unit. At the end of February 1953, the 40th BW had 21 B-29s assigned and 20 KC-97s. By the end of March the number of B-29s had grown to 33 of which 18 were located at Smoky Hill. The B-29 aircraft assigned to the Wing came from two sources: 15 APQ-7 radar type B-29s from Davis-Monthan AFB made excess by the conversion of the 303rd BW to B-47s; and 18 aircraft from the Sacramento Air Materiel Area that had been taken out of mothballs at Pyote AFB, Texas, and sent to McClellan AFB, California, where they were completely refurbished.[43] Through the end of April 1953, the 25th Bomb Squadron was the only operational bomb squadron in the 40th BW. The 44th BS would become operational on 1 June 1953 and the 45th BS in October 1953.

The assigned tail marking for the 40th Bomb Wing was a **Circle S**, which was assigned by the Fifteenth Air Force in October 1952.[44] It is believed this tail marking initially appeared on 40th ARS KC-97s and subsequently on B-29s assigned in early 1953. In addition to the **Circle S** tail marking, the Fifteenth Air Force insignia was placed on the dorsal fin of both B-29s and KC-97s. It is not known if the 40th BW used distinctive squadron identification markings prior to October 1953, several months after tail markings were removed. The October 1953 40th Bomb Wing Unit History mentions color assignments for each tactical

Top: 44th BS B-29A-75-BN (44–62314) shows the full marking scheme for the 40th BG in 1946. The squadron color is red and appears on the fin cap, single fuselage band, engine cowling panels and on nose gear doors. The squadron insignia appears on the left side of the nose. (Photograph by Art Krieger, courtesy P. Stevens) Bottom: Command Decision *B-29–85-BW (44–87657) was assigned to the 40th BW in 1953 after its return from the Korean War and service with the 19th BG. Aircraft is in the black camouflage pattern used during the latter part of the Korean War. (Museum of Flight — Gordon S. Williams Collection)*

unit of the wing — blue for the 25th Bomb Squadron; red for the 44th Bomb Squadron; yellow for the 45th Bomb Squadron; and green for the 40th ARS.[45] There is no evidence the 40th Bomb Wing used wing or squadron insignia on its aircraft in 1952 or 1953.

The 40th Bomb Wing would continue to operate as a B-29 wing until May 1954 when they transferred their B-29s and began converting to B-47s.

43rd Bombardment Group/Wing

The story of the 43rd Bombardment Group, Very Heavy, begins on 1 October 1946 at Davis-Monthan Field, Arizona, when the 444th Bombardment Group (VH) was inactivated

Top: *Two 64 BS B-29s show the squadron identification marking scheme inherited from the 444th BG in October 1946 when the 43rd BG was activated. The squadron markings appear on the fin tip, single fuselage band, nose gear doors, propeller domes and outer cowling panels. The 64th BS color was green. (San Diego Aerospace Museum)* Bottom: *B-29 A-70-BW (44–62234) shows 43rd BG markings in mid-1947. The aircraft displays the 64th BS insignia on the left side of the nose as well as a small plane-in-group number used only in 1946 and 1947. San Francisco Airport, 24 May, 1947. (Courtesy W. Larkins)*

and on the same day the 43rd Bombardment Group (VH) was activated, incorporating the personnel and equipment of the 444th.

Assigned to the Eighth Air Force and equipped with B-29s, the 43rd Bombardment Group spent most of its first year in existence participating in mass training flights with other units of the Eighth Air Force to include the well-publicized mock attack on New York City in May 1947, and deploying squadron-size elements on overseas training missions: the 65th BS to Yokota, Japan, in May 1947, the 64th BS and 65th BS to Germany in August 1947, and the 63rd BS to Yokota, Japan, in September 1947.[46]

In November 1947 the 43rd Bombardment Wing was organized under the new Hob-

Top: Lucky Lady II *on display for July 4 at Chicago's Orchard Place Airport (today's O'Hare Airport). The name* Kensmen *appears on the lower right nose in honor of one of the 43rd BG commanders killed during World War II. (Courtesy National Museum of the USAF) Bottom: December 1948 found the 43rd BW operating from Ladd AFB, Alaska. The 43 BW B-50As were painted in insignia red Arctic markings with the tail markings removed and the radio call number located in a natural metal rectangle. Also, for this deployment, 43rd BW squadron markings only appear on the nose gear door. (USAF, AFHRA)*

son Plan with both the 43rd Bombardment Group and the recently activated 2nd Bombardment Group assigned.

In early 1947 the 43rd Bombardment Group became one of the first Strategic Air Command bombardment groups to use a tail marking. Assigned by Eighth Air Force and approved by SAC, a **Black Hollow Diamond** started to appear on the vertical stabilizer of 43rd BG B-29s. In addition, the Eighth Air Force insignia was applied to both sides of the dorsal fin and an aircraft identification marking (buzz number) consisting of the two letter prefix BF with the last three digits of the aircraft serial number placed aft of the national insignia on the fuselage. These buzz numbers were black on silver finish B-29s and insignia red on black camouflage aircraft. The 43rd Bombardment Group insignia appeared on the right side of the nose on assigned Superfortresses and, in the case of the 64th Bombardment Squadron, its World War II insignia was placed on the left side of the nose. The 43rd BW assigned squadron colors were yellow and black for the 63rd Bombardment Squadron, green for the 64th Bombardment Squadron, and red for the 65th Bombardment Squadron. These squadron identification markings appeared on fin tips, nose gear doors, on the fuselage as a single belly band and on outer cowl-

Gracious Oasis *at Davis-Monthan AFB in 1949.* *(Boeing P9727. © Boeing. Used under license.)*

Most KB-29M tankers of the 43rd ARS had nose art reflecting its air refueling mission with a sense of humor. This example is Sky Octane. *(Boeing P9680. © Boeing. Used under license.)*

ing panels. Also during this time there was a considerable amount of nose art in the 43rd BW, primarily in the 63rd Bombardment Squadron. Examples included: *Lucky 'Leven, Cosmic Clipper, The Uninvited, Celestial Princess, Forever Amber,* and *The Wild Hare.*[47]

Designated to be the first B-50-equipped bombardment wing in the Air Force, the 43rd BW received its first B-50A (46–017) on 20 February 1948. The 43rd BW would continue to operate a mixture of B-29s and B-50As until early 1949 when the 43rd BW would become fully operational with the B-50A. With the introduction of the B-50, the only change to aircraft markings came with the placement of the squadron markings which were reduced to the single fuselage band and nose gear doors.

Top: *As part of its markings scheme, the 43rd ARS placed its newly designed squadron insignia on the right side of the aircraft nose. Davis-Monthan AFB, 1949. (Boeing P9693. © Boeing. Used under license.)* Bottom: *The* City of Tucson *was a 64th BS B-50A christened on Air Force Day 1948. Ground crew in November 1949 at Davis Monthan AFB. (USAF, AFHRA)*

In late 1948, the 43rd deployed to Alaska with its newly assigned B-50s for cold weather training. During this deployment, all tail markings were removed as well as the single fuselage band. Insignia red Arctic markings were applied to the usual surface areas of the tail and on the outer wings. The Eighth Air Force insignia remained on the dorsal fin and squadron identification markings were retained on the nose gear doors.[48]

The 43rd BW would develop an enviable record of flight accomplishments with its B-29s and B-50s in 1948 and 1949. On 22 July 1948, three B-29s, *Lucky Lady*, *Gas Gobbler*, and *Pride of Tucson*, left Davis-Monthan on a planned trip around the world. The

63rd BS B-50A named Nogoodnik *(46–044) was the first B-50 in the Air Force to get 600 hours on all four original engines. Crew chief being congratulated was T/Sgt Alexander F. Hydak. (USAF, AFHRA)*

*In late 1949, the authorized strength of the 43rd BW increased from thirty B-50As to forty-five. As an interim measure, B-29s were brought out of storage until sufficient B-50s became available. BF-310 shows the new **Circle K** tail marking but retains the older style squadron identification markings and buzz marking. (Museum of Flight — Gordon S. Williams collection)*

crash of the *Pride of Tucson* delayed the trip one day, but the other two aircraft completed the trip in a record 15 days. The 20,000 mile flight required eight stops along the way and took 103 hours and 50 minutes of flying time to complete.[49]

On 2 March 1949, *Lucky Lady II*, a B-50A (46–010) completed the first nonstop, round-the-world flight, having covered 23,452 miles in 94 hours and 1 minute. Starting on 26 February 1949, *Luck Lady II* was refueled four times in the air by KB-29M tankers of the 43rd Air Refueling Squadron. The 43rd ARS was divided into four detachments which staged out of the Azores, Saudi Arabia, the Philippines, and Hawaii to provide aerial refueling support for *Lucky Lady II*. For this outstanding flight, the *Lucky Lady II* crew was awarded the MacKay Trophy.[50]

In 1949 the 43rd BW would make the first TDY deployment of a SAC B-50A medium bombardment unit to the United Kingdom. The 43rd BW would operate from Sculthorpe, Lakenheath and Marham during its stay in England from August to November 1949. A number of B-50s possessed nicknames such as *Lucky Lady II*, *Nogoodnik*, *Nifty 50*, *Fat Chance II*, and *Miss Minooki*. Also participating in this deployment were KB-29Ms of the 43rd Aerial Refueling Squadron (ARS), one of the first two aerial refueling squadrons in the U.S. Air Force.[51] 43rd ARS KB-29Ms had squadron colors of blue and white, which beginning in July 1949, were placed in the form of diagonal stripes on the fin tip, fuselage band and nose gear doors. The 43rd ARS squadron insignia was placed on the right side of the KB-29M nose. For several of the tankers, nicknames and nose art appeared on the left side.[52] Examples of KB-29M aircraft nicknames included: *Hosin Hosea*, *Gracious Oasis*, *Sky Octane*, *Homogenized Ethyl*, *Touch and Go*, *Who's Next*, *Short Time Only*, *Bold Venture* and several others.

Squadron line-up with six B-50A tails of the 64th BS. Davis-Monthan AFB circa 1950–1951. (Boeing P10329. © Boeing. Used under license.)

After its return from the UK in late 1949, the 43rd BW received an increase in authorized strength from thirty aircraft to forty-five. Due to delays in B-50A deliveries, the 43rd removed several B-29s from flyable storage to help meet the requirement to provide forty-five aircraft and crews.

In late 1949, the 43rd BW received a new tail marking assignment as part of SAC's newly announced policy on aircraft markings. The new marking—**Triangle D**—was never implemented due in part to the 43rd BW's TDY to the United Kingdom from August until November 1949 and its impending transfer to the Fifteenth Air Force on 1 April 1950. Another new tail marking—**Circle K**—was assigned and started to appear on B-50A and KB-29M vertical stabilizers in May 1950.

*Nogoodnik with the **Circle K** tail marking, Fifteenth Air Force insignia and squadron identification markings now located on fin tip and fuel tank tips in addition to the nose gear doors. (Boeing P10332. © Boeing. Used under license.)*

Another unique marking used by the 43rd BW on B-50s assigned to the 63rd BS was the name *Kensmen* which appeared below the 43rd BW insignia on the right front of the aircraft nose. This marking was used in honor of one of the 43rd BG commanders, Ken McCullar, killed during World War II.

By early 1951, the 43rd BW was completely equipped with B-50As (45) and KB-29Ms (20). B-50A markings would include the **Circle K** tail code, Fifteenth Air Force insignia on the dorsal fin, squadron markings on the fin tip, single fuselage band, nose gear doors and forward portion of the wing fuel tanks, **BK** prefix buzz numbers on the aft fuselage and a small identification number on the fuel tank wing strut. The 43rd BW was the only SAC B-50 unit to continue to use the **BK** prefix buzz numbers after the introduction of the **USAF** and **United States Air Force** markings. A change to the 63rd BS marking scheme was the use of solid yellow on the fin tip, yellow and black diagonal stripes for the fuselage band and nose gear doors, and yellow with a black border on the fuel tanks. The 43rd ARS markings remained basically the same except for KB-29Ms that were TDY to the FEAF in Japan where these tankers displayed a four-digit identification number on the nose gear doors. Also the unit placed scrolls on the aircraft nose that were used to list crewmember names—ground crew on the left, air crew on the right.

These markings remained in force through the 43rd BW deployment to the U.K. from March to June 1953. After its return to the United States, tail codes were removed and aircraft markings in general were toned down.

The 43rd BW would continue to fly B-50s for another year, after which they would convert to B-47s. The KB-29Ms were replaced by KC-97s in 1953.

44th Bombardment Wing

The 44th Bombardment Wing, Medium, was reactivated on 2 January 1951 as part of the USAF expansion program due to the conflict in Korea. Assigned to the Fifteenth Air Force, the 44th Bombardment Wing's assigned bombardment squadrons were the 66th,

Square K *tail marking and squadron markings for the 66th Bombardment Squadron. The 66th BS insignia on the nose is its World War II design. (Courtesy Brig. Gen. H. J. Dalton, Jr.)*

67th and 68th. The initial base assignment was March AFB, Riverside, California. Personnel and organizational support came from the 22nd Bombardment Wing, also located at March AFB.

The first B-29s assigned to the 44th BW came from the 5th SRW at Travis AFB where the 5th SRW was in the process of converting to RB-36s. By March 1951, 26 B-29s had been assigned to the 44th BW.

The first tail marking assignment for the 44th BW was **Circle T**. This was communicated to the Wing in a message from Headquarters, Fifteenth Air Force dated 24 January 1951.[53] In March 1951, the 44th BW inspected its fleet of B-29s and made the following report: "The painted surfaces, including 15th Air Force markings, National Insignias, USAF, Aircraft serial numbers, Decals and miscellaneous markings have been estimated at 60% poor, 30% fair and 10% good. Tactical markings and Group markings have to be applied to all B-29s. An estimate of 140 hours to complete insignia painting, and removal of old insignia for each B-29 is estimated."[54] In May 1951 the 44th BW took action to comply with the SAC directive on removing aircraft tail numbers from rudder surfaces and repositioning the numbers to the vertical stabilizer. As stated in the May 1951 44th BW unit history, "...a SAC directive ordered all radio call numbers to be placed on the vertical stabilizer which necessitated removal of these numbers from the rudder surfaces. As the planes entered the docks the call numbers were removed and repainted in the proper position."[55]

The 44th Bombardment Wing completed its training program at March AFB in July 1951 and was transferred to the 21st Air Division, a direct reporting unit to Headquarters SAC, with duty station at Lake Charles AFB, Louisiana. The first five B-29s from the 44th BW landed at Lake Charles AFB on 31 July 1951.

The 67th BS Flying Pelican *insignia was displayed on all squadron B-29s on the right side of the aircraft nose. The 44th BW insignia was placed on the opposite side of the nose. Lake Charles AFB during Armed Forced Day 1952. (Courtesy F. Fiorentino)*

The mission of the 44th BW after its arrival at Lake Charles was to serve as an Operational Training Unit (OTU) wing to train B-29 replacement crews for the Far East Air Forces. During this program from October 1951 to August 1952, the 44th BW trained and shipped 89 complete combat-ready B-29 replacement crews. Also, in addition to training FEAF replacement crews, the 44th BW served as the parent wing to the 68th Strategic Reconnaissance Wing and guided it through all aspects of operational training from October 1951 through August 1952 when the 68th BW, newly redesignated a bombardment wing, became a fully operational wing.[56]

Shortly after its arrival at Lake Charles, 44th BW B-29s had the **Circle T** tail markings and Fifteenth Air Forces insignias removed.[57] As an OTU aircraft assigned to the 44th BW did not use a tail marking, but the 44th BW did place squadron identification markings on fin tips and nose gear doors. Squadron color assignments were: 66th Bombardment Squadron — Blue; 67th Bombardment Squadron — Yellow; and the 68th Bombardment Squadron — Red.[58] Also, the 44th BW insignia was painted on the left side of the nose and, in the case of the 66th BS and 67th BS, the squadron insignia appeared on the right side of the aircraft nose.

After its training mission, the 44th BW assumed a tactical mission under the control of the 806th Air Division of the Second Air Force. A new tactical tail marking was assigned to the 44th BW — **Square K** — which started to appear on its B-29 fleet in the fall of 1952. The only other change to markings was the placement of the last four numbers of the air-craft serial number on the nose gear doors in contrasting colors. These were the markings used on 44th BW B-29s during its deployment to Sidi Slimane, French Morocco, in January–February 1953.

Upon its return, the 44th BW was notified that it was to convert to B-47s. In the mean-time, the 44th BW removed all tail codes per SAC policy during the spring of 1953. By early July 1953, all 44th BW B-29s had been transferred. The first 44th BW B-47 arrived on 23 June 1953.

55th Strategic Reconnaissance Group/Wing

The 55th Reconnaissance Group, Very Long Range Mapping, was activated 24 Febru-ary 1947 at MacDill Field, Florida, and assigned directly to Strategic Air Command. The first assigned squadron was the 343rd Reconnaissance Squadron, Very Long Range Map-ping. Equipped with modified B-17 aircraft, the 343rd conducted aerial photography, photo-reconnaissance, mapping and charting missions over the United States, Greenland, and the Caribbean. The other reconnaissance squadrons, the 38th and 338th, were subsequently assigned and equipped with RB-17 and RB-29 aircraft. They conducted photo-mapping mis-sions in the Pacific region.[59]

From 1947 to 1949, 55th RG aircraft had no distinctive aircraft markings other than the required national emblem, aircraft tail number and aircraft identification numbers (buzz markings).

In June 1948, the 55th SRG was redesignated the 55th SRG, Photo-Mapping, and was assigned to the newly activated 55th Strategic Reconnaissance Wing. In July 1948, the 55th SRW moved from MacDill Air Force Base, Florida, to Topeka Air Force Base, Kansas, and received an attached RB-29 squadron, the 1st SRS — Photo. In July 1949, the 38th SRS and 338th SRS rejoined the 55th at Topeka (now Forbes AFB) flying RB-29s. The assignment was short-lived as the 55th SRG was deactivated in October 1949 and its aircraft assets were transferred to the 91st Strategic Reconnaissance Wing.

The 55th SRW with its assigned squadrons — the 38th, 338th and 343rd — was reacti-vated in November 1950 at Barksdale Air Force Base, Louisiana. Also at this time the 55th Air Refueling Squadron was activated. The 55th SRW transferred in mid–November 1950 to Ramey Air Force Base, Puerto Rico, and would stay in Puerto Rico for nearly two years. The first aircraft from the 55th SRW arrived at Ramey AFB in December 1950 with the trans-fer of the 38th SRS and its RB-50Bs from Barksdale. This was soon followed in early Jan-uary 1951 with the arrival of the 343rd SRS with its RB-29s, and the 338th SRS also equipped with RB-29s; air crews and maintenance support personnel of the 55th ARS began arriv-ing on 8 January 1951 and operated KB-29M tankers. In short order, the 55th SRW began an active program of strategic reconnaissance, charting, electronic geodetic mapping, and

Top: *RB-29 transferred to the 55th SRW in November 1950 from the 91st SRW at Barksdale. It retained its original markings from the 91st. Since the 91st SRW was re-equipping with B-45 and RB-45 aircraft, the tail marking—**Square V**—was assigned to the 55th SRW and the 91st SRW was given a new tail marking—**Square I**. (USAF) Bottom: A 338th SRS RB-50E-40-BO (47–121) in the shop getting ready to have squadron markings applied at Ramey AFB, P.R.–January 1951. (USAF)*

An RB-50 of the 338th SRS landing at Ramey AFB showing off newly-applied squadron markings on the fin cap, vertical fin, fuel tanks, propeller spinners and nose gear door. January 1951. (USAF)

other related reconnaissance functions for SAC.[60] Aircraft operated in early 1951 included RB-29s, RB-50Bs, KB-29Ms and C-82 transports.

Upon reactivation, the 55th SRW received notification that its official tail insignia would be the letter V inside a **Black Square.** Previously this tail marking had been used by the 91st SRW, but they gave up this marking since it was converting to RB-45C aircraft and most of its RB-29s and RB-50Bs were transferred to the 55th SRW. (91st SRS RB-50Bs went to the 38th SRS; 323rd RB-29s went to the 338th SRS; and 324th SRS RB-29s went to the 343rd SRS)

Beginning in January 1951, the 55th SRW started to replace its B-29s with modified RB-50s. Also during 1951, RB-50Bs of the 38th SRS were modified at Boeing-Wichita with SHORAN navigation radar designed to conduct mapping, charting and geodetic surveys and were redesignated RB-50Fs. The 338th SRS was

Three RB-50s assigned to the 38th SRS. The SAC command insignia started to appear on 55th SRW RB-50s in March 1952 and was applied to the left side of the nose. (USAF)

responsible for photographic reconnaissance and observation missions and received its first RB-50E in January 1951. The 343rd SRS conducted the electronic reconnaissance mission for the 55th SRW and started to operate RB-50Gs in June 1951. The RB-50G platform featured six electronic countermeasures stations and carried a 16-man crew.

KB-29M Tillie the Tanker *had black speed lines on the forward fuselage, which were later removed, and blue and white diagonal squadron markings on nose gear door, wings tips and fin cap. (Courtesy E. Gisbert)*

Squadron identification markings for most 55th SRW aircraft started to appear in early 1951. The exception to this was the 38th SRS which inherited the marking scheme used by the 91st SRS of the 91st SRW. The squadron identification colors for the 38th SRS were green and yellow. The fin tips and propeller domes were painted green and nose gear doors displayed green and yellow diagonal stripes. The wing tanks were decorated in a green tapered stripe outlined by a thin forward-pointing yellow arrow. Aircraft nicknames noted in the 38th SRS included *Laborin Lady* and *Belle of Bourbon Street*. The 38th SRS deployed to the United Kingdom in mid–January 1951 and would stay in England through May 1951.

Based at Bassingbourn, the 38th SRS would carry out many photographic and electronic reconnaissance activities along the East German Border.

In January 1951, the 338th SRS started marking their new RB-50Es with a blue lightning bolt outlined in yellow across the wing tip tanks and down the vertical stabilizer, with blue propeller hubs, and blue and yellow diagonal striped nose wheel doors.[61] *Mac's Effort* was one of the named aircraft in the 338th SRS.

A later photograph of Tillie the Tanker, *a KB-29M of the 55th ARS, her crew chief, M/Sgt. Elmer V. Gisbert Jr., and her assistant crew chief, S/Sgt. Kenneth R. Ainsworth. Nose gear door colors are blue and white. (E. Gisbert)*

Markings for the 343rd SRS were not as bright and conspicuous as its sister SRSs. This squadron performed

Top: *KB-29M-40-MO (44–27340) of the 55th ARS finishing a periodic maintenance inspection at the docks at Ramey AFB just prior to the 55th SRW move to Forbes AFB, Kansas. October 1952. (USAF) Bottom: 338th SRS RB-50 with new markings after the 55th SRW move to Forbes AFB and the Fifteenth Air Force. The arrow trim on the fuel tanks is yellow. (USAF courtesy Combat Air Museum— Topeka)*

the electronic intelligence (ELINT) or CROW missions for the Wing flying RB-29s and later RB-50Gs. Not anxious to identify aircraft or unit identity, 343rd RB-50Gs flew missions from TDY locations around the world. Starting in August 1951, RB-50Gs from the 343rd SRS flew combat missions during the Korean Conflict as a detachment to the 91st SRS out of Yokota, Japan. Squadron colors were red and white and appeared on the nose of the wing fuel tanks and occasionally as diagonal stripes on the nose wheel doors. A stylized crow served as the squadron insignia and was placed on the left side of the aircraft nose. This same emblem in smaller form was used as a combat mission marking for those RB-50Gs that flew combat during the Korean Conflict. Several aircraft nicknames noted in the 343rd SRS were *Caribbean Queen, Ramey Ramblers, Fat Cat, The Horrible Herm,* and *SAC Hobo.*[62]

The 55th Air Refueling Squadron was equipped with KB-29M tankers. Their assigned colors were blue and white. Diagonal striped markings were placed on nose gear doors, fin tips, wing tips and the aft portion of the sealed tail gunner compartment. Nicknames noted in the 55th ARS included *Tillie the Tanker.*

Top: *The 343rd SRS of the 55th SRW had an electronic warfare mission (ELINT) and starting in early 1951 began sending crews TDY to Japan in support of FEAF combat operations. Crew photograph shows* The Fat Cat *of the 343rd SRS with 30 crow combat mission symbols. (USAF-National Archives) Bottom: RB-50 (47–134) still displays its squadron colors — green and yellow — on the nose gear doors and green on the propeller hubs. In this photograph taken in 1953 at Forbes AFB, the tail marking is gone, replaced by insignia red Arctic markings. (Museum of Flight)*

The only change to aircraft markings while the 55th SRW was at Ramey AFB was the placement of the newly authorized official Strategic Air Command insignia on the right side of the nose of 55th RB-50s beginning in March 1952.[63]

In October 1952, the 55th SRW conducted a permanent change of station to Forbes Air Force Base, Kansas, and was assigned to the 21st Air Division of the Fifteenth Air Force. A new tail code—**Circle V**—was assigned to the Wing and both the new tail marking and the Fifteenth Air Force insignia started to appear on the dorsal fin of 38th and 338th RB-50s. Due to its mission, the 343rd SRS continued to fly RB-50s without tail markings.

These markings only lasted until May-June 1953 when all tail insignia and major subordinate command insignia were ordered removed by Headquarters, SAC. The 55th SRW would continue to operate RB-50s and KB-29s until 1954 when it began to re-equip with RB-47s and the 55th ARS was inactivated.

68th Strategic Recon/Bombardment Wing

The 68th Strategic Reconnaissance Wing, Medium, and the 24th, 51st and 52nd Strategic Reconnaissance Squadrons, Medium, were activated on 10 October 1951 at Lake Charles Air Force Base and were assigned to SAC's Second Air Force. The 68th SRW was further attached to the 21st Air Division for training purposes. Their permanent unit at Lake Charles AFB, the 44th Bombardment Wing, would train the crews and personnel of the 68th SRW as part of a 180-day training program prior to its departure to its proposed permanent station—Lockbourne Air Force Base, Columbus, Ohio. The flying training program for the 68th SRW began in late October 1951 using aircraft assigned to the 44th Bombardment Wing.

In May 1952, SAC decided that the 68th SRW would not move to Lockbourne AFB but would stay at Lake Charles AFB as a bombardment wing to be effective 16 June 1952.[64]

*68th BW B-29-A-60-BN (44–62028) with the **Square N** tail marking. Red fin tip and nose gear door indicates assignment to the 52nd BS. Photograph taken at Lake Charles AFB in late 1952. (Courtesy Brig. Gen. H. J. Dalton, Jr.)*

*68th BW B-29A-60-BN (44–62091) shows the remnants of its recently removed **Square N** tail marking. Photograph taken at Hensley AFB, Dallas, Texas, on 18 May 1953.*

During its training phase with the 44th BW, the 68th SRW had no aircraft assigned, but used those of the 44th BW. In preparation for its mission change to bombardment, the 68th SRW received its first B-29 aircraft in May 1952 when nine B-29s were transferred from the 44th BW.[65]

The assigned tail code for the 68th SRW, and later BW, was **Square N**. The 68th BW applied tail markings to its B-29s in the summer and fall of 1952. 68th BW squadron color assignments were yellow for the 24th BS, green for the 51st BS, and red for the 52nd BS[66]. These colors appeared on fin tips as two horizontal stripes separated by the silver finish of the aircraft and on nose gear doors. 68th BW B-29s displayed the last three numbers of the tail number on nose gear doors in a contrasting color. In addition, the aircraft tail number was painted in black on the vertical tail assembly just below the fin cap. There is no evidence that the 68th BW used squadron or wing insignia on its B-29 aircraft.

Like the rest of SAC, the 68th BW started to remove tail codes from its B-29s in April 1953 and finished by early June 1953. Later in 1953, the 68th converted to B-47 medium jet bombers.

72nd Strategic Reconnaissance Wing

The 72nd Strategic Reconnaissance Wing, Heavy, was activated on 16 June 1952 at Ramey Air Force Base, Puerto Rico. The 72nd SRW's assigned squadrons were the 60th, 73rd, and 301st Strategic Reconnaissance Squadrons. The 72nd SRW was not operational until October 1952 when it received residual personnel and equipment assets from the 55th Strategic Reconnaissance Wing which had been transferred to the Fifteenth Air Force and moved to Forbes Air Force Base, Kansas. The 72nd SRW received its first two aircraft, RB-36s, on 27 October 1952, starting a steady flow of aircraft to the Wing. These first two RB-36s were assigned to the 60th SRS; the first aircraft for the 73rd SRS arrived on 8 January 1953, and the 301st received five RB-36s in March 1953.[67]

According to the SAC Tactical Doctrine Manual — Bombardment 55–1, change 3 dated 29 January 1952, the assigned tail marking for the 72nd SRW was **Square L**. For unknown

*72nd SRW RB-36 with its short-lived **Square F** tail marking shares the ramp with a visiting 5th SRW RB-36 from Travis AFB. (USAF, AFHRA)*

*Clear view of **Square F** tail marking of 72nd SRW RB-36 (52–13571) undergoing dock maintenance at Ramey AFB. (USAF, AFHRA)*

reasons, this marking was changed to **Square F** in late 1952 and started to appear on 72nd RB-36s after their arrival in late 1952.

It is not known if squadron identification markings were used prior to the removal of the **Square F** tail marking in the spring of 1953. The only other marking used on 72nd RB-36s were large aircraft identification numbers located on the forward fuselage.

Although the 72nd SRW operated RB-36s and B-36s from Ramey Air Force Base until 1958, the mission of strategic reconnaissance changed to strategic bombardment beginning in 1954. The formal change in mission came on 1 October 1955 when the 72nd Strategic Reconnaissance Wing, together with its 60th, 73rd, and 301st Strategic Reconnaissance Squadrons, was redesignated as a bombardment unit, and the Wing's mission officially changed from reconnaissance to bombardment on a global scale.[68]

90th Bombardment Wing/Strategic Reconnaissance Wing

In early 1951 the 90th Bombardment Wing, Medium, was activated as a B-29 unit at Fairchild AFB, Spokane, Washington, assigned to SAC's Fifteenth Air Force. The 90th BW with its three squadrons—the 319th, 320th and 321st—moved to Forbes Air Force Base, Kansas, in February or March 1951 when it was assigned to the 21st Air Division, a Headquarters, SAC direct reporting unit. The primary mission of the 90th BW was to serve as an Operational Training Unit for newly activated SAC bombardment wings, specifically,

the 376th, 308th and 310th Bombardment Wings. Additionally, the 90th BW served as a Replacement Training Unit to provide replacement combat crews to the Far Eastern Air Forces. On 16 June 1952 the 90th Bombardment Wing was redesignated the 90th Strategic Reconnaissance Wing and received a change in mission from SAC Headquarters, "Effective 1 September 1952, the 90th Bombardment Wing is relieved of its OTU mission. The mission of the 90th Bombardment Wing will then be to train FEAF bombardment crews and continue the Strategic Air Command Shoran Bombing training function. On 1 November 1952, the requirement of training FEAF reconnaissance crews will be added ... relieving the 111th Strategic Reconnaissance Wing of this requirement."[69]

In a message from Headquarters, Fifteenth Air Force dated 24 January

Top: *Crew inspection for the* City of Baton Rouge *assigned to the 319th BS. Notice the World War II–design squadron insignia on the nose. Forbes AFB, 1952. (USAF — Combat Air Museum — Topeka)* Above: City of Baton Rouge *showing the 90th BW* **Circle Z** *tail marking and Fifteenth Air Force insignia. (USAF — Combat Air Museum — Topeka)*

Top: *The* City of Topeka *was christened at Forbes Air Force Base during Armed Forces Day on 17 May 1952. B-29A-55-BN (44–61926) was assigned to the 321st BS and has the squadron color — yellow with black diagonal stripes — painted on the nose gear doors. (USAF — National Archives)* Bottom: *The 90th Bombardment Wing was redesignated a Strategic Reconnaissance Wing in June 1952. RB-29–100-BW (45–21846) of the 90th SRW at Oakland Airport on 15 March 1953. (Courtesy D. Olson)*

1951 the 90th BW was assigned **Circle Z** as its tail marking.[70] However, with its assignment to the 21st Air Division at Forbes AFB and assumption of SAC's OTU mission, the **Circle Z** tail marking was not used until the 90th was redesignated a SRW and reassigned to the Fifteenth Air Force on 16 July 1952. During its time as an OTU the 90th BW did display squadron identification markings which were painted on the fin cap and nose gear doors using a pattern of two diagonal stripes in contrasting color over the squadron color. The 90th BW's squadron colors were: red for the 319th, blue for the 320th, and yellow for the 321st, with diagonal stripes of white for the 319th and 320th BS/SRS, and black for the 321st BS/SRS. The only squadron to use squadron insignia on its aircraft was the 319th which placed its World War II "Asterperious" design on the left side of the aircraft nose. Tail numbers initially were painted in black midway on the vertical stabilizer. Later, beginning in June 1952, when the **Circle Z** tail marking was placed on aircraft tails, the aircraft tail number was moved to the top of the tail fin just below the fin cap. Eventually the aircraft tail number would be moved to only the vertical stabilizer in a forward break of the Fifteenth Air Force **Circle**. Also, after assignment to the Fifteenth Air Force in June 1952, the Fifteenth Air Force insignia was placed on the dorsal fin.

Beginning with Armed Forces Day in May 1952, the 90th BW began a tradition of naming many of its aircraft for cities. On 19 May 1952, five B-29s were sent to several locations to participate in christening ceremonies and to be named for those cities; specifically *City of Fargo*—319th BS; *City of Belleville*—320th BS; *City of Kansas City*—320th BS; *City of Topeka*—321st BS; and *City of Milwaukee*—321st BS.[71] Subsequent names appearing on 90th BW/SRW B-29s in 1952 and 1953 would include *City of Akron*, *City of San Francisco*, and *City of Baton Rouge*. In each case the name of the city would appear on a banner on the left side of the aircraft nose with "City of" written above the banner in script.

The **Circle Z** tail marking started to disappear in the spring of 1953 and by early summer was gone. The same was true for the Fifteenth Air Force insignia and all squadron insignia. The 90th SRW continued to use RB-29s until late 1954 when the wing converted to RB-47Es.

91st Strategic Reconnaissance Group/Wing

The 91st Strategic Reconnaissance Group, Medium, was a cadre organization until the summer of 1948 when the unit was transferred to McGuire AFB, New Jersey, and was brought up to full strength. Equipped initially with B-17, RB-17, TB-29, TRB-29 and RC-54 aircraft, the 91st SRG had two assigned reconnaissance squadrons—the 323rd and 324th.

By the autumn of 1949, the 91st Strategic Reconnaissance Wing had been activated and assumed control of the 91st SRG and its subordinate squadrons, which in addition to the 323rd and 324th Reconnaissance Squadrons, now included the 91st Strategic Reconnaissance Squadron, Photo-Mapping, and the 7th Geodetic Squadron. There continued to be a variety of aircraft assigned to the 91st SRW due to the different squadron missions being performed. The first B-50B aircraft was received in July 1949 and assigned to the 91st Strategic Reconnaissance Squadron, Photo. By August 1949 thirteen B-50Bs were on hand, but soon thereafter the 91st SRW started to send its B-50s to Boeing-Wichita for modification to RB-50B standards. These modifications would include new turbo-superchargers, wing fuel tanks, camera hatches and modifications for aerial refueling. The 323rd Strategic Reconnaissance Squadron, Photo, would continue to operate both RB-17s and RB-29s; the 324th

SRS would operate RB-29s modified to perform its electronic surveillance mission; and the 7th Geodetic Squadron would use both RB-29s and C-82s in its mission to establish geodetic control points.[72]

Through the end of 1949, the 91st SRW carried no distinctive aircraft markings, except for the required national markings, USAF markings and aircraft tail numbers.

A couple of organizational changes would affect the 91st SRW in the second half of 1949. First, the 91st SRW would conduct a permanent change of station from McGuire AFB to Barksdale AFB, Louisiana, in September. Second, the 311th Air Division was redesignated the Second Air Force and would serve as the higher headquarters for the 91st SRW.

In October 1949, SAC announced its new tail marking policy and as a consequence the 91st SRW would receive **Square X** as its tail marking, the **Square** representing the Second Air Force and the letter **X** representing the 91st SRW. But, for reasons unknown, this assigned tail marking never appeared on 91st SRW aircraft.

By early 1950, all RB-17s had been transferred out of the 91st SRW and some distinctive aircraft markings started to appear on B-50Bs and RB-50Bs assigned to the 91st Strategic Reconnaissance Squadron. Squadron colors of green and yellow were adopted by the 91st SRS and appeared in the form of diagonal stripes on nose gear doors. The external fuel tanks were also painted in squadron colors using a scalloped design with green on the forward portion and yellow on the aft portion. The 91st SRS also placed a large squadron insignia on the left side of the aircraft nose. Several aircraft were given nicknames and included *City of Albany*, *City of Knoxville*, and *Laborin Lady*. Many of the RB-29s assigned to the 91st SRW carried the standard insignia red Arctic trim on the outer wing surfaces and tails but no distinctive squadron or wing markings.

April 1950 brought a major realignment of SAC units with the Command being reorganized on a geographical basis. The 91st SRW stayed as a Second Air Force unit, but did receive a new tail marking assignment —**Square V**. April 1950 also saw the activation of the 91st Air Refueling Squadron which would be equipped with the KB-29P boom-type tanker.

The new **Square V** tail marking started to appear in the late spring and early summer of 1950 on 91st SRW RB-50Bs and RB-29s. On those RB-29s with Arctic trim the tail marking was applied in black. It is not known if the **Square V** tail marking was ever placed on 91st ARS KB-29s.

The 91st SRW started to transition to the RB-45C and B-45A aircraft in the summer of 1950 receiving its first two RB-45Cs on 26 August. These were assigned to the 323rd Strategic Reconnaissance Squadron, Photo-Mapping. By the end of August 1950, 91st SRW squadrons were equipped with an unusual variety of aircraft:[73]

B-50B City of Knoxville *with striking 91st SRS insignia as well as the striped nose gear doors, which were painted in the squadron colors of green and yellow. Photograph taken at Barksdale AFB in 1950. Officer standing to the left is the 91st SRS commanding officer, Colonel Thomas W. Steed. (Museum of Flight)*

B-45A (47–038) was assigned to the 322nd SRS. The squadron color for the 322nd SRS was yellow and was placed as a wide band on the top of the tail and on the aircraft lower nose with two thin stripes extending rearward. The squadron insignia on the fuselage is left over from its service with the 85th BS of the 47th BW. (National Museum of the USAF)

91st Air Refueling Squadron — Five KB-29P
91st Strategic Reconnaissance Squadron, Photo— Nine RB-50B
322nd Strategic Reconnaissance Squadron, Photo-Mapping — Six RB-29
                                                                Four C-82
323rd Strategic Reconnaissance Squadron, Photo— Two RB-45C
324th Strategic Reconnaissance Squadron, Electronics— Nine RB-29A
                                                                Three RB-29

In addition to the aircraft previously mentioned, there is photographic evidence showing the **Square V** tail marking on some of the initial RB-45Cs assigned to the 91st SRW. The 323rd SRS also started to place its squadron insignia just aft of the left side crew door on its RB-45Cs.

November 1950 would bring tremendous change to the 91st SRW. As described in the narrative section of the November 1950 unit history for the 91st SRW:

On 1 November 1950 the 55th Strategic Reconnaissance Wing, Medium, was reactivated at Ramey Air Force Base, Puerto Rico, for the purpose of accepting, maintaining, and developing the RB-50 capability of the 91st Strategic Reconnaissance Wing, Medium, presently stationed here at Barksdale Air Force Base. The above-mentioned reactivation has brought about major organization changes within the 91st Wing.

The following units, having been assigned to the 55th Strategic Reconnaissance Wing, were activated at Barksdale Air Force Base on 1 November 1950 and attached to the 91st SRW and further attached to the 91st Strategic Reconnaissance Group, Medium, for all administration and operational control effective, 1 November 1950: the 38th Strategic Reconnaissance Squadron, Medium, Photo; the 338th Strategic Reconnaissance Squadron, Medium, Photo-Mapping; and the 343rd Strategic Reconnaissance Squadron, Medium, Electronics. Personnel and equipment used in the activation of these units were derived from the tactical squadrons assigned to the 91st SRG, according to the following procedure: personnel and equipment of the 38th SRS were absorbed from the 91st SRS; personnel and equipment of the 338th SRS were absorbed from the 322nd SRS; and personnel and equipment of the 343rd SRS were absorbed from the 324th SRS.

Simultaneously with the above actions, on 1 November 1950, the following units assigned to the 91st SRG, were redesignated as indicated below:

Line up of RB-45Cs at Lockbourne AFB shows two 324th SRS aircraft (BE-034 and BE-036) and one 323rd SRS aircraft (BE-021). Squadron color was blue for the 324th SRS and red for the 323rd SRS. The squadron color was on the tip of the tail cone for the 324th SRS aircraft. (Boeing H81–0278B. © Boeing. Used under license.)

Old Designation	**New Designation**
322nd Strat Rcn Squadron,	322nd Strat Rcn Squadron,
Medium, Photo-Mapping	Medium, Photo
324th Strat Rcn Squadron,	324th Strat Rcn Squadron,
Medium, Electronics	Medium, Photo
323rd Strat Rcn Squadron,	323rd Strat Rcn Squadron
Photo	Medium, Photo

Effective 16 November 1950 the 91st Strategic Reconnaissance Squadron, Medium, Photo, was relieved from assignment to the 91st Strat Rcn Group, Medium, and was transferred, less personnel and equipment, from Barksdale Air Force Base, Louisiana, to Yokota Air Base, Japan. The unit remained assigned to Strategic Air Command as a separate squadron. The personnel and equipment to man the 91st Strat Rcn Squadron at Yokota Air Base were made available by the transfer of the 31st Strat Rcn Squadron, less personnel and equipment, from Yokota Air Base to Travis Air Force Base, California."[74]

As a consequence of all B-50Bs and RB-29s being transferred from the 91st SRW to the newly-activated 55th SRW, the **Square V** tail marking — already present on the transferred aircraft — was given to the 55th SRW and the 91st SRW received a new tail marking assignment — **Square I**.

By early 1951 the 91st SRW was nearly fully equipped with its authorized complement of RB-45Cs (323rd & 324th SRS), B-45As (322nd SRS) and KB-29Ps (91st ARS). The **Square I** tail marking appeared on all 91st SRW tactical aircraft and squadron identification marking schemes were implemented. The 91st ARS used blue and white diagonal stripes for squadron identification and these markings appeared on the fin tip, the base of the refueling boom, nose gear doors, and as a single fuselage band. The 91st ARS would also sport

its squadron insignia on the left side of the aircraft nose. The 323rd and 324th Strategic Reconnaissance Squadrons' assigned colors were red and blue, respectively. The squadron identification markings were placed with some variation on the top of the vertical stabilizer as a fin flash, on the fuselage in the form of a single belly band, on the outer wing tanks in the shape of a forward-pointing arrow, and in some instances as a horizontal nose stripe extending back on both sides at mid-fuselage level to the leading edge of the pilot cockpit. As previously mentioned, the 323rd SRS did use its squadron emblem on its aircraft and both RB-45C squadrons had a bloodshot eye representing the Wing insignia painted around the nose camera port. The 322nd SRS flew B-45As and used yellow for its squadron color. Their squadron identification marking was a wide fin flash in yellow outlined in black positioned just above the aircraft tail number on the upper portion of the vertical stabilizer.

The 91st SRW sent its first detachment of RB-45Cs overseas in January 1951 when four RB-45Cs from the 323rd SRS,

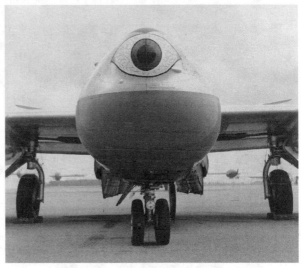

Top: *Aircraft assigned to both RB-45C squadrons (323rd and 324th). The last aircraft in the line, RB-45C (48–033), was the wing commander's aircraft and has all three squadron colors, blue, yellow, and red, represented on the tip of the tail cone. (Boeing H81–278Y-1. © Boeing. Used under license.)* Bottom: *The 91st SRW used a bloodshot eye design on the camera port of its RB-45Cs as an unofficial wing insignia (Boeing H81–278F-1. © Boeing. Used under license.)*

Left: *324th SRS RB-45C (48–036) has a blue belly band and blue tail cone tip and the BE-prefix buzz numbers aft of the national insignia. The* **Square I** *tail marking was reduced in size to accommodate the smaller vertical stabilizer on the RB-45C. (Boeing H81–278T-1. © Boeing. Used under license.)* Right: *91st ARS KB29P shows the* **Square I** *tail marking as well as the squadron markings (blue and white) on the fin tip and boom swivel. In the background on display are several other KB-29Ps of the 91st ARS. Castle AFB, October 1952 — part of the Fox Peter Two mission. (Boeing P12832. © Boeing. Used under license.)*

91st ARS crew waits for its Fox Peter Two mission. The 91st ARS insignia is clearly displayed on the left side of the tanker nose and appeared on all assigned KB-29s. (Boeing P12807. © Boeing. Used under license.)

*Several RB-45Cs supporting FEAF operations were painted gloss black in 1952 and featured an insignia red **Square I** tail marking. This particular example (48–027) was used to test the effectiveness of black camouflage as a means to avoid detection at night by enemy searchlights. Yokota Air Base, 1952. (Photograph by Dorr, courtesy D. Menard)*

accompanied by four KB-29Ps from the 91st ARS, were deployed to the United Kingdom for a 30-day TDY. The 91st SRW would also start sending detachments to Japan in support of FEAF combat operations. It wouldn't be long before nicknames and nose art would start to appear along with combat mission markings in the form of small black cameras. Some of the nicknames noted on RB-45Cs during the Korean War included *Eyes of Shreveport*, *State Side*, *No Sweat*, and *For Sale Inquire Within*. In an interesting variation to RB-45C aircraft markings in the Far East, two aircraft received black camouflage, with the **Square I** tail marking painted in insignia red on the vertical stabilizer.

Perhaps the most publicized RB-45C of the 91st SRW was *No Sweat* whose crew was awarded the MacKay Trophy in 1952 for the most meritorious flight of the year. Their flight was the first nonstop Pacific crossing by a jet bomber. Departing Elmendorf AFB, Alaska, on 29 July 1952, *No Sweat* covered the distance between Alaska and Yokota, Japan, in just less than ten hours (9 hours and 50 minutes). The flight was supported by two KB-29P aerial refuelings.[75]

The 91st SRW would be the only SAC unit equipped with B-45A and RB-45C medium jet reconnaissance bombers; however, the operational history of the RB-45Cs and B-45As would be relatively short-lived in SAC, as the 91st SRW would convert to RB-47s in early 1953 at Lockbourne AFB, Ohio, having departed Barksdale AFB in September 1951.

92nd Bombardment Wing

Although the 92nd Bombardment Group, Very Heavy, was activated at Fort Worth Army Air Field, Texas, on 4 August 1946, it would remain a "paper unit" until June 1947 when it began to organize and equip as a B-29 medium bombardment unit at Spokane Field, Washington. The 718th Bombardment Squadron from the 28th Bombardment Group at Rapid City, South Dakota, was transferred to the 92nd BG at Spokane Field to serve as cadre for the remanning of the group. The first three B-29s where assigned on 31 July 1947 and by the end of the year the 92nd BG would have 27 B-29s on hand.

Top: *Black camouflage B-29A-65-BN (44–62166) shows typical markings used by the 92nd BW in 1948–1949. In addition to the **Diamond W** tail marking and Fifteenth Air Force insignia on the dorsal fin, this aircraft carries its* Alley Oop *326th BS insignia on the forward fuselage. Fin cap is in the 326th BS color — red. (Museum of Flight)* Bottom: *92nd BW insignia on the right side of the aircraft nose, February 1950. The 92nd insignia was used on all Wing B-29s. (USAF, AFHRA)*

The 92nd Bombardment Wing (VH) was activated on 17 November 1947 and assigned to SAC's Fifteenth Air Force. The 92nd BW would assume control of the 92nd BG and its three assigned squadrons: the 325th, 326th and 327th Bombardment Squadrons. Also, the 92nd would serve as the parent wing for the 98th BG which was also organized and manned in September 1947 at Spokane Field.

Top: *Although the 92nd BW had a tail marking change to **Circle W**, the older **Diamond W** is still displayed in this early 1950 photograph at Spokane AFB. It would take until early summer of 1950 for the 92nd BW to complete the conversion to its new **Circle W** tail marking. (USAF, AFHRA) Bottom: Painting the 16-foot insignia on the tail of a 92nd BW B-36 at Fairchild Air Force Base in 1951. This job required approximately 85 man-hours, 1 gallon of black lacquer, 2 quarts of blue lacquer, 1 quart of white lacquer and 2 quarts of zinc chromate. (USAF, AFHRA)*

Until early 1948, 92nd BW B–29s were essentially "plain tails," devoid of any unit markings except for those required by Technical Order 07–1-1 (these markings included the national emblem, identification numbers (buzz numbers), and aircraft tail numbers). In early 1948, when Fifteenth Air Force assigned tactical aircraft markings or tail markings to its subordinate wings, the 92nd BW received the letter **W** in a black **Diamond**.[76] During February and March 1948 this marking as well as the Fifteenth Air Force insignia on the dorsal fin, and squadron identification markings placed on fin tips and nose gear doors started to appear on 92nd BW B–29s.[77] The 92nd BW assigned squadron colors were: red for the 325th BS, blue for the 326th BS, and yellow for the 327th BS. These were the markings in effect when the 92nd BW sent the 326th Bombardment Squadron to Yokota, Japan, in March 1948 and, also, later in the year (August 1948)

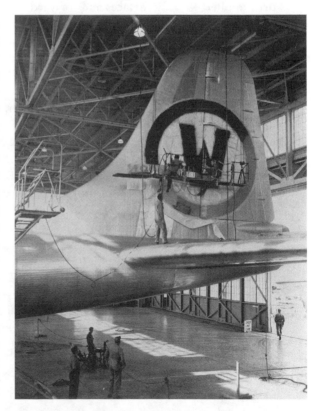

B-36D-40-CF (44–92065) with the full display of tactical markings used by the 92nd BW. The pattern for squadron identification now incorporates the use of diagonal stripes and the aircraft tail number is displayed in a forward break of the tail marking. Detroit-Wayne Airport, August 31, 1952. (Courtesy D. Olson)

when the 92nd BG would deploy as a group to Kadena Air Base, Okinawa for a 90-day training exercise with the Far East Air Forces.

The next iteration of aircraft markings for the 92nd BW would take place in late 1948 and early 1949 and would see buzz markings removed and **USAF** and **United States Air Force** applied to wing surfaces and forward fuselage respectively. Also the 92nd BW began to apply squadron insignia on the left side and the wing insignia on the right side of its B-29's noses. These markings were in place when the 92nd BW deployed to the United Kingdom in February 1949 for a 120-day tour of duty. The 92nd BW would be the first SAC unit stationed at Sculthorpe during its TDY to England.

In late 1949 SAC announced a change to its tactical markings policy which resulted in the 92nd BW receiving **Circle W** as its new tail marking. The transition to the new tail marking would take some time and it wasn't until June 1950 that the painting of the new **Circle W** tail marking on 92nd B-29s was completed.[78]

On 8 July 1950 the 92nd BG was deployed to Yokota, Japan, to support FEAF air operations over the Korean Peninsula. The 92nd BG flew its first combat mission on 13 July 1950. Unlike its sister wing at Spokane AFB, 92nd BG participation in the Korean War would be relatively short-lived. Due to a lack of strategic bombing targets General MacArthur would release two SAC B-29 units to return to the United States in October 1950. The two chosen to return to their home stations were the 22nd BG to March AFB and the 92nd BG which returned to Spokane AFB in late October and early November 1950.

Tactical aircraft markings for the 92nd BG did not change substantially during its relatively short combat tour in Korea except for some variations with displaying squadron colors on nose gear doors; however, there was an increase in the use of unofficial markings such as nicknames, nose art, and mission markings. Nicknames noted on 92nd BG B-29s at Yokota included: *Mac's Effort, Peace Maker, Peace on Earth, Deal Me In, Lake Success Express, Tremlin Gremlins, Miss Spokane, Eight Ball, Chief Spokane, The Wanderer, Laggin Waggon, Fire Ball, Lucky Strike, United Notions,* and *Guardians of Peace.* Many 92nd BG B-29s displayed a map of the Korean Peninsula on the left side of the aircraft nose — the top half of the map was red, with a large bomb superimposed, and the bottom half of the map was white — next to which bomb mission symbols were placed.

When the 92nd BG returned to Spokane AFB and to the control of its parent wing, the 92nd BW, it was earmarked for conversion to the B-36 heavy bomber. The first deliveries were made on 20 July 1951 and coincided with the dedication ceremony to rename Spokane AFB in honor of General Muir S. Fairchild, former Vice Chief of Staff of the USAF.

The 92nd BW continued to use both wing and squadron insignia on its B-36s. The wing insignia was placed on the left side of the nose and the squadron insignia

C-47 assigned to the Base Flight Section of the 92nd BW. It displays the Circle W tactical marking, unusual for base support aircraft. (USAF)

B-36D-40-CF (44–92065) with the 326th BS insignia on the right side of the nose. Detroit Air Show, August 1952. (Photograph by William J. Balogh, Sr., courtesy San Diego Aerospace Museum)

would occupy the right side. The Fifteenth Air Force insignia would continue to be worn on the dorsal fin and the **Circle W** would remain the authorized tail marking for the 92nd BW. The only variation with aircraft markings from the B-29-era was in the application of squadron identification markings. The 92nd BW adopted a diagonal bar pattern in contrasting color over the solid color nose gear doors and fin caps. 92nd BW squadron color assignments remained the same: red for the 325th, blue for the 326th and yellow for the 327th.

The tail markings would continue to be displayed until May-June 1953 when SAC ordered the use of tail markings discontinued. By August 1953, when the 92nd deployed to Guam for Operation Big Stick, the only tactical markings remaining were wing and squadron insignia and squadron identification markings.

The 92nd BW would continue to fly B-36s until 1957 when it would reequip with the B-52 Stratofortress.

93rd Bombardment Group/Wing

Although the 93rd Bombardment Group, Very Heavy, was never deactivated after its World War II service, it remained essentially a paper organization until June 1947 when Strategic Air Command sent the 371st Bombardment Squadron, 307th Bombardment Group stationed at MacDill Field, Florida, to Castle Field, Merced, California, to serve as the cadre for the remanning of the 93rd BG.

The first aircraft assigned to the 93rd were the ten B-29s brought to Castle Field by the former 371st Bombardment Squadron from MacDill Field. An additional three B-29s were transferred from MacDill Field to Castle Field in July 1947. With the reactivation of the 329th Bombardment Squadron in mid–August 1947, seven additional B-29s were obtained from the 509th Bombardment Group at Roswell Field, New Mexico. The final group of B-29s assigned to the 93rd BG came from the 28th Bombardment Group at Rapid City, South Dakota. These airplanes arrived at Castle Field during September and October 1947 and were assigned to the 330th Bombardment Squadron. This final delivery brought the 93rd Bombardment Group to its full authorization of 30 B-29 Superfortresses.[79]

There were no standard group markings for the B-29s assigned to the 93rd Bombardment Group during the first seven months after reactivation. The aircraft in many cases simply retained markings from previous group assignments. The aircraft that came from MacDill Field had the aircraft tail number centered on the vertical stabilizer and buzz numbers located on both sides of the fuselage and under the port wing. These buzz numbers were black for aircraft in silver finish and red for aircraft with black undersides. Some of the aircraft obtained from the 509th Bombardment Group and assigned to the 329th Bombardment Squadron retained the 509th **Circle** and **Arrow** tail marking. Buzz markings for these aircraft, however, were located on both sides of the aircraft nose and also under the port wing. These buzz markings were yellow on black bellied B-29s. The 329th BS also placed its squadron insignia on the port side of the aircraft directly under the pilots' window. The 328th Bombardment Squadron did not have a squadron insignia, but did have aircraft with nicknames—*Hang-Over-Haven* and *WoodenShu*.

The final group of aircraft assigned came from the 28th Bombardment Group at Rapid City and carried only the aircraft tail number on the vertical stabilizer. Buzz numbers on these aircraft were black for silver finish and red for black camouflaged aircraft. A couple of B-29s retained the 718th Bombardment Squadron insignia located on the vertical stabilizer above the aircraft tail number. With this group of B-29s came some of the more colorful nose art in the 93rd: *Forever Amber* (later renamed *Ballerina*) and *Al-Ask-Her* were two B-29s assigned to the 330th Bombardment Squadron that had their nose art applied while on TDY in Alaska with the 28th Bombardment Group.

Organized under the Hobson Plan in August 1947, the 93rd Bombardment Group was assigned to the 93rd Bombardment Wing which was activated on 16 August at Castle Field. On 7 January 1948 the 93rd Bombardment Wing flew its graduation exercise maximum effort mission and was declared a fully operational bombardment wing by SAC. Also on 13 January 1948, Castle Field was renamed Castle Air Force Base in keeping with the U.S. Air Force's new status as a separate branch of service.

Beginning in February, the 93rd BW started to apply its newly authorized tail marking on assigned B-29s.[80] The marking, an M inscribed on a black square or **Block M**, had recently been proposed by Fifteenth Air Force and approved by SAC. In addition to the tail marking, squadron identification colors were assigned; 328th — blue; 329th — red; and 330th — yellow. Placement of squadron identification markings was on the fin cap and nose gear doors for all squadrons; additionally, the 329th BS applied its color marking to propeller domes and nose wheels. The only other marking, besides those authorized by TO 07–1-1 and those previously mentioned, that appeared on 93rd Bomb Group B-29s in the first half of 1948 was the 330th Bombardment Squadron insignia which was applied to the left side of the nose.

Lt. Col. Robert H. Stewart, CO of the 330th BS, being greeted by base commander at Furstenfeld-bruck, Germany. Ballerina *was previously assigned to the 28th Bombardment Group and carried the name* Forever Amber. *The 330th BS insignia on the nose appeared on all squadron B-29s. The insignia resembled a similar unofficial 330th BS insignia used during World War II, but this insignia was actually the official emblem for the 420th BS. (USAF, courtesy Col. R. Stuart)*

The 93rd Bombardment Group was selected by SAC to be the first B-29 bombardment group to perform a four-month TDY out of Kadena Air Base, Okinawa, with the Far East Air Forces beginning in May 1948. In preparation for this exercise, the 329th Bombardment Squadron traded its 10 Albert or Harkin-type B-29s for regular tactical B-29As from the 7th Bombardment Wing, Carswell AFB, Texas, which was in the process of converting to B-36s.[81]

The 93rd BG arrived in Okinawa without any major mishaps, but did experience some difficulty with routing. The original plan called for 27 aircraft to proceed to Okinawa via the southern route (Hawaii, Kwajalein and Guam), while three aircraft (one from each squadron) were to follow an eastern route (Azores, Germany, Saudi Arabia, Ceylon, and the Philippines). The Group was ordered to delay movement for ten days because of activity associated with Operation Sandstone — atomic tests conducted in the vicinity of Kwajalein. As a result, the 93rd BG sent all winterized aircraft via Shemya in the Aleutians and all non-winterized aircraft took the southern route. The three planes that were directed eastward reached Furstenfeldbruck, Germany, but could not continue due to lack of diplomatic clearances, caused in part by the beginning of the first Arab-Israeli conflict. These planes left Germany on 21 May 1948, returned to Castle AFB, and flew the southern route to rejoin the rest of the Group already on Okinawa. The majority of the 93rd BG had arrived at Kadena Air Base by 31 May 1948.[82]

The 330th BS flies past Mt. Fuji en route to Yokota for a refueling stop before returning to Castle AFB after completing a 120-day TDY at Kadena AB, Okinawa, August 1948. (USAF)

Top: *Two 330th BS B-29s, with their squadron insignia on the nose, flying over Northern California in late 1948. The buzz markings are insignia red on the black camouflage and the fin caps are in the 330th BS color — yellow. The second aircraft displays a Fifteenth Air Force insignia on the dorsal fin which was relatively uncommon for 93rd BG B-29s. (USAF, courtesy Castle Air Museum)* Bottom: *329th Bombardment Squadron, Castle AFB, November 1948. The large squadron insignia was placed on squadron aircraft after their return from Okinawa in August 1948. (Photograph by B. Bridgman, author's collection)*

Top: *A 328th BS B-50D at RAF Marham, summer 1950. The A on the fuselage was the letter code for the 328th BS and the two numbers 93 are the last two digits of the aircraft tail number. (Quadrant House)* Bottom: *Two newly assigned receiver-type B-50Ds of the 329th BS flying somewhere over England. Both aircraft are in the process of having markings applied. (USAF, courtesy Col. J. Houlgin)*

A 330th BS B-50D with all four engines turning. Squadron color is yellow, numbers on nose gear door are black, and the three rings on fuel tanks indicate select crew status. (USAF)

While in Okinawa the 93rd BG engaged in radar bombing, live gunnery exercises, long range cruise control missions, and fighter interception exercises. Although the 93rd BG pioneered the rotation of full bombardment groups to the Far East, no major problems were encountered. The biggest challenges had to do with aircraft maintenance especially the short supply of spare parts.[83]

Markings were little changed until after the 93rd BG returned from the FEAF TDY in August 1948. The 329th BS applied a much larger squadron insignia on the port side of the aircraft nose. Also the Fifteenth Air Force insignia began to appear on the dorsal fin of some of the assigned B-29s during the last half of 1948. Finally, the elimination of buzz markings as required by USAF Technical Order 07–1–1 dated 26 July 1948 and the application of **United States Air Force** in small letters on the forward fuselage and **USAF** in larger letters on the lower port main and the upper starboard main started to be implemented in the fall of 1948.

In 1949 the 93rd Bombardment Wing was earmarked to receive the USAF's first operational B-50Ds, receiving their first aircraft in June 1949. Leaking fuel tanks on the newly assigned B-50Ds delayed full implementation of reequipping the 93rd Bombardment Wing, but by January 1950 the 45th B-50D had been assigned to the 93rd BW.

The first marking to appear on 93rd Bombardment Wing B-50Ds beginning in early 1950 was the newly assigned tail code — **Circle M** — which was approved by SAC in October 1949. Squadron colors remained the same: blue for the 328th; red for the 329th; and yellow for the 330th — and were applied to fin caps and nose gear doors. The 93rd BW also used an identification number that was placed on the aft fuselage behind the national insignia. This marking consisted of a letter designator for each squadron followed by the last two numbers of the aircraft serial number. The letter **A** was assigned to the 328th, **B** to the 329th, and **C** to the 330th.

This marking scheme was in effect when, in July 1950, the 93rd Bombardment Group (93rd Bombardment Wing headquarters stayed at Castle AFB) deployed to the United King-

Top: *The 93rd BW started to receive KB-29Ps in early 1951. KB-29P-65-BW (44–69858) has the early markings used by the 93 ARS — green fin cap and nose gear doors, crewmember shield outline,* **Circle M** *tail marking, D-58 aircraft identification number on the fuselage, and the last four numbers of the aircraft tail number at the top of the vertical stabilizer and rudder assembly. (Courtesy R. Notley)* Bottom: *KB-29P-45-BA (44–83907), taken at Oakland Airport, California, October 1952. The squadron color — green — appears on the fin cap and nose gear doors supplemented by two white diagonal stripes. The crewmember shield is also green with white lettering used for crewmember names. (Courtesy W. Larkins)*

dom for an indefinite stay due to the start of the Korean War. While in the United Kingdom, the 93rd BG exchanged all non-receiver-capable B-50Ds for aircraft that were equipped for air refueling operations.

Returning to the United States in February 1951, the only changes to markings from the summer of 1950 were the appearance of the Fifteenth Air Force insignia on the dorsal fin, painting the last three numbers of the aircraft serial number in a contrasting color on nose gear doors, and the placement of concentric rings in squadron colors on the nose of the fuel tanks to indicate the combat readiness status of the crew: one ring indicated a combat-ready crew, two rings for lead crew status, and three rings represented select crew status. The 93rd BW would deploy with these markings on a second TDY to the United Kingdom from December 1951 to March 1952. While in England, the bomb squadrons would be based at Mildenhall and Lakenheath; the air refueling squadron would operate out of Upper Heyford. These B-50D markings would continue to be used until Strategic Air Command required the removal of high visibility markings in April-May 1953.

Although activated much earlier, the 93rd Air Refueling Squadron (ARS) started to receive KB-29s in the spring of 1951. The assigned color for the 93rd ARS was green and the letter designator for the squadron was **D**. The squadron identification markings appeared on the fin tip and on the nose gear doors with two forward diagonal white stripes with the last three digits of the aircraft serial number, also in white, appearing between the diagonal stripes. The 93rd ARS also placed a green shield with crewmember names in white on the left side of the aircraft nose. In addition to the 93rd BW deployment to England from December 1951 to March 1952, the 93rd ARS would participate in Operation Fox Peter Two, the movement of the 31st FEW from the U.S. to Japan in July 1952 by staging 11 KB-29Ps on Guam and Kwajalein to provide aerial refueling support.

B-50Ds and KB-29Ps would continue to serve with the 93rd BW at Castle AFB until 1954 when they were replaced with B-47Es and KC-97s.

97th Bombardment Group/Wing

On 4 August 1946, the 97th Bombardment Group, Very Heavy, was activated at Smoky Hill Army Air Field, Salina, Kansas, receiving personnel and B-29 aircraft from the deactivated 485th Bombardment Group. The 97th BG tactical squadrons were the 340th, 341st and 342nd.

In its first year with Strategic Air Command, the 97th Bombardment Group spearheaded projects and operations that spanned the globe. In addition to its participation in the Harken Project, which tested many types and sizes of bombs against World War II German submarine pens, the 97th BG units participated in TDY deployments to Germany, Japan, and Uruguay as well as an escort mission for the President of Mexico's airplane from Kansas City to Mexico City.[84]

Y-Namit B-29–60-BA (44–84094) preparing to depart Andrews Field, Maryland, 3 June 1947, for training flight to Europe (UK). This B-29 was assigned to the 340th BS. Fin cap is in the 340th squadron color — red. Buzz numbers on the fuselage and under the left wing are yellow. The 97th Bombardment Group insignia is partially visible on the tail under the radio call number. (AP/Wide World Photo)

B-29–60-BA (44–84096) of the 340th BS lands at Marham, UK, in June 1947. The small Fifteenth Air Force insignia on the aircraft tail started to replace the 97th BG insignia in May or June 1947. (Courtesy Quadrant House)

There were no standard tactical markings for 97th BG aircraft until early 1947 when the Group began to apply its insignia on the tail fin below the tail number and squadron identification colors were placed on the fin cap. Squadron color assignments were red for the 340th, blue for the 341st and yellow for the 342nd. All B-29s bore buzz markings under the left wing and on the fuselage behind the national insignia, black for silver finish and yellow for black camouflage. Aircraft nicknames noted during this period included: *Hang-Over-Haven*, *Stork Club*, *Lena the Hyena* and *Y-Namit*.

During the summer of 1947 the 97th Bombardment Group started to place a small Fifteenth Air Force insignia on the tail below the aircraft tail number in lieu of the 97th BG insignia.

The next change in aircraft markings came in October 1947 when the 97th Bombardment Wing traveled from Salina, Kansas, to Mile 26, (today's Eielson AFB) Alaska, for six months of training in the Arctic region. All B-29s had the insignia red Arctic markings applied to tails and outer wings with a silver rectangle encasing the aircraft tail number. Mission symbols in the form of polar bears were painted on the left side of the aircraft nose, each polar bear representing a mission flown over the polar ice cap. *Arctic Indoctrinated* was the nickname for one of the 97th's B-29s deployed to Alaska.

Shortly after its return to the Continental United States from Alaska, the 97th BW was transferred to Biggs Air Force Base, El Paso, Texas, and came under the jurisdiction of the Eighth Air Force. Also additional aircraft were transferred into the 97th BW to bring it up to its authorized strength of 30 B-29s.

The change from the Fifteenth Air Force to the Eighth Air Force left the 97th BW without an assigned tail marking. In September 1948, the 97th BW requested approval of a proposed tail marking, the urgency of which was driven by an impending TDY to the United Kingdom.[85] No approved tail marking was forthcoming due, in part, to SAC's desire to adopt a standard aircraft tail marking policy throughout the command. The result for the 97th BW was plain tail B-29s, and later B-50s, with only the aircraft tail number on the vertical tail and the Eighth Air Force insignia on both sides of the dorsal fin. The 97th BW now

Top: *The* City of San Fernando *B-50D-80-BO (48–067) shows it all — nickname, wing insignia, and squadron markings on nosewheel door, fuel tanks, and vertical fin cap — as well as a lead crew identification band on the aft portion of the fuselage. (USAF) Bottom: Many B-50Ds in the 97th BW were named for cities and used a standard format of placing the name of the city on a banner located next to or above the Wing insignia. A nice example is the* City of Chattanooga *B-50D-90-BO (48–087) of the 340th BS. (USAF)*

placed squadron identification colors on fin tips and nose gear doors. The nose gear doors were also marked with a forward pointing arrow broken in the middle with the squadron numerical designation. With the assignment of B-50s in the first half of 1950, the 97th BW included squadron identification colors on the B-50 long-range fuel tanks in the form of a tapered cheat line. Additionally, beginning in late 1948 and early 1949, the **USAF** and **United States Air Force** started to appear on assigned aircraft, replacing the older **BF**-prefix aircraft identification numbers.

The 97th BG would conduct an operational deployment to the United Kingdom from November 1948 to February 1949. The 340th BS would operate from Marham and the other two squadrons — the 341st and 342nd — would be based at Waddington. A large part of

Top: *The City of Missoula B-50D-110-BO (49–2734) was assigned to the 341st BS. (USAF)* Bottom: *Detroit B-50D-95-BO (48–101) was assigned to the 342nd BS and has yellow squadron markings on the fin tip, wing tank, propeller domes and nose gear doors. Notice the shark mouth painted on the wing tank. (Photograph by Burt Kemp, courtesy P. Stevens)*

*By April–May 1953, most of the tail markings had been removed. B-50D-95-BO (48–095) shows the outline of its former tail marking — **Triangle O**. Nicknamed* Milwaukee, *this 342nd BS aircraft still retains yellow trim on the fin cap, wing tanks, propeller domes, and nose gear doors. (Photograph by Burt Kemp, courtesy P. Stevens)*

*Left: All 97th BW KB-29s carried the Wing insignia on the nose. Nose gear door is painted in the 97th ARS color — green. (Boeing P11429. © Boeing. Used under license.) Right: The 97th ARS received the first USAF KB-29P in March 1950. All KB-29Ps carried the **Triangle O** tail marking and Eighth Air Force insignia on the dorsal fin. Flags on the flying boom were used on the ground to increase visibility of the boom. (Boeing P11431. © Boeing. Used under license.)*

their training program while in England would be to conduct fighter affiliation exercises with the RAF.[86] Later in 1949, after the 97th BG returned from the UK, the 97th BW would start to receive Silverplate B-29s from the 509th BW at Roswell AFB. A total of 28 Silverplate B-29s would arrive at Biggs AFB during July-August 1949 and would give the 97th BW an atomic delivery capability. The Silverplate would remain in the 97th BW's arsenal until May 1950 when they were replaced by more modern B-50Ds.[87]

With the outbreak of war in Korea in late June 1950, part of SAC's response was to send several atomic-capable wings to the United Kingdom as a precaution to any Soviet response in Europe. The 97th BW was one of the wings dispatched to England for an indefinite period. Arriving in July 1950, the Wing would be dispersed over many East Anglia airfields. The 97th BW would return to Biggs AFB in February 1951.[88]

With the assignment of B-50D bombers in 1950, the 97th Bombardment Wing started to place its insignia on the left side of the nose. The 97th BW also named many of their B-50s after cities using a standard policy of painting the name of the city on a banner on the nose forward of the wing insignia. Named examples included: *City of El Paso*, *City of Big Spring*, *City of Missoula*, *City of San Fernando*, *City of Chattanooga*, *City of Hutchinson*, and *Detroit*. Several 97th Bombardment Wing B-50s had an aft fuselage band which may have indicated lead or select crew status.

The 97th Air Refueling Squadron was activated on 2 February 1949 and started to be manned and equipped with the Air Force's first KB-29P tanker in September 1950. The designated color for the 97th ARS was green and was placed on the fin caps and nose gear doors. The Eighth Air Force insignia was placed on the dorsal fins and the 97th Bomb Wing insignia on the left side of the nose.

Although the 97th BW received its first assigned tail marking of **Triangle O** when SAC announced new tactical aircraft markings in October 1949, this marking didn't begin to appear on 97th Bomb Wing B-50Ds and KB-29Ps until late 1950/early 1951. This was due, in part, because the 97th BW was transitioning from B-29s to B-50s during the first half of 1950, was starting to equip the 97th Air Refueling Squadron beginning in September 1950, and deployed to the United Kingdom from July 1950 to February 1951. All 97th aircraft displayed the **Triangle O** tail marking by the end of the first half of 1951.

The 97th BW would deploy to the United Kingdom once again in 1952 for a much shorter stay—from March to May 1952. The squadrons were less dispersed than the 1950–51 deployment; the 340th and 341st Bombardment Squadrons were based at Lakenheath, the 342nd Bombardment Squadron was based at Mildenhall, and the 97th Air Refueling Squadron was stationed at Upper Heyford.[89]

The 97th Bombardment Wing was the last wing in the Air Force to employ the B-50 in a bomber role, retaining B-50s until 1955 when they were replaced by B-47s. The 97th BW lost its KB-29s in January 1954 when they converted to newer KC-97s.

98th Bombardment Group/Wing

The 98th Bombardment Group, Very Heavy, became operational on 24 September 1947 when it was assigned to the Fifteenth Air Force and stationed at Spokane Field, Washington. The Group was formed with a cadre from the 436th Bombardment Squadron, 7th Bombardment Group (VH), Fort Worth Air Force Base, Texas.[90] The 98th BG's three tactical squadrons were the 343rd, 344th and 345th Bombardment Squadrons. The 98th BG was attached to the 92nd Bombardment Wing, also at Spokane, and would share a wing commander with the 92nd BW until April 1950.

Equipped with B-29s, the 98th BG spent all of 1947 and most of 1948 organizing and training to become a fully operational SAC B-29 unit.

Early in 1948, Fifteenth Air Force assigned the 98th BG its first tail marking—a **Black Diamond** with the letter **Y** inside. The new tail marking started to appear on 98th BG Superfortresses in February-March 1948 along with the Fifteenth Air Force emblem on the dorsal fin. Squadron colors were placed on fin tips and nose gear doors. Squadron color assignments were: red for the 343rd BS; green for the 344th BS; and white with black stripes for the 345th BS. The 98th BG operated both black camouflage and silver finish B-29s. Buzz numbers were painted in the customary insignia red for B-29s wearing black undersides and black for those in silver. Besides the Fifteenth Air Force insignia, the only other insignia

Top: *B-29–55-BW (44–69667)* Snugglebunny *still shows the outline of the previously used* **Circle B** *tail marking and the Fifteenth Air Force insignia on the dorsal fin. The colors on the fin tip and nose gear doors are reddish-orange and represent the 343rd BS. In 1951 the 98th began using large plane identification numbers on the aft fuselage composed of a squadron letter followed by the last three digits of the radio call number.* Snugglebunny, *July 1951, getting ready to return to the United States for depot overhaul. (USAF— 80531 A.C.) Bottom: The 98th Bombardment Wing deployed to the Far East with the* **Square H** *tail marking which reflected its assignment to the Second Air Force and a planned change of station to Ramey Air Force Base, Puerto Rico. War in Korea cancelled the 98th's transfer to the Caribbean. B-29–95-BW (45–21822)* Heavenly Laden *of the 344th BS still displays its markings, with the exception of the nose art, from the summer of 1950. Squadron colors were green with white stripes. April 1951:* Heavenly Laden *has just returned from its 60th consecutive combat mission over Korean targets. (USAF— 81636 A.C.)*

appearing on 98th BG B-29s was the Group insignia which was displayed on the left side of the aircraft nose.

The 98th BG displayed the above-mentioned markings when it deployed on its first overseas training mission to the United Kingdom from April to August 1949. Based at Sculthorpe, the 98th BG trained with the RAF's No. 12 Group. As with previous SAC B-29 groups in England, the 98th BG engaged in many fighter defense exercises, a major one being Exercise Foil conducted in June — July 1949 and was the second major post-war UK

air defense exercise.[91] The only change to 98th BG aircraft markings during this time was the replacement of buzz markings with the now mandatory **USAF** and **United States Air Force**.

In December 1949, Fifteenth Air Force notified the 98th Bombardment Wing that, due to SAC's revision of its tactical doctrine manual and establishment of a standard aircraft marking policy, the new tactical tail marking for the 98th BW would be the

Top: *Pre–Korean War 98th BG markings with the nose gear door painted a solid color — in this case red for the 343rd — and the Group insignia on the nose. Spokane AFB, 1950. (USAF, courtesy Travis Air Museum)* Bottom: *A July 1952 pre-flight inspection prior to boarding aircraft for another bombing mission over North Korea. Although 98th BW B-29s sported black camouflage by mid–1952, the use of 98th BW insignia,* **Circle H** *tail marking, and squadron identification marking on fin tip continued. Communist flags painted on the ship's nose denote 154 missions flown against the North Koreans. (USAF — AF-2161-7)*

Top: *Following a 98th BW mission to bomb a railroad bypass bridge at Sunchon, North Korea, October 24, 1951. Assigned to the 343rd BS, B–29–40–MO (44–27341) Dreamer is shown after landing at Taegu, South Korea. (Courtesy Max D. Nelson) Bottom: In the early part of 1952 the 98th BW changed the* **Square H** *tail marking to its authorized* **Circle H** *marking.* Ready Willin Wanton *shows the* **Circle H** *tail marking and the 345th BS squadron colors of white with black diagonal stripes on fin tip and nose gear doors. The* **C** *prefix of the plane identification number also indicated the 345th BS. Photograph shows "2106" on its assigned hardstand at Yokota, 1952 (Courtesy B. Banks)*

Circle B.[92] The 98th began painting the new tail marking and by April 1950, 80% of the assigned B-29s wore the new **Circle B** on their vertical stabilizer. However, April 1950 brought forth another organization change within SAC as well as notification to the 98th BW that it was to be assigned to the jurisdiction of the Second Air Force and would undergo a permanent change of station to Ramey AFB, Puerto Rico, in the near future. The impact of these changes on 98th BW tail markings is made clear in the following letter.

"...Action has been taken to comply with subject letter and at the present time compliance is eighty per cent (80%) complete." The above mentioned letter stated that 98th Bombardment Wing aircraft would be marked with circle "B."

On 11 April 1950 letter, Headquarters Fifteenth Air Force, file 452.1, dated 3 April 1950, same subject, was received this Headquarters. This letter required that tactical markings be changed to circle H.

In the interest of economy of manhours and material and due to anticipated move of 98th Bombardment Wing (M) to jurisdiction of the Second Air Force, which will require completely new markings on aircraft, request this station be exempt from compliance with Fifteenth Air Force letter, file 452.1, dated 3 April 1950.

Aircraft presently marked with diamond and letter will have this marking removed and left clear pending outcome of this request."[93]

It appears that the 98th BW was exempted from the requirement to paint the **Circle H** on its aircraft since the **Square H** tail marking was placed on 98th B-29s in May and June of 1950 in anticipation of its move to Ramey AFB and the Second Air Force.

World events would intervene to prevent the 98th BG from serving with the Second Air Force. The outbreak of war on the Korean Peninsula in June 1950 would result in the 98th BG (combat echelon of the 98th BW) being deployed to Yokota Air Base, Japan. Departing Spokane Air Force Base between 2 and 4 August 1950, the 98th BG flew its first combat mission from Yokota Air Base on 7 August, and for the next three years would fly combat missions in support of FEAF operations.

Top: *Some of the best nose art during the Korean War came out of the 98th BW operating from Yokota.* Miss Minooki *was assigned to the 343rd BW. (USAF, courtesy Col. R. Ireland)* Middle: Los Angeles Calling *belonged to the 344th BS. The nose gear doors are green with white stripes and numbers. The nose also has some very interesting artwork. (USAF, courtesy Col. R. Ireland)* Bottom: Wolf Pack, *a 345th aircraft, has added some additional artwork to the nose. (USAF, courtesy Col. R. Ireland)*

The 98th BG would go to war wearing the **Square H** tail marking and this marking would remain on Group B-29s until 1951 when the 98th BG changed to its authorized **Circle H** tactical marking (The 98th BG was reassigned to the Fifteenth Air Force effective July 1950).

The 98th BG squadron markings would be slightly modified during the Korean War. The 343rd BS would adopt a reddish-orange color while the 344th BS would add two white diagonal stripes on its green nose wheel door. The 345th BS would continue to use white with black diagonal stripes on both the fin cap and nose gear doors. The 98th BG insignia continued to be worn on the left side of the aircraft and in the case of the 343rd BS was joined by a large squadron insignia. The right side of the aircraft nose was reserved for aircraft nicknames and nose art that were plentiful during the 98th BW's stay at Yokota.

In January 1952, to avoid daylight interception by enemy fighters, the 98th BW began to fly night missions almost exclusively. This would result in all B-29s being painted black with the irregular pattern terminating above mid-fuselage and extending to the rear of the aircraft ending just below the tail marking and aircraft tail number. In 1953 the black camouflage would be extended to include the entire vertical stabilizer and, as a result, all tail markings would be covered.

The wing's last combat mission was flown on 25 July 1953. The 98th BW would be permanently assigned to the Far East Air Forces (FEAF) in August 1953 and would remain at Yokota until 1954. In the summer of 1954 the 98th BW returned to the United States and SAC. The 98th BW would move to Lincoln AFB, Nebraska, needed and soon receive B-47 Stratojets and KC-97 tankers.

106th Bombardment Wing/320th Bombardment Wing

As part of the expansion of Strategic Air Command during the Korean War, the 106th Bombardment Wing, Light, a New York Air National Guard B-26 unit, was inducted into

Line-up of 106th B-29s on the March AFB ramp includes aircraft of the 114th BS and 135th BS. Fin tips are yellow for the 114th BS and blue for the 135th BS. The 106th BW placed squadron identification colors only on the fin tip. (USAF, AFHRA)

Top: *A red tipped B-29 of the 102nd BS awaits replacement of the national insignia on the fuselage. March AFB, January 1951. (USAF, AFHRA)* Bottom: *Proudly displaying the 106th BW insignia, this B-29 and its crew prepare for inspection during ORI preparation, August 1952. (USAF, AFHRA)*

federal service on 1 April 1951. The 106th BW came into SAC designated as a B-29 medium bombardment unit and was assigned to March AFB, California, as part of the 12th Air Division, a Fifteenth Air Force organization.

The newly-activated 106th BW spent its first four months engaged in training activities to prepare itself for the delivery of B-29 aircraft scheduled for mid-summer 1951. Nucleus crews were sent to B-29 Combat Crew Training School at Randolph AFB, Texas. Other crew members (bombardiers, navigators, flight engineers and radio operators) were sent to service schools, and maintenance personnel were trained in B-29 maintenance operations by the 22nd BW, a sister wing also stationed at March AFB.[94]

Top: *In September 1952, the 106th BW underwent an Operational Readiness Inspection (ORI). Shown here is Airman First Class William K. Wilbert of Halifax, Pennsylvania, checking his tail gunner position. The red fin tip indicates a B-29 assigned to the 102nd Bombardment Squadron. (USAF–K6558)* Bottom: *The 106th ARS, and later 320th ARS, was one of the few KC-97 units to display tail codes. The tankers were marked just like the B-29s they supported —* **Circle A** *tail marking, Fifteenth Air Force insignia on the dorsal fin and Wing insignia on the nose. Photograph taken in March AFB, 1952. (USAF, courtesy Col. J. Decker)*

The first B-29 was delivered to the 106th BW at March Air Force Base on 28 July 1951. In June 1951, prior to receiving its first aircraft, the 106th BW was assigned **Circle A** as its tactical tail marking.[95] In August 1951, the 106th BW decided on color assignments for its bombardment squadrons: red for the 102nd Bomb Squadron; yellow for the 114th Bomb Squadron; and blue for the 135th Bomb Squadron.[96] The 106th BW painted squadron identification markings only on the fin tip of its B-29s. The only other marking to appear on 106th BW B-29s during 1951 was the Fifteenth Air Force insignia which was displayed on the dorsal fin.

In January 1952, the 106th BW started to paint its newly authorized insignia on the left side of the nose of its B-29s.[97] There is no evidence to indicate squadron insignia was ever used by the 106th BW.

In addition to being a fully operational medium bombardment wing by mid–1952, the 106th BW added an air refueling capability with the activation of the 106th Air Refueling Squadron in July 1952. The 106th ARS operated the KC-97 tanker and received its first three KC-97s in August 1952. By the end of October 1952, the 106th ARS had 20 KC-97 aircraft assigned. The **Circle A** tail marking was applied to 106th ARS KC-97s along with the Fifteenth Air Force insignia. The assigned squadron color for the 106th ARS was green and was painted on the fin tip, initially, and later, in mid–1953, was displayed in the form of two diagonal stripes at the top of the vertical stabilizer.

On 1 December 1952, the 320th Bombardment Wing, Medium, was activated and assigned to Fifteenth Air Force, March AFB, California, as a unit of the Strategic Air Command. On that date, the 320th BW took control of all personnel and equipment of the 106th Bombardment Wing which reverted to Air National Guard status effective 30 November 1952. The three bombardment squadrons of the 106th Bombardment Wing — the 102nd, 114th and 135th — were inactivated and the 441st, 442nd and 443rd Bombardment Squadrons were activated and assigned to the Wing. Additionally, the 320th Air Refueling Squadron replaced the 106th Air Refueling Squadron and took over its KC-97 tankers.

As the 320th BW, all aircraft markings remained the same — the **Circle A** tail marking; squadron colors (441st — red, 442nd — yellow, 443rd — blue, 320th ARS — green); and the 106th BW insignia by mutual consent of both units became the insignia of the 320th Bombardment Wing, Medium, on 5 December 1952.

The spring of 1953 brought the removal of all high visibility markings as required by SAC Headquarters. According to the 320th BW history for May 1953, the 320th ARS removed all tail markings and Fifteenth Air Force insignia from their KC-97 aircraft.[98]

The 320th BW began transferring B-29s in February 1953, but would continue to operate B-29 bombers until July 1953 when they were replaced with Boeing YRB-47 service test bomber/reconnaissance aircraft. The primary mission of the wing remained strategic bombardment, but the 320th BW added a reconnaissance capability that enabled the Wing to perform a dual mission.[99]

111th /99th Strategic Reconnaissance Wing

The 111th Bombardment Wing, Light, a Pennsylvania Air National Guard unit, was called into federal service on 1 April 1951. As an Air National Guard organization, the 111th BW was stationed at Philadelphia's International Airport and was equipped with B-26 light bombers. Shortly after activation, the 111th BW received orders assigning it to Fairchild Air

*RB-29A-35-BN (44–61531) was originally assigned to the 103rd SRS and was one of three RB-29s selected to represent the 111th SRW in the 1951 SAC Bomb/Nav Competition. In early 1952, this RB-29 was transferred to the 129th SRS. This photograph shows all the tactical markings used by the 111th SRW— checkerboard pattern squadron identification markings on fin tip and nose gear doors, **Circle I** tail marking, and Fifteenth Air Force insignia on the dorsal fin. (USAF— ARHRC)*

Force Base, Spokane, Washington. On 24 April 1951, the 111th was reassigned from the First Air Force to the Fifteenth Air Force of the Strategic Air Command (SAC).[100] The three tactical squadrons assigned to the 111th BW were the 103rd, 129th and 130th.

The first RB-29s were assigned to the 111th BW in June 1951 when six aircraft were received from Travis AFB, California, and Forbes AFB, Topeka, Kansas.[101] These RB-29s were assigned to the 103rd BS which was the only operational squadron of the Wing until late 1951.

Although the 111th BW was training as a strategic reconnaissance wing, it wasn't until 1 August 1951 that it was officially designated the 111th Strategic Reconnaissance Wing.

On 11 June 1951, **Circle I** was assigned to the 111th SRW as their official tail marking.[102] On 26 June 1951, the 111th SRW sent a letter to Fifteenth Air Force requesting a change in the letter identification for the Wing. As stated in the letter, "Authority is requested to use the letter **P** instead of **I** if letter **P** is not presently assigned to an existing organization. The 111th is composed mainly of Pennsylvania Air National Guardsmen and in the interest in esprit de corps it is requested that the letter **P** be used."[103] The reply from Fifteenth Air Force Headquarters was, "Request contained in basic letter not favorably considered. Headquarters Strategic Air Command has been advised of the previously assigned letter which has been included in the revised Strategic Air Command Tactical Doctrine, scheduled for distribution in near future."[104] The **Circle I** tail marking first appeared on four 111th RB-29s selected to represent the Wing at the Strategic Air Command Bombing and Navigation Competition held at MacDill AFB, FL from 10 August and 18 August.[105]

Beginning in September 1951, the 111th SRW began applying squadron identification markings on their RB-29s. Using an unusual checkerboard pattern, these markings were painted on the fin tip and nose gear doors. Also placed on the nose gear doors were the last four digits of the aircraft serial number. It is believed, but has not been confirmed, that the color assignment for each squadron was: black and white for the 103rd SRS; red and white for the 129th SRS; and black and yellow for the 130th SRS. Since most of the RB-29s came from other Fifteenth Air Force units, they already carried the Fifteenth Air Force insignia

25G-92BPL-20 OCT51- 111TH S.R.W.-REST.

*Parking space was a problem at Fairchild with two wings assigned (92nd and 111th). The 111th acquired Hangar No. 3, and this photograph taken in October 1951 shows the practicality of parking five RB-29s inside the hangar. Of note is RB-29–95-BW (45–21761) with the insignia red Arctic tail still showing the outline of the X used by the 5th SRW at Travis and the use of a contrasting yellow for the **Circle I** tail marking. (USAF, AFHRA)*

on the dorsal fin. Several 111th SRW RB-29s had insignia red Arctic markings and in their case the **Circle I** tail marking was painted in a contrasting yellow on the insignia red surface. There is no evidence to indicate the 111th SRW used wing or squadron insignia on any of its RB-29s.

In January 1952, the 111th SRW redistributed RB-29s from the 103rd SRS to the other two squadrons to provide a more equitable maintenance workload and by the middle of February each squadron had five RB-29s. The 111th SRW would continue to receive additional RB-29s during 1952 but would never operate at its authorized strength of 36 aircraft. The 111th SRW would participate in its first overseas TDY in August 1952 when it sent a four-plane detachment to the United Kingdom for a 90-day deployment.

The 111th SRW continued to operate RB-29s until late 1952 when it started to convert to RB-36s. The 111th received its first RB-36F-1-CF (49–2709) from the 5th SRW at Travis AFB. The **Circle I** tail marking was immediately applied to newly assigned RB-36s. It is not known if the 111th SRW ever painted squadron identification markings on its RB-36s prior to its relief from active federal service and return to Air National Guard status, which was effective on 1 January 1953.

The 99th Strategic Reconnaissance Wing, Heavy, was activated at Fairchild Air Force Base, Spokane, Washington, on 1 January 1953 and inherited the assets of the 111th SRW. The assigned squadrons of the 99th were the 346th SRS, 347th SRS, and 348th SRS; how-

RB-36 (49–2709) was the first RB-36 assigned to the 111th SRW (soon to be 99th SRW) on 18 December 1952. The fin tip squadron marking is left over from the 5th SRW, but the 111th **Circle I** *tail marking is newly applied. (USAF, AFHRA)*

ever, due to space considerations, the 347th SRS would initially operate from Travis AFB where it was attached to the 5th SRW. In January 1953, the 99th SRW transferred its remaining five RB-29s and by May 1953 was fully equipped with 23 RB-36Ds and RB-36Fs for the two squadrons stationed at Fairchild. It is not known when squadron identification markings were applied to 99th SRW RB-36s. Also in compliance with a policy change from SAC, the **Circle I** tail marking was removed from the RB-36 fleet during the spring of 1953.

The 99th SRW would continue to operate as a RB-36 wing until 1956 when it began to reequip with B-52s as an Eighth Air Force unit assigned to Westover AFB, MA.

301st Bombardment Wing

Although the 301st Bombardment Group, Very Heavy, along with its three bombardment squadrons— the 32nd, 352nd and 353rd — was assigned to SAC on 4 August 1946, the unit initially was a "paper" unit with no aircraft assigned.

In the fall of 1947, SAC started to man and equip the 301st BG with B-29 Superfortresses. The 301st Bombardment Wing was activated in November 1947 and assumed control of the 301st BG and its three tactical squadrons. The 301st shared Smoky Hill Army Air Field (later AFB) with the 97th BG. By the end of 1947, the 301st had 31 B-29s assigned.

Early 301st BW B-29 markings were relatively plain with only the national emblem, aircraft tail number and buzz numbers appearing on aircraft. Squadron identification mark-

Top: *301st BW B-29s parked behind snowbank at Goose Bay, Labrador, 14 April 1948, prior to their departure for Germany. Tail markings have yet to be painted on several 32nd BS B-29s. (USAF— 9645 A.C.)* Bottom: *B-29A-60-BN (44–62090) shows its buzz markings on the nose in yellow. Sioux City Airport, April 4, 1948. (Photograph by Bob Stolze, courtesy D. Olson)*

ings initially were painted only on fin tips. The 301st BW squadron color assignments were: yellow for the 32nd BS, red for the 352nd, and blue for the 353rd BS. A majority of the B-29s assigned to the 301st BW in early 1948 had black undersurfaces with buzz numbers painted in yellow. All silver finish aircraft had black buzz numbers mostly on the aft fuselage but a few carried their buzz numbers on the aircraft nose.

In February 1948, the Fifteenth Air Force assigned the 301st BW its first tail marking—**Triangle V**. These tail markings started to appear on Wing aircraft in March 1948. In addition to the new tail marking, the Fifteenth Air Force insignia was placed on the dorsal fin. Squadron colors were applied to nose gear doors and each squadron used its own design on nose gear doors to further enhance squadron identification. The 32nd BS used a Black Arrow with the numerals 32 in the center; the 352nd BS used a forward pointing lightning bolt running through a shield with the numerals 352 inside; and the 353rd used a cross-hatched flat diamond symbol on both sides of the designation "353rd."[106]

Operationally, 1948 would be a very busy year for the 301st BW. As part of SAC's mission as a worldwide striking force, a regular rotation plan was established to give SAC a

Top: *The **Circle A** tail marking was very short-lived and appeared on only a few 301st BW B-29s during the first few months of 1950. Notice the 301st BW insignia on the nose. (USAF, AFHRA)* Bottom: *301st BW B-29A-75-BN (44–62325) at Toronto Airport, 1952. An ex–43rd BW B-29 shows remnants of its former fuselage band and **BF-325** marking. (Photograph by Peter Troop, courtesy D. Olson)*

forward presence in both Europe and the Far East. The 301st BG would deploy to Furstenfeldbruck, Germany, in April 1948 for a short visit, but would have one of its squadrons on station in Germany through June 1948. With the beginning of the Berlin crisis in June 1948, the 301st BG was ordered to send its two other squadrons to Goose Bay, Labrador, for possible movement to Germany to join the 353rd BS. Finally ordered to Germany, the rest of the 301st BG arrived at Furstenfeldbruck by 2 July 1948. In August, it was decided by higher military command to remove the B-29 group in Germany considering it to be too vulnerable in the event of hostilities; consequently, the 301st BG returned to Smoky Hill AFB.[107]

Two months later, the 301st BG would deploy once again to Europe, only this time to the United Kingdom for a 90-day TDY from October 1948 through January 1949. All three squadrons would operate from Scampton, England, and train with the RAF in fighter interception exercises.[108]

In October 1949, the 301st BW began a change of station from Smoky Hill AFB to Barksdale AFB. On 7 November 1949, the 301st BW officially became operational at its new station.[109]

In late 1949, the 301st BW received a tail marking change to **Circle A**. The **Circle** geometric figure represented the Fifteenth Air Force and the letter **A** identified the 301st BW. This new tail marking was

Top: *The 301st BW began placing the last four digits of the aircraft serial number on the nose gear doors starting in 1952 as shown on this 301st ARS KB-29M. (USAF, AFHRA)* Bottom: Gas Panic Wagon, *a KB-29M-65-BW (44–69815) of the 301st ARS upon its return from the United Kingdom, November 1951. (USAF, AFHRA)*

Top: *KB-29M (44–61858) was assigned to the 301st ARS and carries the squadron's red and white markings on the nose gear doors and fin cap, in addition to displaying the 301st BW* **Square A** *tail marking. (Courtesy A. Lloyd)* Bottom: *Two Saddletree modified B-29s (atomic-capable) assigned to the 301st BW at Barksdale AFB. The orange-trimmed B-29–60–BW (44–69678) was assigned to the 32nd BW; the blue-trimmed B-29–75–BW (44–70072) belonged to the 352nd BS. (Courtesy A. Lloyd)*

painted on several 301st B-29s, but this project was not completed due to another tail marking change in April 1950 caused by SAC's reorganization — which resulted in the 301st BW being transferred to the Second Air Force. The 301st BW received **Square A** as its new tactical tail marking.

As the 301st BW prepared for another temporary duty assignment to the United Kingdom, the new **Square A** tail marking was painted on Wing aircraft. The 301st BW deployed to the UK in May 1950 and in addition to its B-29s also deployed KB-29Ms from the 301st Air Refueling Squadron. The 301st ARS squadron identification markings were red and white diagonal stripes on the fin tip and nose gear doors. The 301st BW deployment to the UK also saw some changes to squadron color assignments. The 32nd BS's color changed to

*A mobility exercise at Barksdale AFB, May 1953. The KB-29M in the background shows the outline of the recently removed **Square A** tail marking. (USAF)*

orange from yellow and added squadron markings to propeller domes; the 352nd Bombardment Squadron's new color was green while the 353rd BS retained blue. A considerable number of B-29s displayed the 301st BG shield on the left side of the aircraft nose. Several B-29s and KB-29Ms had nicknames and nose art — *Wild Goose, Triflin Gal, Dee-Fence Buster, Flying Rumor* of the 32nd BS; *Antagoniser, Little Wheels,* and *Per Diem* of the 353rd BS; and *Lonesome Polecat* of the 352nd.[110] The 301st BW would have their stay in the UK extended until November 1951 as a result of the Korean War. During this TDY the squadrons of the 301st BW would be based in several different locations: 32nd BS — Lakenheath; 352nd BS — Sculthorpe, then Lakenheath; 353rd BS — Sculthorpe, then Lakenheath and Bassingbourn; and the 301st ARS — Lakenheath.[111]

In 1952 the 301st BW removed the individual squadron marking on nose gear doors and replaced it with the last four digits of the aircraft serial number. Another change to 301st BW aircraft markings involved the aircraft tail number which was relocated from the top of the vertical fin to mid-way on the vertical stabilizer positioned in a break to the forward edge of the black square of the tail marking. These markings would be displayed on 301st BW aircraft for their final TDY to England as a Superfortress unit from December 1952 to March 1953.[112]

By May 1953, the tail markings were gone from 301st BW B-29s and KB-29Ms and the only markings left were squadron identification markings. The 301st continued to fly B-29s and KB-29Ms until mid–1953 when they were exchanged for B-47s and KC-97s.

303rd Bombardment Wing

As part of the USAF's expansion plan during the Korean War, the 303rd Bombardment Wing, Medium, and its three Bombardment Squadrons — the 358th, 359th and 360th — were activated on 4 September 1951 at Davis-Monthan Air Force Base, Tucson, Arizona, and assigned to SAC's Fifteenth Air Force.

The 303rd BW received its first B-29 from the Grand Central Aircraft Company on 12

October 1951.[113] By May 1952, a full complement of 30 B-29s was on hand and, shortly thereafter, the 303rd BW achieved combat-ready status.

The assigned tail insignia for the 303rd BW was **Circle T**. The Fifteenth Air Force insignia was worn on the dorsal fin and squadron identification colors were worn on fin caps and nose gear doors. Additionally nose gear doors had the last three numbers of the aircraft serial number painted in contrasting color on the forward portion and a double-kink lightning bolt on the aft portion. In the case of the 360th, the double-kink lightning bolt also appeared on the fin cap.

The aircraft tail number appeared in black in a forward break of the Fifteenth Air Force Circle. The 303rd BW squadron color assignments were: black for the 358th, blue for the 359th, and red for the 360th. All 303rd BW B-29s had the Wing insignia painted on the left side of the nose with the motto

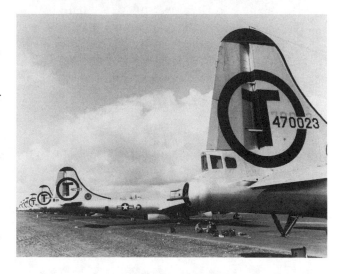

Top: *A closer view of the nose of B-29–40–MO (44–86255) shows an interesting front wheel design and the name* Hells Angels *in red under the Wing shield. Also to the right of the 303rd BW insignia is a list of crewmember names painted on the aircraft. Davis-Monthan AFB, November 1952. (Courtesy of Special Collections and Archives, Wright State University)* Middle: *B-29–60–BA (44–84066) was assigned to the 360th BS and carries the lightning bolt motif on the fin cap. Notice the empty circle on the dorsal fin waiting for the Fifteenth Air Force insignia. Davis-Monthan AFB. 1952. (USAF, courtesy March Field Museum)* Bottom: *Squadron line up shows the black-tipped tails of the 358th BS. This squadron was unique in selecting black as their squadron color. Davis-Monthan AFB, 1952. (USAF, courtesy March Field Museum)*

B-29A-50-BN (44–61864) carries the small lightning bolt on the fin cap. It appears that the 360th BS was the only squadron in the Wing to place the lightning bolt on both nose gear doors and fin cap. (USAF, courtesy March Field Museum)

Hells Angels painted in red below the insignia. These insignia were painted almost immediately after B-29s arrived at Davis-Monthan for assignment to the 303rd BW.

On 15 January 1952, the 9th Air Refueling Squadron was attached to the 303rd Bombardment Wing for administration and operational control.[114] The 9th ARS had previously been attached to the 43rd BW, also at Davis-Monthan AFB. This action brought an additional 22 aircraft — KB-29s — into the Wing. The markings used by the 9th ARS have not been confirmed; however, photographic evidence shows green as a squadron color applied to fin cap, nose gear doors, and as a single belly band. It is believed that the 9th ARS used the **Circle T** tail marking, but this has not been verified.

In September 1952 the 303rd BW was alerted for its first movement overseas to Sidi Slimane, French Morocco. The Wing deployed in early October and by 6 October 1952 all 303rd BW B-29s had arrived at Sidi Slimane. The Wing would leave North Africa in early November and by 10 November 1952 all 303rd BW aircraft had arrived back at Davis-Monthan.[115] In December 1952, the 303rd BW began conversion activities to reequip with B-47s. In January 1953, all 303rd BW B-29s were transferred to the 40th Bombardment Wing at Davis-Monthan, placed in storage facilities, or sent to depots for modification.[116]

305th Bombardment Wing

In January 1951, the 305th Bombardment Wing, Medium, was activated at MacDill Air Force Base, Florida. The first few months of the Wing's reactivation were spent in assigning and training personnel many of whom were recalled reservists. The 305th BW received its first B-29s in February 1951 and had a not-so-grand total of nine by the end of March 1951.[117] Most B-29s came from its sister wing at MacDill AFB, the 306th Bombardment Wing, which had started to convert to B-47s becoming the first B-47 wing in the U.S. Air Force.

By the end of April 1951, the 305th was nearly fully manned with 27 assigned B-29s

Top left, top right, and right: *Sequence shows the painting of the first **Square G** tail marking in the 305th BW on 20 March 1951. The letter **G** had been used by the 305th BG during World War II and, when the 305th BW was reactivated in early 1951, was requested by the 305th BW as its assigned letter for wing identification. (USAF, AFHRA)*

and participated in its first extensive training mission, a long-range penetration mission into Canada from MacDill AFB for the purpose of testing tactics and working with the Air Defense Command.

The authorized tail marking for the 305th Bombardment Wing was **Square G**. The 305th BW had requested the letter **G** be assigned as their wing identification since this letter had been used during World War II to designate the 305th Bombardment Group.[118] The first marking was applied on 20 March 1951 on an aircraft belonging to the 364th BS,[119] and soon started to appear on all assigned aircraft to include T-33 support aircraft which were assigned to support the transition to B-47 aircraft. In addition to required USAF markings and assigned tail marking, squadron identification markings were applied to fin caps and nose gear doors. The marking of Wing aircraft in squadron colors began in early April.[120] The 305th BW assigned squadron colors were: orange for the 364th BS; red for the 365th BS; and blue for the 366th BS.[121]

The summer of 1951 saw the activation of the 305th Air Refueling Squadron and the

Top: *Several T-33s were assigned to the 305th BW to provide jet familiarization prior to receiving B-47 bombers. The T-33s were marked with the* **Square G** *tail marking and also carried a small 305th BW insignia on the tip tank.* (*USAF* — *AFHRA*) Bottom: *305th BW B-29s had squadron identification markings on fin caps and nose gear doors as shown on these aircraft on the MacDill flight line. Squadron colors were orange-yellow for the 364th, red for the 365th, and blue for the 366th.* (*USAF, AFHRA*)

assignment of cargo-type C-97s until KC-97s could be assigned. The **Square G** marking was placed on the newly assigned tanker aircraft and the 305th ARS was assigned the color green for identification. The squadron identification marking was placed on the fin cap. The first KC-97 aircraft with boom attached was delivered to the Wing in December 1951.

In July 1952, the 305th would participate in Operation Signpost, a major air defense exercise of key cites in the United States and Canada. This exercise mobilized resources from Strategic Air Command, Air Defense Command, Tactical Air Command, US Navy and Marine Corps, and the Royal Canadian Air Force. While operating from a forward base at Selfridge AFB, 305th BW B-29s served as part of the "enemy armada." During this exercise, 305th BW aircraft displayed a temporary exercise marking — a wide red belly band.[122]

In the fall of 1951, the USAF decided to convert the 305th Bombardment Wing from a B-29 wing to a B-47 wing; however, the first B-47 wouldn't arrive in the 305th until 30

Top: *305th BW B-29s at Selfridge AFB, Michigan, during Operation Signpost. During this exercise a temporary red band on the mid-fuselage was applied and can be seen on B-29-60-BA (44–84100). July 1952. (USAF, AFHRA)* Bottom: *The 305th BW was one of only two bombardment wings that used tail markings on B-47s. At this Wing review the **Square G** tail marking is clearly visible on three 305th BW B-47s. The nearest B-47B-5-BW (50–008) is nicknamed* The Real McCoy *and was assigned to the 364th BW.* The Real McCoy *was the first B-47 delivered to the 306th BW on 23 October 1951 by the 306th BW commander, Colonel Michael N.W. McCoy. The two other B-47s (50–049 and 50–031) were assigned to the 364th BS and 365th BS, respectively. (USAF, AFHRA)*

October 1952. The first B-47 assigned to the 305th BW was named *The Warrior* as a tribute to the 305th BW Commanding Officer, Col. E. Vandevanter Jr., who received this nickname during his early World War II service with the 19th Bombardment Group. The only form of squadron identification on B-47s was a horizontal flash in squadron color on the vertical fin. The **Square G** tail marking did appear on many 305th BW B-47s until the spring of 1953, when all tail markings were removed from SAC's bomber, tanker, and strategic reconnaissance-type aircraft.

306th Bombardment Group/Bombardment Wing

Carried by SAC in an inactive status since June 1947, the 306th Bombardment Group, Medium, came to life in August 1948 when it started to reman with B-29s and was assigned to the 307th Bombardment Wing at MacDill AFB, Florida.

Equipped with 29 B-29s by the end of September 1948, the 306th Bomb Group was assigned the mission of B-29 combat crew transition training in January 1949. Also in January, the 306th Bomb Group, as part of the 307th Bomb Wing, participated in the 1949 presidential inauguration fly-over for President Truman.

For nearly six months, the 306th Bomb Group flew B-29s devoid of any unit markings—only the national insignia on both sides of the aft fuselage and on the upper left wing and lower right wing, **USAF** on lower left and upper right wing surfaces, **United States Air Force** on both sides of the forward fuselage and the aircraft tail number on the vertical stabilizer appeared on 306th Bomb Group aircraft.

In December 1948, the 306th Bomb Group submitted a proposed tail marking for approval and also requested authorization to paint squadron colors on the fin cap and nose gear doors of assigned aircraft.[123] A month later, Headquarters, Fifteenth Air Force disapproved the proposed tail marking for the 306th Bomb Group stating "the unit aircraft design is not consistent with the policy of this Air Force in utilizing geometric designs for wings and assigned letters for group identification." A design in accordance with the Fifteenth Air Force Tactical Doctrine was submitted to the 306th BG for its consideration.[124]

The 306th BG was attached to the 307th BW until 1950. From activation until early 1950, the 306th BG was not assigned a tactical tail marking. Shown at MacDill AFB is a plain-tail B-29A-20-BN (42–93976) of the 369th BS. This B-29 was assigned to the 306th BG on 7 September 1948. (Museum of Flight)

*A 306th BW B-29A-60-BN with a partial **Square P** tail marking in the process of being transferred to the 305th BW. By April 1951 all B-29s had been transferred from the 306th BW in preparation to receive the USAF's first operational B-47s. (USAF, AFHRA)*

In March 1949, the 306th BG resubmitted its request using the proposed design recommended by the Fifteenth Air Force, and, once again, requested permission to apply squadron identification markings. On 2 April 1949, Headquarters SAC provided a response to the 306th Bomb Group: "All Strategic Air Command aircraft markings and identifications are under consideration. In the near future the new SAC Tactical Doctrine will be published, including all approved aircraft markings."[125]

For the remainder of 1949, tactical markings for the 306th Bomb Group included squadron identification markings on fin caps and nose gear doors and the Fifteenth Air Force insignia on both sides of the dorsal fin (The 306th BG as part of the 307th BW was transferred to the Fifteenth Air Force in December 1948). One squadron, the 369th Bomb Squadron, applied its World War II insignia *Fightin' Bitin'* on the left side of its B-29s. The 306th BG assigned squadron colors were — yellow for the 367th Bomb Squadron; blue for the 368th Bomb Squadron; and red for the 369th Bomb Squadron.

With the publication of SAC's new tactical doctrine manual in October 1949, the 306th BG was assigned **Circle H** as its first tail marking. The marking for its parent wing — the 307th — also at MacDill AFB, was **Circle Y**. It is assumed but has not been verified that the **Circle H** appeared on 306th BG aircraft.

In early 1950, as part of its combat crew-training mission, the 306th BG started to receive B-50 aircraft and by May 1950 had ten B-50s assigned.

A new tail marking —**Square P**— was assigned to the 306th BG when, in April 1950, the group along with the 307th Bombardment Wing was transferred to the jurisdiction of the Second Air Force. The new tail markings started to appear on 306th Bombardment Group B-29s and B-50s in May 1950.

When the Korean War started in June 1950, the combat echelon of the 307th Bomb Wing was called to respond to the crisis on the Korean Peninsula. The 307th Bombardment Group departed MacDill AFB in late July 1950, leaving the 307th Bombardment Wing Headquarters and the 306th Bombardment Group at MacDill. This precipitated an organizational change with the 306th BG in September 1950 when it was reorganized as the 306th Bombardment Wing and its authorized strength was increased to 45 aircraft. The mission remained combat crew training, but the 368th Bombardment Squadron performed SAC's lead crew evaluation while the 367th and 369th Bombardment Squadrons handled B-29 and B-50 transition training for aircraft commanders, pilots and flight engineers.

The 306th BW continued to operate B-29s until April 1951 when all Superfortresses were transferred to the recently activated 305th Bombardment Wing, also at MacDill, as the 306th BW prepared to become the Air Force's first operational B-47 bombardment wing. The first B-47 was delivered on 23 October 1951 and christened *The Real McCoy* in honor of the 306th BW Commander, Colonel Michael N.W. McCoy.[126]

The 306th BW was one of two SAC units to place tail markings on B-47s. However, in early March 1952, while trying to comply with existing directives from Strategic Air Command and Second Air Force, the 306th BW encountered a problem with the size of the B-47 vertical stabilizer being too small to accommodate both the **Square P** tail mark-

Left: *Two ground crewmen check the two 50-caliber machine guns in the tail of B-47B-40-BW (51–2225) prior to a training mission. This B-47 was assigned to the 367th BS and carries a tail band in the squadron color — yellow. MacDill AFB, February 21, 1953. (USAF — 47119 A.C.)* Right: *The first B-47B-5-BW (50–008) for the 306th BW arrived on 19 November 1951 and was flown by the Wing CO, Col. Michael N.W. McCoy. The aircraft was appropriately named* The Real McCoy! *(USAF, AFHRA)*

ing, aircraft tail number, and a twelve-inch strip in squadron color. The 36th Air Division, higher headquarters for both the 306th BW and 305th BW, recommended to both Second Air Force and SAC that a reduced tail marking size, similar to that used by the 91st SRW with its RB-45Cs, be approved and that the squadron color identification strip be lowered to a point two inches below the installed antenna. On 21 May 1952 SAC approved the recommended changes.[127] In addition to the **Square P** marking on the tail, squadron identification was indicated by a tail band just below the fin tip. The 306th Bomb Wing insignia was placed on the left side of the aircraft nose and

Getting ready for 90 days temporary duty in England, Capt. Jack Harper, in Cherokee Indian headdress, looks at the name Sa-Gua, *which means "first" in the tribal language. The squadron insignia is that of the 369th* Fitin Bitin *BS. (USAF, AFHRA)*

*The 306th ARS was the first unit in the USAF to operate the KC-97. KC-97E (51–200) with the **Square P** tail marking of the 306th BW, MacDill AFB, 1952. (USAF, courtesy Col. John Decker)*

squadron insignia appeared on the right side. The **Square P** tail marking also appeared on T-33 aircraft assigned to the 306th Bomb Wing for jet transition training.

In July 1951 the 306th ARS was activated and became the first air refueling unit in the Air Force to be equipped with KC-97s. The 306th ARS used green as its squadron color which appeared on KC-97 fin tips. Also the **Square P** tail marking was placed on KC-97 tails.

The 306th Bomb Wing continued to use the **Square P** tail marking until May-June 1953 when most tail markings were removed from all assigned aircraft. A few tail markings survived to be seen in the United Kingdom where the 306th BW deployed in June 1953 bringing the first B-47 operational deployment to England as part of SAC's overseas rotation program. But by their return to the United States in August 1953, the 306th BW **Square P** tail marking had been removed from all aircraft.

307th Bombardment Wing

On 4 August 1946, as part of the U.S. Army Air Forces post–World War II reorganization, the 498th Bombardment Group, Very Heavy, was inactivated at MacDill Field, Tampa, Florida, and the 307th Bombardment Group (VH) was reactivated along with its assigned squadrons— the 370th, 371st and 372nd Bombardment Squadrons. Personnel and B-29 aircraft assets were inherited from the inactivated 498th BG.

Initially affected by the Army Air Forces demobilization, the 307th Bombardment Group (VH) was designated as the initial SAC bomb group to engage in anti-submarine and sea search operations and was tasked to develop tactics, operating procedures and training requirements for this program. As a result, the 307th BG received a higher priority on personnel and equipment. In December 1946, the 307th Bombardment Group had 13 B-29 aircraft assigned. By the end of January 1947 the 307th Bombardment Group had its full authorization of 30 B-29s.[128]

In addition to the anti-submarine program, the 307th participated in nation-wide Army Week flights in April 1947 and in May 1947 started over-water navigation flights to bases in the Caribbean as well as Panama. The 307th Bombardment Group also participated in the highly publicized Operation Big Town, SAC's maximum effort raid on New York City conducted on 16 May 1947.

From the time of activation to mid–1947, the 307th Bombardment Group did not use any tactical markings on its aircraft. All markings were those required by Technical Order 07–1-1, Aircraft Camouflage, Markings and Insignia and included: the national insignia, aircraft tail number, and buzz numbers. On 307th Bombardment Group aircraft, buzz numbers appeared on the aft portion of the fuselage behind the national insignia and under the left wing; silver finish B-29s had black buzz numbers and those with matte black undersurfaces had red buzz numbers. No group or squadron insignia appeared on 307th B-29s during this time. One 307th aircraft was named *Hang-Over Haven,* but this B-29 was transferred to the 93rd Bomb Group at Castle Field, California, in June 1947 when the 371st Bomb Squadron was transferred to California to serve as cadre for remanning the 93rd BG.

In the spring of 1947 the 307th BG ordered bomb squadron insignia decals to be placed on the left side of the aircraft nose.[129] Group identity was a blue azure fin shield bearing a four petal dogwood bloom painted on a white disc located on the vertical stabilizer above the aircraft tail number. The 307th BG squadron identification colors were: red for the

Top: *371st BS B-29–90-BW (44–87772) on a visit to Dhahran, Saudi Arabia, January 1948. Notice the white disc with the 307th BG insignia on the tail. (Photograph by Crull, courtesy W. Thompson)* Bottom: *Undergoing maintenance near Hangar 5 at MacDill AFB, B-29A-25-BN (42–94045) was assigned to the 307th BG on 14 May 1948. The fin tip is green, which was the 371st BS color in 1948. The **Arrowhead** tail marking started to appear on 307th BG aircraft after their return from England in November 1948. (Museum of Flight)*

370th BS; green for the 371st BS; and blue for the 372nd BS.[130] These squadron identification markings were painted on aircraft fin tips and nose gear doors.

These markings were observed on 307th Bombardment Group B-29s during the rest of 1947 and through the fall of 1948 as the 307th embarked on squadron-size TDYs to Germany in 1947 and a full group deployment to the United Kingdom in July 1948 as part of

The 307th BW **Circle Y** marking authorized in late 1949. (USAF)

the U.S. response to the crises in Berlin. During its stay in England, the 307th BG operated from two bases: Marham which housed the 370th and 371 Bombardment Squadrons and Waddington where the 372nd Bombardment Squadron was stationed.[131]

Upon its return to MacDill in November 1948 the 307th received its first tail marking assignment — a **Hollow Black Arrowhead** design. A month later the 307th Bomb Wing was relieved from direct assignment to Strategic Air Command Headquarters and reassigned to the Fifteenth Air Force. In addition to its new tail marking, the 307th BW soon applied the Fifteenth Air Force insignia on the dorsal fin of its B-29s.

Late 1948 and early 1949 was a busy time for the 307th BW. Another bomb group — the 306th — had been activated in August 1948 and was assigned to the 307th Bomb Wing. The 306th BG was assigned the role of B–29 combat crew transition training beginning in January 1949. Also in January 1949, the 307th BW was one of two SAC B-29 bombardment wings to participate in the USAF flyover for President Truman's inauguration. (The 93rd Bombardment Wing from Castle AFB was the other B-29 unit).

In February 1949 the 307th BW commenced its second TDY in the United Kingdom which would last through May 1949. This time the 307th would occupy two bases: Marham and Lakenheath. Two squadrons— the 371st BS and 372nd BS — would use Lakenheath, and the 370th would use Marham.[132] Changes to 307th BW aircraft markings from the previous TDY to the UK in 1948 would include the addition of the arrowhead tail marking, Fifteenth Air Force insignia on the dorsal fin, and for the 371st Bomb Squadron a change in squadron color from green to yellow. Most B-29s were silver but several B-29s still retained their black camouflage. Buzz numbers still appeared on assigned aircraft (most in red but a few in yellow), but would soon give way to the **USAF** and **United States Air Force** mark-

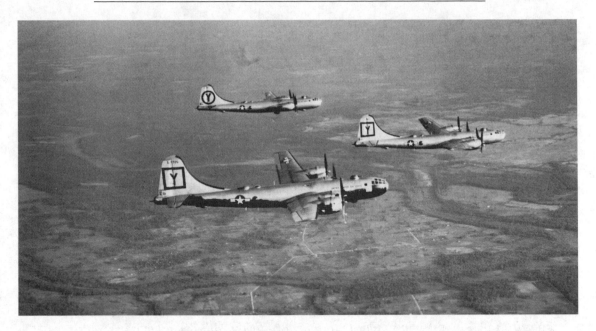

*The 307th BW received another tail marking change — **Square Y** — in April 1950. This formation shot shows the transition from **Circle Y** to **Square Y** tail marking, May 1950. (USAF, courtesy G. Erkes.)*

ings on wings and forward fuselage, respectively. Squadron insignia continued to be used and appeared on the left side of the nose.

SAC's implementation of a standardized tail marking policy in October 1949 brought another tail marking change to the 307th — **Circle Y**. The **Circle** represented the Fifteenth Air Force and the letter **Y** the 307th Bomb Wing. According to the 307th Bomb Wing Unit History for December 1949, "necessary stencils were cut and paint was requisitioned to start painting the new tail code beginning in mid–January 1950."[133]

Shortly after implementing the newly-assigned tail marking, SAC's realignment of units on a geographical basis in April 1950 found the 307th BW now assigned to the Second Air Force and, once again, assigned another tail marking — **Square Y**. The removal of the **Circle Y** and placement of the **Square Y** on 307th BW B-29 tails was started in May 1950 and completed in June 1950.

The outbreak of war on the Korean Peninsula in June 1950 had a near immediate effect on the 307th BW. Its combat echelon, the 307th Bomb Group, deployed with 31 B-29s to Kadena Air Base in Okinawa, and on 8 August 1950 began combat operations against the North Koreans by bombing the marshalling yards at Pyongyang. The 307th would fly combat missions until the end of the Korean War in July 1953.

Although most squadron insignias were removed prior to the 307th BG deployment to Okinawa, markings remained little changed until 1951 when the 307th started to use a different scheme for squadron identification markings. The fin cap color marking was extended downward to the upper horizontal bar of the **Square Y** tail marking, and squadron colors were also placed on the lower lip of the nose assembly, on wing tips, and in the form of a rectangle at the intersection of the main wing with the fuselage.

In late 1952, the 307th B-29s were painted black to help make them less vulnerable to enemy air defenses during the night bombing missions over North Korea. The black

370th BS B-29 at K-9 strip in Korea. Red squadron markings on lower nose lip started to appear in 1951 in a system similar to the one used by the 19th BG of the FEAF which shared Kadena with the 307th BG. (Photograph by Lamoreux, courtesy W. Thompson)

camouflage was painted in an irregular pattern up to the mid-level of the fuselage extending to the top of the tail assembly. The fin cap still displayed squadron colors and the nose gear doors displayed the last three numerals in white of the aircraft serial number. Also during this phase, all 307th B-29s were marked with the Wing insignia placed on the left side of the aircraft nose in addition to mission markings.

The 307th BW would remain on Okinawa as part of the Far East Air Forces until 1954 when the Wing returned to the United States, turned-in its B-29s and was assigned to Lincoln AFB, Nebraska as a B-47 unit.

308th Bombardment Wing

The 308th Bombardment Wing, Medium, was activated at Forbes Air Force Base, Topeka, Kansas, on 10 October 1951. The three tactical squadrons assigned to the 308th BW were the 373rd Bombardment Squadron, the 374th Bombardment Squadron, and the 375th Bombardment Squadron. Although assigned to the Second Air Force, the 308th BW initially was attached to the 21st Air Division and trained under the guidance of the 90th Bombardment Wing at Forbes. The 308th participated in a six-month training program with the 90th BW and used their aircraft until it left for its permanent station, Hunter Air Force Base, Georgia, in April 1952. While at Hunter AFB, the 308th BW would be assigned to the 38th Air Division and join the 2nd BW, a B-50D unit also stationed at Hunter AFB.

The 308th BW received its first reconditioned B-29s in May 1952 from Dobbins Air Force Base and by the end of May would have seven gleaming Superfortresses on hand.[134] The Wing was completely equipped with B-29 medium bombers by the end of September 1952.[135]

The 308th received the letter **O** for its letter designator in a Second Air Force message

Top: *Col. M.A. Preston, 308 BW commander, and crew awaiting briefing prior to flight to Sidi Slimane, French Morocco, February 1953. (USAF, AFHRA)* Bottom: *B-29 #959 taking off from Hunter AFB for French North Africa — February 1953 (USAF — AFHRA)*

dated 18 July 1952 and the tail marking—**Square O**—started to appear on 308th B-29s almost immediately.[136] In addition to its tail marking, 308th B-29s displayed squadron identification colors on tail tips and nose gear doors. The squadron colors for the 308th BW were: blue for the 373rd BS, red for the 374th BS, and yellow for the 375th BS. Besides the required national markings, the last four digits of the aircraft tail number were displayed in black on the vertical stabilizer and in contrasting color on the front portion of the nose gear doors. The only unit in the 308th BW to apply squadron insignia on its B-

Top: *Line up of 308th BW B-29s before maximum effort mission, 26 February 1953. (USAF, AFHRA)* Bottom: *A 374th BS B-29 taking off on maximum effort mission from Sidi Slimane Air Base on 26 February 1953. Notice the 374th BS insignia on the forward fuselage. (USAF, AFHRA)*

29s was the 374th BS. Photos of 374th BS B-29s during the 308th BW TDY to Sidi Slimane, French North Africa, show the insignia on the right side of the aircraft nose. On 29 August 1952, the 308th Bombardment Wing insignia was approved by Headquarters, USAF; however, it appears the Wing insignia never was applied to its B-29 aircraft, but made its debut on 308th B-47s.

In July 1952 the 308th BW participated in Operation Signpost which was a joint USAF and RCAF maneuver. All participating 308th B-29s wore a red band around the fuselage as temporary identification.[137] Further operational activities for the 308th BW would include: support of West Point cadet B-29 familiarization training at Maxwell AFB in August 1952; participation in a fly-over for the American Legion in New York City, also in August; and a Wing TDY to Sidi Slimane AB, French Morocco from 20 February 1953 to 30 March 1953.

The 308th BW continued to operate B-29s until mid–1953 when the unit converted to B-47s.

310th Bombardment Wing

The 310th Bombardment Wing, Medium, was activated as a B-29 wing on 28 March 1952 at Forbes Air Force Base, Topeka, Kansas. The three assigned tactical squadrons were the 379th, 380th and 381st Bombardment Squadrons, Medium. The 310th BW was trained as an entire unit by SAC's OTU at Forbes AFB — the 90th BW. Using the "Parent-Wing" concept, the 310th BW would undergo an operational training unit program for 180 days prior to moving to its permanent station — Smoky Hill Air Force Base, Kansas.

No aircraft were assigned to the 310th during its training phase at Forbes. All pilot transition and crew training were conducted using 90th Bombardment Wing B-29s. The 310th BW completed its training program in early August 1952 and on August 8th movement orders were received directing the transfer of all units of the 310th Bombardment Wing from Forbes AFB to Smoky Hill AFB.[138]

On 2 August 1952, the 310th BW received the assignment of the letter **B** as the tail designation letter. This was changed to the letter **V** in a message from Fifteenth Air Force Headquarters on 5 August 1952. However, the letter designator was changed, once again, to the letter **B** on 8 August 1952 due to the reassignment of the 55th Strategic Reconnaissance Wing, which was already using the letter **V** with the Second Air Force, to the Fifteenth Air Force.[139]

Beginning in September 1952, the first B-29s started to arrive at Smoky Hill AFB to equip the 310th BW. The first B-29 arrived on 11 September 1952 and was assigned to the 379th BS. Aircraft came from various SAC bases like Walker AFB and Fairchild AFB as well as from an aircraft refurbishing company, The Grand Central Aircraft Corporation at Tucson, Arizona. Almost immediately the **Circle B** tail marking was placed on 310th B-29s along with squadron identification markings on fin caps and nose gear doors. The 310th BW color assignments for its bombardment squadrons were: red for the 379th; blue for the 380th; and yellow for the 381st. The tactical markings were complemented by the required

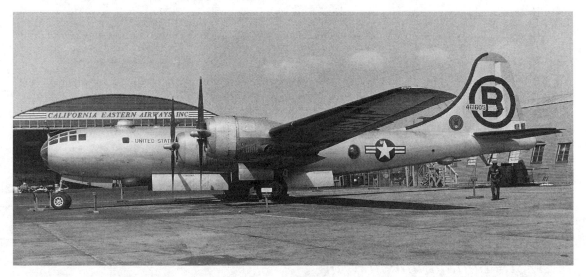

*This 310th BW B-29A-35-BN (44–61605) was assigned to the 381st BS. Fin cap and nose gear door are painted in the 381st color — yellow. **Circle B** tail marking was authorized for the 310th BW in August 1952. Oakland Airport, March 15, 1953. (Courtesy D. Olson)*

The second crew selected to represent the 310th at the 1952 SAC Bombing-Navigation Competition came from the 381st BS. Squadron color is yellow. (USAF)

national insignia, **USAF,** on the lower left wing and upper right wing and **United States Air Force** in smaller letters on both sides of the forward fuselage. The aircraft tail number appeared on the vertical stabilizer in a forward break of the Fifteenth Air Force **Circle**. The Fifteenth Air Force insignia was applied to its usual position on both sides of the dorsal fin.

The 310th Air Refueling Squadron was activated in October 1952 and started receiving KC-97 tanker aircraft in Jan 1953 when five aircraft were delivered from Seattle.[140] The 310th ARS used green as their assigned squadron color which was painted on aircraft fin caps. It is believed, but not yet verified, that the **Circle B** tail marking was used on 310th KC-97s. The 310th BW did not apply wing or squadron insignia to its B-29s or KC-97s.

An additional unit, the 40th Air Refueling Squadron, was attached to the 310th BW in October 1952. The 40th ARS would receive its first KC-97 on 18 October 1952 and would have its full complement of 20 KC-97s by the end of January 1953. The 40th ARS would remain under the operational control of the 310th BW until 1 May 1953.[141]

The 310th BW continued to operate B-29s until early 1954 when it converted to B-47E Stratojets.

376th Bombardment Wing

The 376th Bombardment Wing, Medium, was activated 1 June 1951 and assigned to the 90th Bombardment Wing at Forbes Air Force Base, Topeka, Kansas, for a 120-day oper-

*376 BW B-29 with **Square X** tail marking on the runway at Sidi Slimane, French Morocco. The 376th BW was TDY to Sidi Slimane from 15 April 1952 through 1 May 1952. (USAF, AFHRA)*

ational training program. Assigned squadrons were the 512th, 513th, and 514th Bombardment Squadrons. All B-29 aircraft used to conduct training at Forbes AFB belonged to the 90th Bombardment Wing.

In October 1951, the 376th BW completed its training program with the 90th BW and moved to its permanent station at Barksdale Air Force Base, Louisiana, where, as part of the Second Air Force, it began a mission centered on operational testing and evaluation of Electronic Countermeasure (ECM) tactics and equipment.

Initially, with no B-29 aircraft assigned, the 376th BW borrowed aircraft from its sister unit at Barksdale the 301st Bombardment Wing; however, by November 1951, each squadron had four B-29s of their own and were steadily receiving more from the Grand Central Aircraft Company of Tucson, Arizona, which had a contract with the U.S. Air Force to recondition mothballed B-29s.[142]

The tail marking assigned to the 376th BW was **Square X**. The aircraft tail number appeared in black on the vertical stabilizer in a forward break to the Second Air Force **Square**. The 376th BW squadron color assignments were: blue for the 512th BS, yellow for the 513th BS and red for the 514th BS. These squadron colors were painted on fin caps and nose gear doors. The last three numerals of the aircraft serial number in contrasting color appeared on the nose gear doors as well. The 376th BW did not use wing or squadron insignia on its B-29s. Several 376th BW B-29s carried insignia red Arctic trim on the outboard wing panels and on the tail. Their **Square X** tail marking was painted in identification yellow to offer better contrast and visibility.

During April and May 1952, the 376th BW took part in its first overseas deployment when it sent ten B-29s to Sidi Slimane in French Morocco. The 376th BW would also train with the RCAF in Montreal, Canada, in June 1952; send aircraft to the Air Proving Ground Center at Eglin AFB, Florida, for testing and evaluation of electronic countermeasures equipment and tactics; and in November 1952 deploy ten of its B-29s to Elmendorf AFB, Alaska, for cold weather testing of ECM components. The 376th BW would spend most of

*Tail insignia of three Strategic Air Command wings — 106th BW (**Circle A**), 376th BW (**Square X**), and 310th BW (**Circle B**) — are prominent along the flight line at Davis-Monthan AFB, Tucson, Arizona, during the fourth annual SAC Bombing and Navigation Competition being held 12–19 October 1952. The Boeing B-29s are being readied for another 12-hour mission that will take them over the target cities of Kansas City, Dallas and Phoenix. (USAF, National Archives)*

1953 participating in various exercises to test the effectiveness of their ECM capabilities as part of SAC's offensive tactics.[143]

The 376th BW continued to use B-29s until March 1954, when in preparation to receive new B-47E bombers, its B-29s were delivered to the Military Aircraft Storage and Disposition Center at Davis-Monthan Air Force Base, Arizona.

509th Bombardment Group/Wing

As the Group that flew two atomic missions against Japan during World War II, the 509th Composite Group along with its 393rd Bombardment Squadron and 320th Troop Carrier Squadron, was transferred to Strategic Air Command effective 21 March 1946 and to the Fifteenth Air Force effective 31 March 1946.[144]

From March 1946 until its return to Roswell Army Air Field in August 1946, the 509th CG was stationed at Kwajalein Island in the Pacific immersed in preparing for the atomic bomb drop as part of Operation Crossroads. As part of Task Group 1.5, the Army Air Forces component of Task Force One, the 509th Composite Group provided aircraft to evaluate the effects of nuclear detonations in the air and water — and on 1 July 1946 provided the drop aircraft, *Dave's Dream*. Although the 509th CG continued to use its **Black Arrow** in a **Black Circle** tail marking from World War II (the **Black Circle** representing the 313th Bombardment Wing and the **Arrow** the 509th Composite Group), special aircraft markings were used during Operation Crossroads. (See Chapter 8 for a discussion of Operations Crossroads aircraft markings)

On 30 July 1946, the 509th Composite Group was redesignated the 509th Bombardment Group, Very Heavy, and the 715th Bombardment Squadron, formerly of the 448th Bombardment Group at Ft. Worth, Texas, and the 830th Bombardment Squadron, formerly

Top: *B-29–55-MO (44–86401) was modified to Silverplate configuration in 1946 and assigned to the 509th BG in March 1947. The markings reflect those used for the first half of 1947 with the arrow painted in squadron color and the tail number on the dorsal fin. (USAF, courtesy M. Foley)* Bottom: *During Operation Big Town in May 1947. A mix of 393rd and 715th BS Silverplates in formation. Notice that B-29–36-MO (44–27302), nicknamed* Top Secret, *retains its markings from Operation Crossroads. (USAF, courtesy M. Foley)*

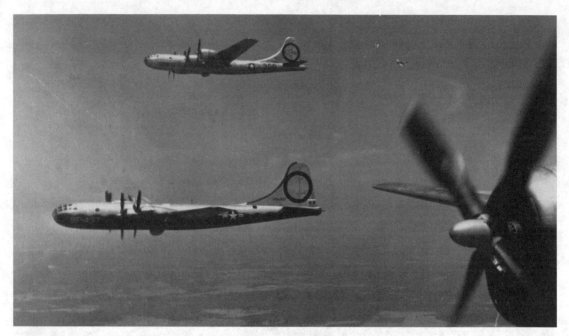

Top: *Two different marking schemes for the 509th BG. The new scheme, illustrated on 393rd BS B-29–36-MO (44–27300), was adopted during the summer of 1947. The new markings would include the Eighth Air Force insignia on the dorsal fin and the tail number relocated from the dorsal fin to inside the arrow. (USAF, courtesy M. Foley)* Bottom: *Standard markings for the 509th BG implemented in July–August 1947 are displayed on B-29–60-MO (44–86430). The arrow is in the 393rd BS color — yellow — with the numbers in black. The buzz numbers on the nose and under the wing are in yellow. (USAF, courtesy M. Foley)*

of the 485th Bombardment Group at Smoky Hill, Kansas, were assigned to the 509th Bombardment Group at Roswell AAF in June and became operational in August 1946 when the 509th BG returned from Kwajalein.[145]

In November 1946, the 509th Bombardment Group was transferred from the Fifteenth Air Force to the Eighth Air Force, and by February 1947 the 509th BG was a fully operational SAC bombardment group equipped with a full complement of 30 B-29s, nearly all of which were Silverplates or atomic bomb carriers.

Top: *B-29–30-MO (42–63577) carries the yellow squadron markings of the 393rd BS inside the arrow and on the fin cap. Roswell Field, 1947. (National Museum of the USAF)* Bottom: *In early 1949, the 509th BW removed all tail markings and painted all B-29s in insignia red Arctic markings. This black-bellied B-29–90-BW (45–21733) is a Saddletree modified aircraft and carries only the Eighth Air Force insignia and painted nose gear doors as distinctive markings. (Museum of Flight)*

The 509th BG was the only SAC unit to use a tail marking, **Forward Pointing Arrow** inside a **Black Circle**, as group identity until early 1947 when the Eighth Air Force assigned geometric symbols to the 7th Bombardment Group (**Triangle**) and 43rd Bombardment Group (**Diamond**). However, a variation to the tail marking from its World War II usage was painting the arrow inside the circle in the squadron color — yellow for the 393rd, green for the 715th, and red for the 830th.[146]

Other markings appearing on 509th BG B-29s during the first half of 1947 included the 509th insignia on the right side of the nose, buzz markings — yellow for black camouflage, black for silver finish aircraft were located on the nose, lower left wing surface and, for some aircraft, upper right wing surface. The 509th BG also placed the last three digits of the aircraft serial number aft of the national insignia on the fuselage for local identification.

The 509th BG displayed a considerable number of aircraft nicknames during its first year and a half with SAC. Most of these aircraft were Silverplates that served with the unit

Top: *This 509th BW B-50D-110-BO (49–274) shows a variation in the size of the letter C inside the Triangle and in the placement of the aircraft tail number on the vertical stabilizer. (USAF, AFHRA)* Bottom: *B-50D-100-BO (48–112) displays squadron colors on fin tip, nosewheel doors, nose of the wing tanks, and the arrow inside the black circle (old 509th insignia) on side of fuel tank. The 509th BW also used smaller Eighth Air Force insignia on the dorsal fin. (USAF, AFHRA)*

during World War II and during Operation Crossroads in 1946. Examples of named aircraft in the 509th BW included: *Dave's Dream* (44–27354), *Straight Flush* (44–27301), *Top Secret* (44–27302), *Luke the Spook* (44–86346) and *Up An Atom* (44–27304).[147]

In July 1947, the 509th BG changed the marking scheme for its B-29s. As stated in the July 1947 unit history for the 509th BG, "B-29 aircraft assigned to this field are being painted with circles and arrows, denoting the group, on the vertical stabilizer and rudder. The circle is black and the forward pointing arrow within the circle is in Squadron color. The serial number of the aircraft is painted within the arrow. In addition the Eighth Air Force

In 1950–51 the 509th BW adopted a diagonal stripe design to be painted in squadron colors on the nose gear doors. B-29–95-BW (45–21840) has insignia red Arctic trim on the tail and outer wing surfaces, black camouflage underside, and yellow and red diagonal stripes on nose gear doors. (USAF)

Insignia is being painted just outside the circle at five and seven o'clock position in blue and gold on each side of the stabilizer. Base Maintenance Shops estimated completion by the middle of August 1947."[148]

Organizational changes affecting the 509th BG would include being redesignated a bombardment wing under the Hobson Plan in November 1947, an increase in authorized aircraft from 30 to 45 in 1948, and the activation of the 509th Air Refueling Squadron with an authorized strength of 20 KB-29Ms in June 1948.

There were few changes to 509th BW aircraft markings until early 1949 when tail codes were removed and insignia red Arctic trim was applied to the tail and outboard wing surfaces. Buzz markings were gone and replaced by the required **USAF** and **United States Air Force** markings. These modified B-29s were devoid of all unit insignia. The aircraft tail number appeared in a silver rectangle on the Arctic tails. These markings were noted during the 509th BW training mission to the United Kingdom from April 1949 to August 1949.[149]

The 509th received a new tail marking—**Triangle C**—in late 1949, but implementation of the new marking took some time as the 509th BW continued to use insignia red Artic markings on its B-29s and in 1950 started to convert to B-50D bombers.

When the 509th BW returned to the United Kingdom in February 1951, the unit deployed with a mix of modified B-29s, B-50Ds and KB-29Ps. Aircraft markings included many aircraft with insignia red Arctic trim and a number of B-29s with striped diagonal nose gear doors (either a combination of yellow and red or blue and red); in the case of B-50s, the **Triangle C** marking on the vertical fin, solid color nose gear doors (yellow—393rd, blue—715th, and red—830th) and squadron color trim on the fuel tanks.[150]

By the time the 509th BW returned to the United Kingdom for its third TDY from

Top: *The 509th ARS on the flightline ready to support the movement of the 27th FEW to Japan as part of Fox Peter Two. October 1952. (Boeing P12880. © Boeing. Used under license.)* Bottom: *A KB-29P shows the newly designed 509th BW insignia on its nose, 1953. (USAF)*

June to September 1952, all B-29s were gone and the 509th was fully-equipped with 45 B-50D bombers and 20 KB-29 tankers. Markings were standardized with B-50s having the **Triangle C** on the tail, squadron markings painted on the fin tip, nose gear doors and on the nose of the wing fuel tanks. The fuel tanks also displayed the old 509th emblem — circle with a forward pointing arrow — on the outboard side of the wing tank with the arrow painted in squadron color. Nose gear doors had the standard **No Smoking Within 100 Feet** warning in contrasting color. KB-29P tankers of the 509th ARS displayed the **Triangle C** tail marking and squadron identification markings painted on the fin tip and nose gear doors in their squadron color — green. As on B-50s, the **No Smoking** warning appeared on nose gear doors. Beginning in 1953, the 509th BW started to paint a new 509th BW insignia on the left side of the aircraft nose on all assigned B-50Ds and KB-29Ps.

The 509th BW continued to fly B-50Ds until early 1953 when it began its conversion to B-47s. The 509th ARS started to replace its KB-29Ps with KC-97s in the first half of 1954.

6

Fighter Wings

1st Fighter Wing

On 1 May 1949, the 1st Fighter Wing was transferred from the Continental Air Command to Strategic Air Command and the Fifteenth Air Force. Stationed at March AFB, California, and equipped with F-86As, the 1st Fighter Wing, along with the 1st Fighter Group and its three squadrons—the 27th, 71st, and 94th—was attached to the 22nd Bombardment Wing, also at March AFB, on 1 July 1949.

Due to the limited range of the F-86 and numerous mechanical and logistical challenges of a new airframe, the 1st FW was not considered part of the SAC escort fleet, and its tenure in SAC would be less than a year, since it would be transferred back to Continental Air Command on 30 June 1950 with an air defense mission.[1]

The 1st Fighter Wing (later redesignated 1st Fighter-Interceptor Wing on 16 April 1950) F-86 aircraft markings were quite striking and incorporated the use of wing and squadron insignia as well as squadron identification markings. The 1st FW assigned

Side view of a 71st Fighter Squadron F-86A (47–633) shows the striking aircraft marking scheme of the 1st Fighter Wing. Stylized flash on fuselage and upper tail band are in the squadron color—red. Squadron insignia is on a white disc and the lower tail band represents flight assignment—in this case probably red. (Courtesy of Special Collections and Archives, Wright State University)

squadron colors were — yellow for the 27th FS, red for the 71st FS, and royal blue for the 94th FS. The squadron colors were displayed in a narrow band on the upper vertical stabilizer and in a stylized flash on each side of the fuselage starting just below the cockpit and extending to mid-fuselage. Superimposed on this flash was the squadron insignia on a white disc with the 1st Fighter Group/Wing insignia located on the upper right edge of the squadron insignia. Pilot and crew chief information appeared on a large rectangle in squadron color on the right side just below the forward windshield. Each squadron also employed flight identification markings using the color red, blue, white or black. These markings appeared as a horizontal band on the lower portion of the vertical stabilizer just above the **U.S. Air Force** lettering and the aircraft serial number. In addition to squadron identification markings, all 1st FW F-86s carried the standard national and USAF markings required by Technical Order No 07–1-1, Aircraft Camouflage, Markings, and Insignia dated 10 October 1949. These markings included the use of the **FU** prefix in buzz markings that appeared in black on the aft fuselage between the national insignia and the leading edge of the horizontal stabilizer.

4th Fighter Group/Wing

The 4th Fighter Group was the third fighter unit assigned to SAC when it was activated on paper at Selfridge Army Air Field on 9 September 1946. Initially scheduled to be equipped with P-47N aircraft, the 4th FG was selected in November 1946 to become one of the first SAC fighter units to receive the P-80A jet fighter. However, it wouldn't be until April 1947 when the 4th FG and its three fighter squadrons — the 334th, 335th, and 336th — moved to Andrews Field, Maryland, and were assigned directly to SAC Headquarters, that their first P-80 aircraft would be assigned.[2] On 15 August 1947, the 4th Fighter

An early 335th FS P-80A (45–8335) displays its squadron color — white — on the nose, tip tanks, and vertical stabilizer. The painting of squadron insignia was completed in late March 1948. The 4th FG color — black — would replace the squadron color on the nose in March–April 1948. (Courtesy, D. Menard)

Top: *P-80A (45–8334) shows the marking scheme implemented by SAC in February 1948. Squadron color is red and appears on the aft portion of the tip tanks, wing and horizontal stabilizer tips, and vertical fin above the aircraft's tail number. Group color is black and appears on the nose. Idlewild Airport, New York, May 15, 1948. (Courtesy, W. Larkins)* Left: *A group of pilots from the 335th FS upon their return to Andrews AFB after participating in the Miami Air Races, January 1948. The flight from Miami to Andrews AFB took just two hours and three minutes. The squadron color, white, can be seen on the tail band as well as on several of the flight helmets. (USAF, AFHRA)*

Wing was activated and assumed control of the 4th Fighter Group and its three tactical squadrons. Initially operating a combination of P-47 and P-80 aircraft, by the end of 1947 the 4th FW would have 54 P-80s in its inventory and no P-47s.[3]

Early P-80 markings for the 4th FW included **PN** aircraft identification markings located on the mid-section of the fuselage. The 4th FG painted squadron identification markings on the aircraft nose in a scallop design, on the vertical fin as a medium width band just above the aircraft serial number, on the horizontal stabilizer as medium width bands, and on the tip tanks as a horizontal band. The 4th FG assigned squadron colors were red for the 334th FS, white for the 335th FS, and blue for the 336th FS. All three squadrons in the 4th FG painted their insignia on both sides of the aircraft nose just inside the curve of the scallop.

According to the November 1947 unit history for the 4th FG, half of the 335th P-80As had their squadron insignia painted on both sides of the nose section, but the exchange of

An F-80A (44–85431) of the 335th FS has insignia red Arctic markings on the tail and outboard wing surfaces. Notice the tail number framed by the natural metal rectangle. (USAF, courtesy D. Menard)

then current P-80As for modified P-80A-10s halted further painting.[4] It would take until the end of March 1948 for the painting of squadron insignia on all 335th FS P-80A-10s to be completed.[5]

On 10 February 1948, SAC announced its new policy on fighter aircraft markings in which each fighter group was assigned a high visibility color and recommended squadron colors as well as their placement.[6] The 4th Fighter Group identification color of black was painted on the nose of its P-80A-10s and also appeared on the forward portion of the tip tanks. Squadron colors continued to appear on wing tips, horizontal stabilizer tips and as a medium band on the vertical fin and were placed on the aft portion of the tip tanks. Squadron insignias were painted on both sides of the aircraft nose inside the curved portion of the nose scallop. The 4th FG used command markings on its P-80s in the form of fuselage bands: one for flight leaders, two for squadron commander, three for group commander, and four for wing commander. The group commander aircraft also used all three squadron colors for markings located on wing tips and vertical fins.

Late 1948 saw the addition of **USAF** and **U.S. Air Force** lettering on aircraft and a change in the buzz number prefix from **PN** to **FT**. This was required by Technical Order 07–1-1, Aircraft Camouflage, Markings, and Insignia dated 26 July 1948. Additionally, in October 1948 the 336th FS began a five-month deployment to Alaska for training in cold weather operations. All 336th FS F-80s had their outer wing surfaces and tail painted in insignia red Arctic trim for greater visibility. This resulted in the tail band being removed and the squadron color — blue — being placed on the fin cap.

The 4th FW's association with SAC ended on 1 December 1948 when it was assigned to the Continental Air Command to assume an air defense mission. The 4th would continue to fly F-80s until the summer of 1949 when they would convert to F-86A Sabre Jets.

12th Fighter-Escort/Strategic Fighter Wing

The 12th Fighter-Escort Wing along with its assigned squadrons— the 559th, 560th and 561st — was activated on 1 November 1950 at Turner AFB, Georgia, and assigned to the Second Air Force. Shortly thereafter, on 5 December 1950, the 12th FEW was transferred to Bergstrom AFB, Texas, and assigned to the Eighth Air Force. The 12th FEW received its first F-84E aircraft on 13 December 1950 and would continue to fly the E model until December 1951 when it would convert to F-84Gs.

Major operational highlights for the 12th FEW from 1951 through 1953 would include: deployment to England from July 1951 through December 1951; participation in the Operation Ivy atomic test program at Kwajalein from March through December 1952; and, as a Strategic Fighter Wing, pulling a rotational tour at Misawa Air Base and Chitose Air Base, Japan from May to August 1953, replacing the 508th SFW as part of the Northern Area Air Defense Command.

In mid–July 1951, the 12th FEW relieved the 31st FEW at RAF Manston in England. Having left its own fighter aircraft at Bergstrom AFB, the 12th FEW used the aircraft that the 31st FEW had signed over. Operations would begin during the latter part of July 1951 and for the next five months the 12th FEW would conduct training operations in the United Kingdom and on the continent of Europe. Major highlights of this TDY deployment for the 12th FEW would include participation in an exercise to measure the air defenses of Norway and gunnery practice at Wheelus Field, Libya. At the end of their TDY deployment to the UK, much like the 31st FEW previously, the 12th FEW left their aircraft for their replacement at Manston, the 123rd Fighter-Bomber Wing; personnel of the 12rh FEW would return to Bergstrom AFB on 22 December 1951.[7]

The markings on 12th FEW aircraft consisted of painted wing tip tanks, a colored band around the intake lip with a smaller 45 degree extension at the midsection of the band, and a diagonal stripe on the vertical stabilizer and on both sides of the horizontal stabilizer. The 12th FEW assigned squadron colors were red for the 559th, yellow for the 560th,

F-84G (51–1004) displays the 12th FEW insignia on the fuselage and squadron markings on the nose, tip tanks and vertical fin. Detroit-Wayne Major Airport, September 2, 1952. (Courtesy, D. Olson)

Top: *F-84G (51–1054) was part of the 12th FEW Detachment sent to support Operation Ivy —
U.S. atomic tests conducted from Kwajalein Island in the second half of 1952. The insignia on
the tail is for Air Task Group 132.4, the U.S. Air Force Element of Operation Ivy. The tip tanks
are sampling tanks used to gather radioactive particles from the atomic tests. (Courtesy D.
Menard)* Bottom: *The 12th Fighter-Escort Wing at Sola, Norway, in 1951. Apart from the 12th
FEW insignia on the F-84Es, markings are relatively plain due to the transfer of aircraft among
rotational units to the UK. (USAF, AFHRA)*

and blue for the 561st.[8] In addition, all aircraft carried the 12th Fighter-Escort Wing insignia on both sides of the fuselage mid-way between the leading edge of the wing and the cockpit. Factory applied buzz numbers appeared on each side of the aircraft nose. Squadron insignia was not used on 12th FEW F-84Gs; however, those aircraft deployed for Operation Ivy displayed the Air Task Group 132.4 insignia on the vertical stabilizer above the **U.S. Air Force** lettering.

These basic markings stayed in effect until early 1954 when the F-84F made its debut and the 12th SFW started to use the SAC command insignia on its aircraft.

The 12th SFW would continue to operate F-84Fs as part of SAC until 1 July 1957 when it was transferred to Tactical Air Command.

27th Fighter Group/Fighter Escort/ Strategic Fighter Wing

The 27th Fighter Group and the 522nd, 523rd and 524th Fighter Squadrons were initially assigned to SAC and Andrews Field on 25 June 1947 without personnel and equipment. On 16 July 1947 the 27th FG and its three squadrons were assigned to the Eighth Air Force and transferred to Kearney Army Air Field, Nebraska. The 27th FG had an authorized strength of 75 P-51 Mustangs. The 27th FG received its first aircraft in August 1947 and had a grand total of 25 Mustangs by the end of the month. The number of P-51Ds would grow to 79 by the end of December 1947.[9]

Initially, 27th Fighter Group squadron colors were red for the 522nd, yellow for the 523rd and blue for the 524th. During the P-51-era squadron colors were painted on aircraft propeller spinners and possibly on fin caps. An additional colored band marking on the aft fuselage may have indicated flight assignment, but this information has not been verified.

F-82E (46–334) is a 522nd FS aircraft with a red squadron identification color on the wing tips, vertical stabilizer in the form of tail bands, and a flared design on the front portion of the wing drop tanks. Also clearly shown is the Eighth Air Force insignia, which was displayed in the same location on all 27th FG F-82Es. (Museum of Flight — Gordon S. Williams Collection)

The 27th FW transferred to Bergstrom AFB outside of Austin, Texas, in March 1949. These blue-trimmed F-82Es on the tarmac at Bergstrom AFB belong to the 524th FS. (Boeing NAA3502. © Boeing. Used under license.)

On 15 August 1947, the 27th Fighter Wing was designated, organized, and assigned to SAC and the 27th Fighter Group was assigned to the Wing. Concurrently, the wing was redesignated "twin engine" from "single engine" and the 27th FW was selected to receive the P-82E "Twin Mustang."[10] By the end of 1947, however, the 27th FW possessed one P-82B Twin Mustang and this aircraft was used for maintenance instruction.

The 27th FW converted to the P/F-82E throughout the first half of 1948 and by the end of the year they were rated combat ready.

The year 1949 saw the 27th Fighter Wing participate in many long-range missions and special events. Some of the more notable events were the 1949 Presidential Inaugural Review, a long-range over-water navigation flight to Howard AFB, Panama Canal Zone, and in March 1949, a permanent change of station from Kearney to Bergstrom AFB, Texas.

The deployment to the Caribbean by the 27th FG began on 1 February 1949 when 55 F-82s took off from Kearney AFB. Refueling and maintenance stops were made at MacDill AFB and Ramey AFB. The 27th FG arrived at Howard AFB on 5 February 1949 and three days later departed for the flight home with stops in Jamaica and at Carswell AFB. The 27th FG with 49 F-82s would land at Kearney AFB on 10 February 1949. This flight flew a record-breaking 6,800 miles and put the 27th FG in the record books as the first fighter group to make a long distance, unescorted flight using only celestial navigation.[11]

The aircraft markings for the F-82Es of the 27th FW were some of the most colorful in SAC. The assigned group/wing color was blue[12] and the assigned squadron colors were red for the 522nd, white for the 523rd, and blue for the 524th. The group color was painted on the propeller spinner and the underside of the forward fuselage. Squadron colors were painted on wing tips, as horizontal bands across the upper third of the vertical fin, along the middle portion of the horizontal stabilizer, and on the forward portion of the external wing tanks. The **PQ/FQ** buzz numbers were carried on the aft portion of the fuselage behind the national insignia and under the left wing surface. The 27th FG/FW insignia was displayed aft of the cockpit on the left side of the fuselage and the Eighth Air Force insignia was carried on the right side of the fuselage. The pilot and crew chief's names were painted in white letters on a small blue rectangle on the outer lower frame of each cockpit. In late 1948, the **U.S. Air Force** lettering started to appear on both sides of the vertical stabilizer and rudder assembly as well as the **USAF** lettering on the lower surface of the left wing and upper surface of the right wing as required by Technical Order No. 07–1-1, Aircraft Camouflage, Markings and Insignia dated 26 July 1948.

Perhaps the most striking F-82E assigned to the 27th FG was *Ole 97* (46–297) which belonged to the 27th FG Commander, Col. Cy Wilson. His aircraft had *Ole 97* painted on both sides of the nose section. The group color — blue — was displayed on the spinner and lower fuselage as well as the fin tips. Group commander markings in red, white, and blue appeared on the forward portion of the wing drop tanks, vertical fin and on the horizontal stabilizer. Additionally, the 27th FG insignia and Eighth Air Force insignia were painted on the left and right sides of the fuselage, respectively. The 27th FW Commander, Col. Ashley B. Packard, flew F-82E (46–261) and had similar markings to *Ole 97* except the wing commander markings displayed on drop tanks, wing tips, tail fin, and horizontal stabilizer consisted of a wide blue band bordered on each side by thin white and red stripes.

The 27th FG color was blue and was assigned to the Group in February 1948. The 27th FG placed the group color on the propeller spinners and nose undersides. (Boeing NAA 3511. © Boeing. Used under license.)

The approved color scheme and markings for 27th FW aircraft to include squadron markings, group commander and wing commander markings, as well as approved design and location for pilot's name on the aircraft were forwarded in a letter with photo enclosures to SAC in February 1949.[13]

The 27th Fighter Wing was redesignated Fighter-Escort on 1 February 1950 and soon thereafter began the conversion to the F-84E. Early 27th FEW F-84E markings were relatively subdued compared to those used during the F-82-era. Gone was the group color, but squadron colors remained the same except for the 523rd FES that now used yellow. Squadron identification markings were now painted on the nose intake lip, on the vertical fin as a single diagonal band sloping rearward with a break in the middle for the **U.S. Air Force** lettering and aircraft serial number, and on both upper and lower surfaces of the horizontal stabilizer as diagonal bands mirroring those on the vertical fin.

The 27th FEW participated in one of the most significant Atlantic crossings by a SAC fighter unit in September and October 1950. Called Fox Able Three, pilots of the 27th FEW were required to ferry 180 F-84Es from Bergstrom AFB to the 36th and 86th Fighter-Bomber Groups in Germany. For successfully planning and executing this ferry mission, the 27th FEW was awarded the MacKay Trophy for 1950.[14]

The next iteration of 27th FEW markings came into effect during its deployment to the Far East in November 1950 to participate in combat operations over Korea. Operating initially from Taegu, Korea, and later Itazuke, Japan, the 27th FEW flew over 23,000 combat sorties while TDY in the Far East. The 27th FEW F-84Es basically retained the previous marking scheme with a few variations. The nose intake tip marking was modified to include a 45-degree rearward extension. Also, a medium width forward pointing arrow was

In early markings, these two F-84Es are from the 522nd FES (red tail stripe) and 524th FES (blue tail stripe). The arrow on the fuel tank and the 45-degree extension of the nose ring would be added later. Both would be turned over to the 136th FBW for continued service in Korea. (Photograph by W. Thompson, courtesy D. Menard)

placed on the outer surface of the tip tanks and extended to the tip tank rear fin. The only insignia appearing on 27th F-84s during its Korea tour was the 524th FES squadron insignia. Its emblem was the silhouette of a hound that was placed on both sides of the fuselage just above the first letter of the buzz marking. The only other markings appearing on 27th FEW F-84s during its tour in Korea were individual nicknames. Examples from the 27th Fighter-Escort Wing 1951 yearbook include *The Irish Lass, Gypsy-Po'Keepsie, China Doll,* and *Baby Fay.*[15]

When the 27th FEW returned to Bergstrom AFB beginning in July 1951, its F-84s were turned over to the 136th Fighter-Bomber Wing in Japan. In turn, the 12th FEW transferred all assigned F-84s at Bergstrom to the 27th and deployed to the United Kingdom. There, the 12th FEW used aircraft left behind by the 31st FEW. Beginning in September 1951, the 27th FEW started to receive F-84Gs. The 27th FEW insignia reappeared on the left side of the fuselage below the cockpit and squadron insignia was applied to the same location on the right side of the aircraft. The major change to 27th FEW markings was replacing the diagonal stripe on the vertical fin with a wider diagonal fan design. These were the markings carried by 27th FEW F-84Gs during Operation Fox Peter Two which was the second mass flight of F-84 Thunderjets across the Pacific Ocean. The 27th FEW would deploy to Misawa, Japan in October 1952 to replace the 31st FEW who had been performing the air defense mission for Japan since its arrival in July 1952.

On 20 January 1953, all SAC Fighter-Escort Wings were redesignated Strategic Fighter, consequently, the 27th FEW became the 27th Strategic Fighter Wing. The 27th SFW would incorporate the use of the SAC command insignia beginning in 1953. The 27th continued flying the F-84G until early 1954 when it started to convert to the F-84F. In 1957, the 27th SFW would become the only SAC unit to operate the F-101A; however, the assignment would be brief, as the 27th would be transferred to Tactical Air Command on 1 July 1957, only 27 days after receiving its first F-101As.

31st Fighter-Escort /Strategic Fighter Wing

When the 1st Fighter-Interceptor Wing was transferred to CONAC on 1 July 1950, the 31st Fighter-Bomber Wing and the 307th, 308th and 309th Fighter-Bomber Squadrons were assigned as a replacement to SAC. Assigned to the Second Air Force at Turner AFB, Georgia, the 31st FBW was fully equipped with F-84Es. On 16 July 1950, the 31st Fighter-Bomber Wing was redesignated the 31st Fighter-Escort Wing

Early 31st FEW F-84 markings continued to be those used by the 31st FEW while assigned to the Continental Air Command. These markings consisted of a checkerboard pattern on the nose in silver finish with black squares that served as a 31st FW identifier. The 31st FEW assigned squadron colors were red for the 307th FES, yellow for the 308th FES, and blue for the 309th FES, and were painted on the nose, fin cap and wing tip tanks. The piping around the checkerboard pattern was also in squadron color. The **FS** prefix buzz number was placed on the forward portion of the aircraft nose between the scalloped pattern checkerboard and the leading edge of the wing. The 31st FG insignia appeared on both sides of the fuselage just below the cockpit and above the wing's leading edge. In addition to the **U.S. Air Force** lettering and aircraft serial number on the fin, a letter designating flight assignment was placed between the fin cap and **U.S. Air Force**. These markings were in effect when the 31st FEW participated in Fox Able Ten — the deployment of the 31st FEW to the United Kingdom in December 1950. Departing on 26 December 1950, 74 F-84Es and four T-33s took off from Turner AFB, Georgia, and after refueling stops at Otis AFB, Massachusetts; Goose Bay, Labrador; Narsarssuak Air Base, Greenland; and Keflavik, Iceland, arrived on 6 January 1951 at Manston, England. The 31st FEW remained TDY in England until July 1951. Then, all of their F-84s were left for the next rotational unit to

Wing Commander Col. Don Blakeslee's aircraft F-84G (51–1027) during Fox Peter Two. All three squadron colors — red, yellow and blue — are displayed on the nose wing, tip tanks, vertical fin and speed brake. (USAF, courtesy D. Menard)

Top: *A fully armed F-84G (51–821) of the 308th FES has yellow squadron markings on the nose extending rearward at a 45 degree angle to the middle of the nose gear door, on the wing tip tanks as a wide band extending to the fin tips, and on the vertical stabilizer as three tail sunbursts. (Photograph by R. Williams, courtesy D. Menard)* Bottom: *An F-84E (49–2097) is trimmed in yellow. It displays a nose ring and triple fuselage bands in all three 31st FEW squadron colors, indicating a group commander's aircraft. (Photograph by Lt. Col. C. Toynbee, courtesy D. Menard)*

deploy to England — the 12th FEW.[16] Upon their return to Turner AFB, the 31st FEW began its conversion to the F-84G.

The 31st FEW aircraft markings for its F-84Gs were considerably different from those used on the previously assigned F-84Es. Squadron markings now appeared in the form of a nose flash, three tail sunbursts on the vertical fin and single sunbursts on both horizontal stabilizer surfaces, and as a side strip on the tip tanks outlined in trim with a contrasting color. The 31st FEW insignia was placed on the right side of the aircraft fuselage just above the leading edge of the wing. In preparation for Fox Peter One — the first mass inflight fighter refueling mission to take place over the Pacific Ocean — the 31st FEW added squadron emblems on the left side of its F-84Gs and the words **Fly Safely** were added to some of the bands on the tip tanks.

F-84G (51–1029) displays the 31st FEW insignia, the single fuselage band of a flight commander, and the newer style markings on the nose, tip tanks and vertical tail. FS-029-A was assigned to the 308th FES. (Photograph by Brig. Gen. N. Gaddis, courtesy D. Menard)

From 4 to 16 July 1952, the 31st Fighter-Escort Wing executed Fox Peter One. The initial leg was from its home station, Turner AFB, Georgia, to Travis AFB, California. The 31st FEW flew nonstop from the U.S. to Hickam AFB, Hawaii, with the assistance of aerial refueling. From Hawaii, the 31st FEW made stops at Midway, Wake, Eniwetok, Guam, and Iwo Jima before arriving in Japan covering a distance of 10,670 miles.[17] This transpacific flight produced a number of new records for the USAF and the 31st FEW: First mass movement of a complete jet fighter wing by air; longest mass nonstop over-water flight by jet fighters (2400-mile leg from Travis AFB to Hickam AFB); and first mass inflight refueling movement of jet fighters.[18] The experience gained from Fox Peter One demonstrated the feasibility and mobility of moving large numbers of fighters over long distances by air refueling and enhanced SAC's capabilities to project its combat power.

The 31st Strategic Fighter Wing (changed from Fighter-Escort in January 1953) would participate in another long distance venture in August 1953 as part of Operation Longstride. This operation was the first nonstop crossing of the Atlantic by a SAC fighter unit. In this case, aircraft from both the 31st SFW and the 508th SFW took part in the operation. The 31st flew the Central Atlantic route with a final destination of Nouasseur Air Base, French Morocco, while the 508th used the Northern Atlantic route to England. These two nonstop mass flights were rated outstanding and resulted in the award of the MacKay Trophy for 1953 to the parent headquarters of both wings, the 40th Air Division.[19]

F-84G markings during the latter part of 1953 saw the colorful squadron markings removed and replaced with a single medium width tail band in squadron color with an aircraft identification number applied in the center of the band in a contrasting color. This number was repeated on the top of the nose forward of the cockpit to assist the boom operator on KC-97s in identifying receiver aircraft. The tail band was placed just below the fin cap and above the **U.S. Air Force** lettering. The SAC "stars and bar" stripe was placed on both sides of the aircraft nose with the SAC command insignia centered on the stripes.

The 31st SFW would convert to F-84Fs in 1954 and remained a part of SAC until 1 April 1957 when it was transferred to Tactical Air Command.

33rd Fighter Wing

The 33rd Fighter Wing was assigned to the Eighth Air Force and organized at Roswell Field, New Mexico, on 5 November 1947. The 33rd Fighter Group and its three fighter squadrons—the 58th, 59th, and 60th—were assigned to the Wing on 7 November 1947. The 33rd FG would have 53 P-51Ds on hand at the end of November 1947 and be fully equipped with 73 P-51Ds by the end of 1947.[20]

On 17 November 1947, the 33rd FW was attached to the 509th Bombardment Wing also located at Roswell Field.

The 33rd Fighter Wing did not use any identification markings on its P-51s except for those required by Technical Order 07–1-1, Aircraft Camouflage, Markings and Insignia, dated 29 September 1947. The status of 33rd FW P-51 aircraft markings was the subject of a letter dated 20 April 1948 from the 509th BW (the 33rd FW was attached to the 509th BW for administration and operations) to Eighth Air Force Headquarters:

> In reference to 1st Indorsement, your Headquarters, file A3O 452.05 (20 Feb 48), to Strategic Air Command letter, file 452 (20 Feb 48), subject as above, necessary action has been delayed due to the 33rd Fighter Group changing from P-51 type aircraft to P-84 type aircraft.
>
> Markings, in accordance with Par 17b, Section III, Technical Order 07–1-1, dated 29 September 1947, have been accomplished on the P-51 type aircraft. Other markings have not been accomplished due to the shortage of paint and changing of aircraft. Markings on the P-84 type aircraft will be accomplished with the least practical delay upon receipt of these aircraft.
>
> Correspondence referred to in Par 1 above will be retained until action is completed, at this time your Headquarters will be advised.[21]

Beginning in June 1948, SAC's first F-84Cs were assigned to the 33rd Fighter Wing with the first five arriving on 9 June 1948.

In a SAC letter to the Chief of Staff of the Air Force dated 10 February 1948, SAC assigned green as the group color for the 33rd Fighter Group.[22] The 33rd FG assigned squadron colors were red for the 58th FS, yellow for the 59th FS, and blue for the 60th FS.

F-84C (47–1479) displays the 33rd FG color — green — on the tip tanks and the 58th FS color — red — on the nose in a scalloped design, nose gear doors, and on the vertical fin in a rearward sloping diagonal stripe design as well as on the tailpipe rim. (Photograph by C. Graham, courtesy D. Menard)

Photographed at Chicago's Orchard Place Airport on 4 July 1949, F-84C (47–1431) of the 33rd FW has green trim on the tip tanks and the 58th FS color — red on the nose and a diagonal stripe on the tail. (National Museum of the USAF)

As previously mentioned, 33rd FG P-51s were never marked using group and squadron colors. However, once equipped with F-84s, the 33rd FG applied these markings almost immediately. The marking scheme for 33rd FG F-84s would include the green trim on the tip tanks as a group marking; squadron markings, some of the most colorful in SAC, were displayed on the nose in a scalloped design that extended to the leading edge of the cockpit and underneath the nose downward through the nose gear doors. The vertical fin had six rearward sloping diagonal stripes in squadron color that were mirrored on the horizontal stabilizer. The final element in the marking scheme was the exhaust rim painted in squadron color. Photos do show use of wing insignia; however, it is not known if the insignia appeared on 33rd FG F-84s while still assigned to SAC.

The 33rd Fighter Wing would move from Roswell AFB to Otis AFB, Massachusetts, in November 1948 and on 1 December would be transferred from Strategic Air Command to the Continental Air Command with an Air Defense Command commitment.

56th Fighter Group/Wing

The 56th Fighter Group was assigned to the Strategic Air Command and the Fifteenth Air Force on 1 May 1946 and activated at Selfridge Field, Michigan, with an authorized strength of 75 P-51s. The three fighter squadrons assigned to the 56th FG were the 61st, 62nd and 63rd Fighter Squadrons. The first aircraft used by the 56th FG were a combination of P-47Ns and P-51Ds borrowed from the base unit at Selfridge Field, the 146th Base Unit, which had 20 P-47Ns and six P-51s assigned as of the end of May 1946.[23] The first officially assigned aircraft, P-51Hs, began to arrive in September 1946 as part of the Air Force's program to provide flyaway aircraft to its high priority combat units. In the case of the 56th FG, their newly-assigned P-51Hs had undergone winterization modifications at Spokane Field prior to delivery to the Group at Selfridge Field.[24] By the end of the year, there were 82 P-51Hs and 17 P-47s assigned to the 56th FG which represented the entire SAC fighter fleet since the other two assigned fighter groups, the 4th FG and 82nd FG had no aircraft assigned.[25]

Aircraft markings for the first aircraft used by the 56th were outlined in a letter dated 12 July 1946 submitted by the 56th Fighter Group Commander, Col. David C. Schilling, to Headquarters, Army Air Forces. The letter appears below:

> ... Approval is requested for aircraft markings of squadrons of the Fifty Sixth Fighter Group as described in paragraph 4 below.
>
> The above mentioned markings are desired as squadron identification colors and as a morale factor for ground personnel. In addition to combat training these aircraft are used for air shows and demonstrations and are considered an aid in the AAF recruiting program.
>
> Desired design of markings:

Sixty-First Fighter Squadron:

(1) P-47 type aircraft:

    (a) An insignia red band around circumference of ring cowl, one third of the distance from leading edge of cowl to trailing edge of cowl to trailing edge of cowl with a forty-five degree angle extending to trailing edge of cowl on the left and right center section of the cowl.

    (b) Vertical stabilizer and dorsal fin: insignia red.

    (c) Rudder: conventional design of an insignia blue vertical stripe on leading edge with horizontal alternating insignia red and white stripes to rear of the blue and extending to the trailing edge of the rudder.

Sixty-Second Fighter Squadron:

(1) P-47 type aircraft:

    (a) An insignia yellow band to be installed as described in paragraph 4 a(1)(a) above.

    (b) Vertical stabilizer and dorsal fin: insignia yellow.

    (c) Rudder: as described in paragraph 4 a(1)(c) above.

For a short time in 1946, the 56th FG used the striped rudder marking on both P-47s and P-51s reminiscent of the pre–World War II Air Corps. Squadron colors were red for the 61st FS, yellow for the 62nd FS, and blue for the 63rd FS. (Courtesy D. Menard)

(2) P-51 type aircraft:

   (a) Propeller spinner: insignia yellow
   (b) Vertical stabilizer and dorsal fin: insignia yellow
   (c) Rudder: as described in paragraph 4 a(1)(c) above.

Sixty-Third Fighter Squadron:

(1) P-47 type aircraft:

   (a) An insignia blue band installed as described in paragraph 4 a(1)(a).
   (b) Vertical stabilizer and dorsal fin: insignia blue.
   (c) Rudder: as described in paragraph 4 a(1)(c) above.[26]

These bright, colorful markings were replaced with a simpler scheme adopted in the fall of 1946. A large plane-in-group number was painted in black on the upper half of the vertical stabilizer, in part to help with parking on an ever expanding parking ramp at Selfridge.[27] Large aircraft identification numbers with the **PF** prefix appeared on the fuselage just forward of the national emblem. The 56th FG painted its squadron colors on propeller spinners, medium width wing bands on some aircraft and on the top of the vertical stabilizer. During the 1946 deployment of the 62nd Fighter Squadron to Alaska, a number of P-51s displayed their WWII air combat record through the use of kill markings; however, this practice would be discouraged and soon eliminated. Many 56th FG P-51Hs would sport nicknames, some examples were *Jackie*, *Little Annie* and *Ah'm Available*.

Beginning in April 1947 the 56th Fighter Wing started its conversion from P-51Hs to P-80As, and by the end of 1947 had 66 P-80As. The initial group of P-80s assigned to the 56th were painted in gloss light gray and carried squadron identification markings in the form of a medium width band on the vertical stabilizer just above the aircraft serial number with an aircraft identification number painted on the band in a contrasting color, and a large arrow design on the tip tanks. The squadron insignia was displayed just forward of

P-80 (44–85464) was flown by Col. David Schilling and displays group commander markings on the vertical fin and fuselage using the three squadron colors — red, yellow, and blue. Additionally, the 62nd FS insignia is displayed and the PN-464 buzz number still appears on the nose. Col. Schilling's World War II scores for both aerial victories and air-to-ground kills are shown. These kill markings would be removed during Fox Able One while in Germany. (Courtesy of Special Collections and Archives, Wright State University)

P-80A (44–58319) is assigned to the 61st Fighter Squadron and its squadron markings are red with the identification number 16 in white. (Courtesy D. Menard)

the cockpit on the port side and large buzz numbers (initially **PN** prefix followed by **FT** in mid–1948) on the middle portion of the fuselage in black. The 56th FG squadron colors remained the same — red for the 61st, yellow for the 62nd, and blue for the 63rd.

The next major change to 56th FG aircraft markings took place in March 1948 when it began to implement SAC's new policy for fighter aircraft markings. A group color — red — was assigned and painted on the aircraft nose in a scallop design, on the forward portion of the tip tanks, and on the lower diagonal of the nose gear doors. The squadron color was painted on the aft portion of the tip tanks, upper diagonal of the nose gear doors, wing tips,

horizontal stabilizer tips and as a medium width band on the tail just above the aircraft serial number. The tail bands contained an aircraft identification number in a contrasting color (white for the 61st and 63rd; black for the 62nd). This contrasting color also appeared as trim on the tail band and tip tanks. Buzz markings appeared in black on both sides of the fuselage centered above the wing. A large squadron insignia was painted on the left side of the nose just behind the group color and the 56th FG/FW emblem was carried on the right side. Diagonal bands around the fuselage in squadron colors were used to indicate flight leader — one stripe; squadron commander — two stripes; group commander — three stripes; and wing commander — four

Maj. Donavan F. Smith, 56th FG Operations Officer, flew one of the first F-80s to touchdown at RAF Odiham. Squadron insignia is that of the 63rd Fighter Squadron. Nose and forward portion of the tip tank are in the group color — red. (USAF — 34657 A.C.)

stripes. In late 1948, the buzz number designation was changed to **FT** from **PN**; however, for a short time the 56th displayed an **FN** prefix buzz number (noted during Fox Able One). Also in late 1948, **U.S. Air Force** lettering was placed on the tail between the tail band and aircraft tail number, and **USAF** on wing surfaces.[28]

In 1948 the 56th FW along with the 4th FW pioneered overwater flying and long-range navigation flights for the F-80. The major event for the 56th FG was called Fox Able One, the first trans-Atlantic crossing by a USAF jet unit. Sixteen F-80Bs let by Col Dave Schilling, departed Selfridge AFB on 14 July 1948 with a final destination of Furstenfeldbruck, Germany.

The first stop was Bangor, Maine, and then the 56th FW detachment flew to Goose Bay, Labrador followed by stops at Narsarssuak, Greenland; Keflavik, Iceland; RAF Stornoway, Scotland, before reaching RAF Odiham and finally on 25 July 1948, Furstenfeldbruck, Germany. The 56th FG would spend two weeks in Germany flying show of force

While at Furstenfeldbruk, the 56th FG started to paint flags of the countries they had visited just below the crew blaze and in front of the buzz number on the left side of the aircraft. A German fraulein hand-paints the flags on an F-80. (Library of Congress)

missions and visiting many U.S. installations. The 56th FG would depart Europe on 14 August 1948 and would arrive back at its home station, Selfridge AFB, on 21 August 1948. All returning F-80s displayed small flags of the countries they had visited on the left side of the aircraft just below a customized blaze painted in squadron color with pilot and crew chief names.

Based on test sorties conducted by the 56th FG in late 1947 at Carswell AFB which clearly showed that the range capacity of the P-80 fighter, even with the addition of wing-tip tanks, was far less than desired for an escort fighter, SAC decided to phase P/F-80s out of its fighter fleet. On 1 December 1948, the 56th FW was relieved from assignment to SAC and transferred to the Continental Air Command for air defense purposes.[29]

82nd Fighter Group/Fighter Wing

Although the 82nd Fighter Group was assigned to SAC and Bolling Field in an inactive status on 27 June 1946, it wouldn't be manned until April 1947 when it was assigned to the Fifteenth Air Force with duty station at Grenier Field, New Hampshire. The 82nd FG assigned squadrons were the 95th, 96th and 97th Fighter Squadrons. The first P-51H aircraft began arriving in May 1947 with a total of 25 P-51s delivered by the end of the month.[30] The number of Mustangs assigned to the 82nd FG would grow to 72 by the end of the year.[31] On 15 August 1947 the 82nd Fighter Wing was activated under the Hobson Plan and the 82nd Fighter Group and its three fighter squadrons were now assigned to the Wing. Also at this time, the 82nd FW was relieved from assignment to the Fifteenth Air Force and assigned directly to Strategic Air Command.

Line up of 96th FS P-51Hs at Ladd Air Force Base, Alaska, in August 1948. Squadron color for the 96th was white and can be seen on the wing tips, horizontal stabilizer tips, and as horizontal bands on the vertical fin. Propeller spinners are in the group color — yellow. Notice the variance in sizing for the buzz numbers. (USAF, courtesy National Archives)

Early P-51H markings included the **PF** buzz marking in black on both sides of the fuselage and the lower left wing. The aircraft serial number in black was placed on the lower portion of the vertical stabilizer just above the horizontal stabilizer; also, a large plane-in-group number was painted in black on the upper vertical stabilizer. These P-51Hs had come from the 56th FG at Selfridge Field and bore their markings.

Due to the frequent heavy snowfalls at Grenier AFB, most of the operational training activities in early 1948, primarily gunnery training, were conducted at MacDill AFB, Florida. On 1 April 1948, the 82nd Fighter Wing began a deployment to Ladd Field, Alaska, for tactical training and an air defense mission that required the 82nd FG to remain on 24-hour alert, seven days a week.[32] Weather delays kept the entire unit from arriving in Alaska until 17 April when the final aircraft from the 97th FS arrived on station. Although the 82nd FW was scheduled to stay in Alaska for six months, their TDY would be shortened to three months, and from 27 to 30 June 1948 the 82nd FW would stagger flight-size elements at 15-minute intervals from Ladd AFB for the return to Grenier AFB. A request from the Canadian government that no mass flights be conducted in their airspace was the reason the 82nd FW used flights of four aircraft to return to New Hampshire.[33]

Prior to the 82nd FW deployment to Alaska, action had been taken to implement

Top: *P-51H (44–64506) had been the personal Mustang of Lt. Col. Gerald Johnson when he was commanding officer of the 82nd FW. Little Annie has a yellow spinner — group identification for the 82nd FG — and red trim on the wing tips, horizontal stabilizer tips and fin tip indicating assignment to the 95th FS. The aircraft number on the fin tip is white. (Courtesy D. McLaren)* Bottom: *Pilots of the 96th Fighter Squadron. Notice the squadron patches on the flight jackets and flight suits. Grenier AFB, New Hampshire, 1948. (USAF)*

SAC's new policy on fighter aircraft markings approved in February 1948; however, the 82nd FW would not fully implement SAC's directive on fighter markings until after their return from Alaska.[34] The high visibility color assigned to the 82nd FG was yellow and was painted on the aircraft nose. The 82nd FW assigned squadron colors were red for the 95th FS, white for the 96th FS, and blue for the 97th FS.[35] Squadron colors were displayed on the top of the vertical fin and on the lower portion of the vertical fin just above the aircraft serial number; on the tips of the horizontal stabilizer; and on aircraft wing tips. In the case of 95th and 97th Fighter Squadrons, the fin tip also carried a plane identification number in a contrasting color to that of the squadron. There is no photo evidence or documentation that shows the 96th FS using an aircraft identification number on the fin tip.

Upon the 82nd FG's return from Alaska, the group started to replace its F–51H fleet with F–51Ds, many of which had come from the 27th FG at Kearney AFB and the 33rd FG at Roswell AFB. Squadron insignia was carried on many of the 82nd FG P–51Ds. The 95th insignia was displayed forward of the cockpit on the left side of the fuselage; the 96th insignia appeared on the vertical fin and, with some aircraft, on the lower fuselage in front of the leading edge of the wing; and the 97th insignia was displayed in similar fashion to that of the 96th on the lower fuselage.[36]

In late 1948 and early 1949, 82nd FW F–51s added the required **U.S. Air Force** and **USAF** markings and also modified the buzz number from the **P** prefix to the **F** designation for fighter. Additionally, during this time, the lower band in squadron color on the vertical fin was removed.

On 22 August 1949, the 82nd FW would be relieved from assignment to SAC and transferred to the Continental Air Command with an Air Defense Command mission.

506th Strategic Fighter Wing

On 24 January 1953, Strategic Air Command activated the 506th Strategic Fighter Wing (SFW) along with its 457th, 458th and 462nd Strategic Fighter Squadrons (SFS). The 506th SFW was assigned to the Eighth Air Force and stationed at Dow AFB, Maine.

The 506th received its first F–84Gs in March 1953 when eight aircraft were assigned to the Wing.[37] By April 1953, the 458th SFS became fully operational and the 506th SFW had 46% of its authorized F–84s. In addition to its F–84s, the 506th SFW also had seven T–33s assigned. By May 1953, the 506th SFW would have its full complement of F–84s.[38]

So far the author has been unable to locate any photos of 506th SFW aircraft showing unit markings. However, the 506th SFW Mobility Plan published in May 1953 listed squadron color assignments as follows: 457th SFS — red; 458th SFS — orange, and 462nd SFS — blue.[39]

The 506th SFW would deploy to Misawa Air Base, Japan, in August 1953 for a 90-day TDY stay where it served as part of the Japan Air Defense Force alert mission. They would return to the United States in November 1953 after being replaced by the 31st SFW.[40]

In early 1954, the 506th SFW became the first unit in SAC to receive the F–84F. Flying the Thunderstreak, the 506th SFW would win SAC's one and only fighter weapons competition held in 1956 at Offutt AFB, Nebraska. In mid–1957, the 506th SFW would be transferred to the Tactical Air Command.

508th Fighter-Escort/Strategic Fighter Wing

The 508th Fighter-Escort Wing was activated on 1 July 1952 and assigned to SAC's 40th Air Division (Second Air Force) at Turner Air Force Base, Georgia. The mission of the 508th FEW as stated in Second Air Force Regulation 24–25 dated 14 August 1952 was "...protection of the SAC Bombing Force by long-range fighter escort and air defense in any part of the world at any time."[41] The 508th FEW assigned squadrons were the 446th FES, 447th FES and 448th FES. Due to a shortage of F-84Gs, the 508th started to receive aircraft in July 1952, but with a reduced authorization of 30 instead of the normal UE of 75. The first F-84Gs would be received from Republic Corporation in September 1952, and by the end of October 1952, the 508th FEW would have 60 F-84Gs and six T-33s assigned. On 20 Jan 1953 the 508th FEW was redesignated the 508th Strategic Fighter Wing. Later, in February 1953, the 508th SFW deployed to Misawa Air Base, Japan, as part of SAC's rotational commitment for the defense of Japan. The 508th SFW would stay in Japan until May 1953 when it was replaced by the 12th SFW. In August 1953, the 508th SFW participated in Operation Longstride, a dual mission with the 31st SFW, with 20 F-84Gs flying a northern route to Lakenheath, England. 508th SFW F-84Gs were refueled twice by KB-29Ps of the 100th ARS and KC-97s of the 26th ARS, and reached Lakenheath in a total elapsed time of 11 hours and 20 minutes. According to SAC, Operation Longstride's success clearly demonstrated the following: the ability of jet fighter aircraft to deploy anywhere needed in a very short period of time; that weather and communications are far better over the Central route than the Northern route; and that the tanker support and MATS support were the most cooperative and effective ever used.[42] The 40th Air Division, the parent headquarters for both the 508th SFW and 31st SRW, was awarded the MacKay Trophy in 1953 for Operation Longstride. The 508th would continue to fly F-84Gs until mid–1954 when they reequipped with F-84Fs and would remain in SAC service until 1956 when it was inactivated.

The 508th SFW possessed some of the most colorful fighter aircraft markings in SAC's fighter fleet, using squadron colors of red for the 466th SFS, yellow for the 467th SFS, and

F-84G-20-RE (51–1262) at Dayton Airport in September 1954. Each SAC F-84 wing used a different pattern for markings on the vertical stabilizer. For the 508th SFW three forward diagonal stripes in squadron color was the design. (Photograph by Shipp, courtesy D. Olson)

All 508th SFW F-84Gs used the white spear as wing identification and displayed it along the fuselage and along the tip tanks superimposed on the squadron color. Squadron color assignments in the 508th were red for the 466th, yellow for the 467th, and blue for the 468th. (USAF, courtesy D. Menard)

blue for the 468th SFS.[43] The 508th SFW marking scheme consisted of both aircraft nose and forward portion of the tip tanks being painted in squadron color with a speed line, also in squadron color, extending rearward on both the fuselage and wing-tip tanks. A forward break in the white arrow design found factory applied buzz numbers painted in black. Superimposed on these markings was a white forward pointing arrow. The rest of the marking scheme consisted of three color bands arranged diagonally on the vertical fin and upper surfaces of the horizontal stabilizer. Additionally, the pilot and crew chief's names were displayed in white on a rectangle in squadron color located just below the pilot canopy.

Prior to the adoption of this marking scheme, 508th SFW F-84Gs wore the wing insignia on the top of the vertical stabilizer above the **U.S. Air Force** lettering. The wing marking disappeared with the implementation of the squadron color marking pattern with the white arrow. The 508th SFW didn't place squadron insignia on its F-84Gs but did start using the SAC command insignia in 1953, which was located on both sides of the fuselage just under the aft portion of the cockpit. The 508th SFW would continue to use these markings until its deactivation in 1956.

SAC Air National Guard/Reserve Fighter Units

Prior to the Korean War, SAC had one fighter USAF Reserve Corollary Unit — the 87th Fighter Group at Bergstrom AFB. The 87th FG had no aircraft assigned, but trained with the 27th Fighter Wing. The 87th would be inactivated in June 1951.

As part of the U.S. Air Force expansion program during the Korean War, four Air National Guard fighter wings would be assigned to SAC in March and April 1951. The specific units assigned to SAC were: the 131st Fighter Wing, a F-51D unit initially stationed

Top: *Line-up of 108th FBW Wing F-47s at MacDill AFB, Florida. Squadron color appears on engine cowling; fin tips display flight assignment color. (USAF, AFHRA)* Bottom: *The same group of 108th FBW Wing F-47s in front of Hangar No. 5 at MacDill AFB, Florida, September 1951. (USAF, AFHRA)*

F-47s of the 108TH FBW Wing on the MacDill AFB flightline in September 1951. (USAF, AFHRA)

at Bergstrom AFB with the Eighth Air Force Air Force; the 108th Fighter Wing, a F-47D (119th FBS and 141st FBS) and F-47N (142nd FBS) unit stationed at Turner AFB, GA, with the Second Air Force; the 132nd Fighter Wing which operated both F-84B/Cs and F-51D aircraft and was stationed at Dow AFB, Maine, as part of the Eighth Air Force; and the 146th Fighter Wing, a F-51D unit stationed at Moody AFB, GA, and assigned to the Second Air Force.

All ANG fighter wings assigned to SAC were redesignated fighter-bomber wings in April 1951.

Aircraft markings for these units have been very difficult to document due to the lack of primary source information and photo evidence. Squadron identification markings were used, but the specific squadron color assignments are not known.

Before any meaningful contribution to SAC could be made, the four ANG fighter wings were transferred to Tactical Air Command in November 1951 to support Army ground training.

7

Separate Squadrons

46th/72nd Reconnaissance Squadron

When SAC was first organized on 21 March 1946, the 46th Recon Squadron was part of the 449th Bomb Group stationed at Grand Island, Nebraska. Selected by SAC to spearhead a top-secret project code named Project Nanook, the 46th Reconnaissance Squadron would deploy to Ladd Field, Alaska, over the period June–September 1946 and operate with 18 modified F-13 photo reconnaissance aircraft. Their mission in support of Project Nanook would be to: "develop an accurate system of navigation for flying over the polar cap using

The Barrow Sparrow *was the name for RB-29–97-BW (45–21742). The Royal Canadian Air Force participated in aerial flights over Canada made by the 46th/72nd RS from 1946 to 1949. (USAF, courtesy Brig. Gen. Don Stout)*

Top: The Forlorn Turkey, *RB-29–95-BW (45–21775), carries the standard insignia red Arctic markings on the outer wings, aft fuselage and tail used on all squadron F-13/RB-29 aircraft. This RB-29 was lost in a crash on the Seward Peninsula on 23 December 1947. (USAF)* Below: *RB-29–95-BW (45–21766) was nicknamed* Bucket a Bolts *by its crew chief, M/Sgt Cecil Allain, and like most 46th/72nd RS aircraft had very colorful nose gear doors — in this case red and yellow. The lettering in the name is red outlined in yellow.*

existing equipment, assessing the extent of the Soviet threat in the Arctic, surveying and mapping the Arctic, ... testing the endurance and efficiency of men and equipment under the stress of extreme arctic conditions, and ... training SAC bombardment units in polar navigation and arctic operations."[1]

The 46th would operate from Ladd Field under the most difficult of circumstances until 13 October 1947 when the squadron was inactivated and all personnel and equipment assets were transferred with no change of station to the 72nd Reconnaissance Squadron (Very Long Range) Photographic. The 72nd would continue to support Project Nanook until June 1949 when orders were received transferring the 72nd to Mountain Home AFB, Idaho, and assignment to the 5th SRW.

The 46th/72nd RS would leave a tremendous record of accomplishment after nearly two years in Alaska, but not without cost — 4 RB-29s would be lost.[2]

All 46th/72nd Recon Squadron F-13s/RB-29s bore the insignia red trim Arctic markings on the aft fuselage, tail and outer wing surfaces. Although no tactical markings were carried, many 46th/72nd aircraft carried nicknames and brightly colored nose gear doors. Examples included: *Leakin Lena, The Barrow Sparrow, Boeings Boner, The Northern Star, Bucket a Bolts, Kee Bird, Forlorn Turkey, My Achin Back, Over Exposed, Ladies Delight* and *Carmencito Joe*. Also there is no evidence of squadron insignia used on 46th/72nd RS aircraft while in Alaska.

91st Strategic Reconnaissance Squadron

One of the most misunderstood squadrons assigned to SAC was the 91st Strategic Reconnaissance Squadron. On 22 January 1949 the 91st SRS was reactivated and assigned to Strategic Air Command as part of the 91st Strategic Reconnaissance Wing. Initially stationed at McGuire AFB and equipped with F-9/RB-17 aircraft, the 91st would be the first USAF unit to receive and operate the B-50B Superfortress. In October 1949 the 91st SRS would be transferred with the rest of the 91st SRW to Barksdale AFB, LA. Also in late 1949 the 91st SRW started sending its B-50B aircraft to the Boeing plant at Wichita, Kansas, for modification to RB-50B configuration which would include changes to aircraft engines, addition of wing fuel tanks, installation of camera latches, and adding an aerial refueling capability.[3]

Aircraft markings for the 91st SRS B/RB-50Bs in 1950 included the **Square V** tactical tail marking and squadron identification markings in the form of green and yellow diagonal stripes on nose gear doors and green trim on wing fuel tanks (RB-50B), and a large 91st SRS insignia placed on the port side of the aircraft nose.

Effective 16 November 1950, the 91st Strategic Reconnaissance Squadron was relieved

RB-29A-50-BN (44–61854) in 91st SRS markings. Although a separate squadron assigned to SAC's Fifteenth Air Force and attached to FEAF Bomber Command for Operations, the 91st SRS continued to use the **Circle X** *tail marking of the 5th SRW which was the parent wing of the 91st SRS predecessor, the 31st SRS. (San Diego Aerospace Museum)*

RB-29A-50-BN (44–61817) of the 31st SRS during the early months of the Korean War. Notice the 40 mission symbols on the nose. Squadron color is green. The square outline of the previously used Second Air Force insignia on the dorsal fin is still visible. (USAF, courtesy B. Bailey)

from assignment to the 91st Strategic Reconnaissance Group, 91st Strategic Reconnaissance Wing, Second Air Force and assigned to Fifteenth Air Force as a separate squadron and transferred, less personnel and equipment, from Barksdale AFB to Johnson AB, Japan, attached to Far East Command (FEC) for operational control, and Far East Air Forces (FEAF) for logistics support per SAC General Order 78 dated 16 November 1950.[4]

The personnel and equipment to man the 91st SRS in Japan came from the transfer of the 31st Strategic Reconnaissance Squadron, less personnel and equipment, from Johnson Air Base back to its parent wing, the 5th Strategic Reconnaissance Wing at Travis Air Force Base, California.

In physical terms, the personnel and RB-50Bs of the 91st SRS at Barksdale went to the 38th SRS of the newly-formed 55th SRW; the personnel and RB-29s of the 31st SRS at Johnson Air Base stayed in place as the newly designated 91st SRS; and the 31st SRS at Travis AFB began to be manned and equipped with RB-29s from the other two squadrons in the 5th SRW, the 23rd SRS and the 72nd SRS.

Moving to Yokota in December 1950, the 91st SRS would soon change their aircraft markings to reflect their new identity — the green nose gear doors would see a white flash added broken by the last four digits of the aircraft serial number and the squadron emblem would be painted on the port side of the aircraft nose. The fin tips retained its green color and the Fifteenth Air Force insignia stayed on the dorsal fin. The **Circle X** tail marking was left over from its days as the 31st SRS where, although attached to FEAF, it was assigned to SAC's 5th SRW and the **Circle X** was the 5th SRW assigned tail marking. The tail marking was not removed when the 31st SRS became the 91st SRS, however, the **Circle X** tail marking at this point had no official connection to the 91st SRS.

The 91st SRS would retain many of the nicknames and nose art inherited from the 31st. Examples included: *AH Soooo*; *So Tired, Seven to Seven*; *Butterfly Baby, Where Next*; *Tiger Lil*; *Our L'Lass, Honey Bucket Honchos*; and *Moon's Moonbeam*.

In 1952, like the rest of the FEAF B-29 units, the 91st SRS would adopt a black camouflage scheme that nearly covered the entire aircraft. The fin cap would continue to be painted in squadron color and the squadron insignia would remain on the nose, but everything else, except for mission markings, would be gone.

The 91st SRS would play host squadron to SAC detachments of RB-50Gs (55th SRW) and RB-45Cs (91st SRW) sent TDY to support FEAF combat operations.

In 1953, the 91st would have assigned both RB-29 and RB-45C aircraft and would stay in Japan until 1954.

SAC Strategic Support Squadrons

In 1949, the term "Strategic Support Squadron" was created to describe a unit in Strategic Air Command (SAC) with the unique role of supporting SAC overseas deployments and providing nuclear weapon transportation support for SAC heavy bomber operations. There were four strategic support squadrons in SAC.

1st Strategic Support Squadron

The first unit of this kind, the 1st Strategic Support Squadron (SSS), started its operational career as the 320th Troop Carrier Squadron assigned to the 509th Composite Group. Initially equipped with C-54s when assigned to SAC in March 1946, the unit would undergo several name changes: from the 1st Air Transport Unit (ATU) in 1946 to the 1st Strategic Support Unit (SSU) in June 1948, and finally becoming the 1st Strategic Support Squadron in 1949. The C-54s would be replaced by YC-97s and C-97s and the unit would move several times from Roswell Field to Kwajalein Atoll (Operations Crossroads) and back to Roswell in 1946; and from Roswell Field to Fort Worth Army Air Field (later Carswell Air Force Base) in September 1947; and finally to Biggs Air Force Base, Texas, in 1949 where it would eventually receive the Douglas C-124A Globemaster. The 1st SSS would remain at Biggs AFB until January 1959 when it was deactivated.

2nd Strategic Support Squadron

The 2nd Strategic Support Squadron was established in January 1949 at Biggs Air Force Base, Texas, and initially was equipped with former 1st Strategic Support Squadron C-54s as the 1st SSS was converting to C-97s. The 2nd SSS was subsequently moved to Walker AFB, New Mexico, and would receive SAC's first C-124As. In May 1951 the 2nd SSS would be transferred to Castle Air Force Base, California, where it would remain until 1956 when it would be assigned to March Air Force Base, California.

3rd Strategic Support Squadron

On 16 November 1950, the 3rd Strategic Support Squadron was formed at Hunter Air Force Base, Georgia. The 3rd SSS was initially equipped with C-124As transferred from the 2nd Strategic Support Squadron and would reach full strength in early 1951. The 3rd SSS would support numerous SAC operations from Hunter Air Force Base until January 1953 when the squadron would be sent to Barksdale Air Force Base, Louisiana. The 3rd SSS ended its assignment to SAC in 1961 when it was transferred to the Air Materiel Command.

4th Strategic Support Squadron

The last strategic support squadron formed in SAC was the 4th Strategic Support Squadron which was activated on 18 February 1953 at Ellsworth Air Force Base, South Dakota. The squadron had 12 C-124Cs assigned by October 1953 and would remain a SAC unit until 1961.

Strategic Support Squadron Aircraft Markings

The 320th Troop Carrier Squadron of the 509th Composite Group started its service with SAC displaying its squadron insignia with a feathered, stylized wing aft of the squadron insignia followed by a stripe, all in the color green. These markings appeared on both sides of the aircraft as well as the lettering **320th Troop Carrier Squadron.** On the top of the vertical stabilizer, a small green feathered disc would carry a plane-in-group number painted in white. On the lower fin, initially the Fifteenth Air Force insignia was displayed below the aircraft serial number; however, during Operation Crossroads this would change to the 509th Composite Group, 58th Wing insignia.

Upon activation on 8 August 1946, the 1st Air Transport Unit (ATU) was assigned directly to the 58th Bombardment Wing (ending its assignment to the 509th CG) and stationed at Roswell Army Air Field, New Mexico. Personnel and aircraft were assigned from the 320th Troop Carrier Squadron, which had been part of the 509th Composite Group. Known as the *Green Hornets* from its service during Operation Crossroads, a new squadron design of a green hornet started to replace the old 320th TCS insignia on its C-54s. The **First Air Transport Unit** replaced **320th Troop Carrier Squadron** on both sides of the aircraft fuselage. Also, the Eighth Air Force insignia was placed on the lower portion on the vertical stabilizer.[5]

The 1st ATU would undergo a station change to Carswell Air Force Base in September 1947 and in May 1948 would be redesignated for the second time to 1st Strategic Support Unit (SSU). This designation would be reflected in new lettering on the upper fuselage of its C-54s.[6]

Late 1948 and early 1949 would see **United States Air Force** lettering make its appearance on 1st SSU C-54s and also bring the introduction of insignia red Arctic markings on squadron aircraft.

In 1949 the 1st SSS started to

C-54 (42–72616) of the 320th Troop Carrier Squadron, 509th CG during Operation Crossroads. The 58th BW, 509th CG insignia has replaced the Fifteenth Air Force insignia and the plane-in-group number design is red with the number in yellow. (USAF)

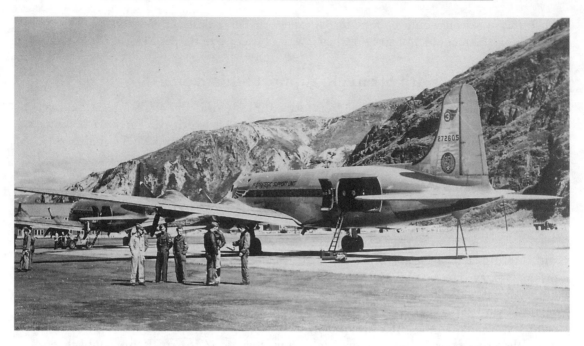

Two C-54s from the 1st Strategic Support Unit. They were part of the support package for Fox Able One, the first transatlantic flight of 16 P-80As of the 56th Fighter Wing from Selfridge AFB to the United Kingdom and Germany. In addition to the Eighth Air Force insignia on the fin, above the radio call number is a flight marking. Greenland, July 1948. (Library of Congress — General LeMay Collection)

receive C-97s. These aircraft retained the very distinctive stylized wing and speed line in green. Insignia red Arctic markings were placed on the outer wing surfaces and the tail. Major subordinate command insignia, in this case the Eighth Air Force, was not used on the C-97s. There is no evidence that any squadron insignia was applied to 1st SSS C-97s.[7]

In January 1949, in response to an expanding SAC operational capability, the 2nd Strategic Support Squadron was formed from a cadre obtained from the 1st SSS at Biggs AFB. Initial aircraft assigned were C-54s from the 1st SSS which was reequipping with C-97s. 2nd SSS C-54s retained the distinctive stylized wing and green color speed line used while in service with the 1st SSS.

After redeployment to Walker AFB in 1950, the 2nd SSS was the first unit in SAC to receive the C-124A. In a special acceptance ceremony on 17 July 1950, C-124A (49–235) arrived at Walker AFB for assignment to the 2nd SSS and was immediately named *Apache Chieftain*.[8] Initially, the plan was to name all C-124s in the 2nd SSS after names of Indian tribes; however, it appears only *Apache Chieftain* was used until 1951 when the 2nd SSS had a permanent change of station to Castle AFB, California, and another C-124A (50–093) was named *Yosemite Chieftain*. The stylized wing in a feathered pattern along with the speed stripe all appeared on assigned C-124s in green along with a nose circle in green inside of which was painted an aircraft identification number. A squadron insignia for the 2nd SSS was approved in March 1951 and started to be placed on 2nd SSS aircraft shortly thereafter. These markings remained in force until late 1953 when all special squadron markings for SAC's C-124s were required to be removed.

The second strategic support squadron in SAC to receive the C-124 Globemaster was

Above: *The C-97 began its SAC career with the 1st Strategic Support Squadron replacing C-54D aircraft. The C-97s would be replaced by C-124As beginning in January 1951. C-97A (48–401) on the ramp at Biggs AFB, El Paso, Texas. (National Museum of the USAF)* Right: *A typical C-124 crew under the Green Hornet squadron insignia for the 1st SSS. Of note is the solid, non-feathered wing pattern in contrast to that of the 2nd SSS (different shape and feathered). Also the outline of the gloss white cockpit area can be seen. (USAF, AFHRA)*

the 1st SSS on 18 January 1951 at Biggs AFB. The 1st SSS used its *Green Hornet* insignia in a stylized wing pattern with the speed line along the fuselage all in green. However, the wing pattern for the 1st SSS was a solid design with no feathering to provide some distinction from the similar marking pattern used by the 2nd SSS. Many of the 1st SSS C-124s used insignia red Arctic markings and also gloss white paint over the cockpit area. As previously mentioned, these special squadron markings were eliminated in late 1953 and early 1954.

The third SAC unit to receive the C-124 was the 3rd Strategic Support Squadron stationed at Hunter AFB, Georgia. Receiving C-124s from the 2nd SSS in December 1950, the 3rd SSS would be fully operational in the first half of 1951. Early markings for 3rd SSS C-124s consisted of a blue speed line on both sides of the fuselage extending to the forward

Top: *The full marking scheme for the 1st SSS squadron insignia, green stylized wing and speed line and insignia red Arctic markings. (USAF, AFHRA)* Bottom: *A 2nd SSS C-124A (49–244) on a visit to the United Kingdom in the fall of 1950 in support of SAC operational deployments. (Courtesy Quadrant House)*

edge of the horizontal stabilizer. Later, a stylized eagle was added to the forward portion of the speed stripe and the speed stripe was outlined yellow. Additionally, propeller hubs were painted yellow, the squadron insignia was displayed on both sides of the nose under the tail feathers of the eagle, and a large two-digit identification number was painted in black on the aircraft nose.[9] To complete the marking and camouflage scheme, the cockpit

Top: *The first C-124A (49–235) to arrive at Walker AFB, New Mexico, being taxied to the ramp by Lt. Col. Avery J. Ladd, CO of the 2nd Strategic Support Squadron, 17 July 1950. (USAF, AFHRA) Below: The first C-124A (49–235) assigned to SAC and the 2nd SSS was christened* The Apache Chieftain. *Here members of the Apache tribe attend the christening ceremony held on 17 July 1950. (USAF, AFHRA)*

area on 3rd SSS C-124s was painted gloss white. Like the other strategic support squadrons previously mentioned, the 3rd SSS eliminated special squadron markings in late 1953.

The final SAC Strategic Support Squadron, the 4th, was formed at Ellsworth AFB, Rapid City, South Dakota, in February 1953. Fully equipped with C-124Cs by October 1953, 4th SSS C-124 aircraft markings were

Top: Apache Chieftain *with the squadron markings (green) and the insignia red Arctic tail. A loading exercise at Walker AFB, 1950. (USAF, courtesy D. Menard) Left: The newly authorized insignia for the 2nd SSS was approved in early 1951. A ground crewman cleaning the insignia, Castle AFB, 1951. (USAF, AFHRA) Below: C-124A (49–240) on jacks gives a good view of the 2nd SSS squadron insignia with the green feathered wing and speed line. Castle AFB, 1951. (USAF, AFHRA)*

Top: *C-124A (49–247) with the 3rd SSS squadron insignia on the starboard side of the aircraft nose and the striking white-capped cockpit area. (Photograph by E. Van Houten, courtesy D. Menard)* Right: *C-124A (49–247) with the markings of the 3rd SSS, which were a colorful blue and yellow, with yellow propeller domes. (Photograph by E. Van Houten, courtesy D. Menard)*

nowhere near as colorful as those of its predecessors. Air Force policy was moving strongly toward standardization and as a consequence 4th SSS C-124s were marked in a standard "plain jane" configuration. Only required **USAF** and **United States Air Force** along with Arctic markings appeared on 4th SSS C-124s. Aircraft numbers were painted on nose gear doors, but no other unit insignia or distinctive markings were used.[10] The 4th SSS would continue to serve in SAC at Ellsworth AFB until 1957 when it was transferred to Dyess AFB, Texas. The 4th SSS would continue on the active rolls of the USAF until 1961 when the squadron was deactivated.

8

Operation Crossroads

Although the United States had detonated three atomic devices during the last years of World War II, our knowledge of atomic energy and its application to warfare was still in its infancy and "clouded in mystery."[1]

To gain better understanding of the atomic bomb, President Truman in January 1946 approved a gigantic peacetime exercise called Operation Crossroads that would involve the efforts of nearly 42,000 Army, Navy and civilian personnel, all operating under a provisional joint command called Task Force One under the direction of Vice-Admiral W.H.P. Blandy.

The purpose of Operation Crossroads was to conduct a review of tests with atomic energy to determine the effect of atomic blasts against naval vessels to help gain an honest appraisal of the strategic implications of the atomic bomb. The project envisioned three atomic detonations to be conducted in the area around Bikini Atoll in the Marshall Islands, chosen as the best operational area which afforded protected anchorage in an unpopulated region under United States control.[2]

The Army Air Forces component of Task Force One was Task Group 1.5 under the command of Brigadier General Roger M. Ramey, Commanding General of the 58th Bombardment Wing. General Ramey's group was responsible for delivering the first A-bomb, an air burst, and providing aircraft to photograph the explosion and collect scientific data.[3]

The B-29s and F-13s assigned to the air component of Task Force One were organized into different units based on function. The Air Attack Unit contained the command, bomb carrying, pressure drop and radiological reconnaissance aircraft; the Air Photographic Unit contained eight F-13 photo reconnaissance aircraft and two C-54s; the Air Weather Unit contained three B-29 weather reconnaissance aircraft; and the Air Orientation Unit possessed one B-29 radio broadcast aircraft and one B-29 press photography aircraft.[4] Although all B-29 and F-13 aircraft were part of the Task Force, not all of the Superfortresses were assigned to the 509th Composite Group. The Air Transport Unit flew C-54s coming mostly from the 320th Troop Carrier Squadron, assigned to the 509th CG, but also supplemented by C-54s from the Air Transport Command. The data collection unit was a B-17 drone unit whose job was to fly pilotless B-17s through the atomic cloud collecting radioactive specimens.

The mainstay AAF tactical unit for Operation Crossroads was the 509th Composite Group, veterans of the two atomic bomb missions against Japan in August 1945. However, in early 1946 the 509th Composite Group was only a skeleton of its former self — to the point they could barely get planes off the ground to provide flight training for rated personnel.

Top: *B-29–40-MO (44–27354)* Dave's Dream *carrying the Operation Crossroads markings for a bomb carrier aircraft. Selected to make the air drop,* Dave's Dream *has yellow and black bands on the fuselage and wings, red fin cap and a large yellow **B** applied to the **Black Square**. In addition, the aircraft has the 58th Bombardment Wing-509th CG insignia on the right side as well as a crew shield. (USAF, courtesy M. Foley)* Bottom: Warm Front *RB-29A-65-BN (44–62128) performed weather reconnaissance tasks during Operation Crossroads as part of the Air Weather Unit. The vertical stabilizer shows a partial **W** tail marking used during Operation Crossroads by weather recon RB-29s. (Courtesy W. Larkins)*

It didn't take long, however, for the 509th CG to see a change in fortune. Due to the highest priority assigned to Operation Crossroads and the short time available to prepare for the project, officers, men, and equipment started to pour into Roswell AAF and the 509th CG from all over the country.

The forming of air crews was done based on skill and experience — the final selection

Left: F-13A-55-BN (44–62000) was named Kamode Head *and was one of eight F-13s assigned to the Air Photograph Unit. Photograph support aircraft carried a **Square F** tail marking, usually yellow on black, but some aircraft like* Kamode Head *had the letter **F** in silver. (USAF) Right: Remotely controlled B-17* Mother Ship *displays a different version of the Operation Crossroads insignia. (USAF, courtesy M. Foley)*

The marking scheme for the B-17 drones included yellow bands on the fuselage as well as yellow wing tips and tail with black fuselage and tail stripes. The B-17s were based on Eniwetok. (USAF)

showing eight crews; four bomber crews and four blast gauge crews. 50% of the crews were attached to the 509th from other groups in the 58th Bombardment Wing to provide them with experience in the procedures and techniques of an atomic bomb mission.[5]

After the crews were formed, the 509th CG conducted competition bombing runs at Roswell to determine which crew was best qualified to drop the world's fourth atomic bomb on the target fleet at Bikini.

The Air Transport Unit (C-54 equipped 320th TCS) began training crews to operate the C-54s tasked with providing airlift support for the project. Their selection was also based on skill and experience on long distance hauls to points in the Pacific and throughout the United States.

By April, the Joint Task Force had moved into the Bikini Areas by a combination of sea and air lift. The B-29s, F-13s, and C-54s were based at Kwajalein and the B-17 drone aircraft were based at Eniwetok.

The bomb carrier selected to drop a Nagasaki-type A-bomb was *Dave's Dream*, a B-29–50-MO (44–27354) assigned to the 509th Composite Group and named for Major David Semple, its original bombardier, who was killed on a training flight before the unit left Roswell AAF. On 1 July 1946, *Dave's Dream* dropped the A-bomb on 73 ships lying off Bikini Atoll. The results were five ships sunk and nine damaged, not exactly the results the AAF was expect-

Top: Kamode Head, *F-13A-55-BN (44–62000), has aircraft identification numbers in white on the nose. (USAF)* Middle: Kamra-Kaze *F-13A-35-BN (44–61583) was one of many aircraft participating in Operation Crossroads with a name and noseart reflective of the nuclear test, but with some humor thrown in. (USAF)* Bottom: Top Secret *was a Silverplate B-29-35-MO (44–27302) and still shows its World War II mission symbols. This aircraft would continue to serve in the 509th BW until June 1949 when it was assigned to the 97th BW at Biggs AFB, Texas. (USAF)*

Top: The Belle of Bikini, *F-13A-50-BN (44–61822)*, in addition to some nice artwork, carries the Yagi antenna on the forward fuselage. (USAF) Bottom: *F-13A-55-BN (44–61999)* with a yellow letter **F** on the tail and white identification numbers on the aft fuselage. (USAF, courtesy M. Foley)

ing. The Air Force also supported the second phase of Operation Crossroads, the underwater explosion on 25 July 1946, by providing air support for photographic and other support functions.[6]

According to Alwyn T. Lloyd's *B-29 Superfortress in detail & scale — part 2 Derivatives,* the specialized markings used by various B-29/F-13 aircraft participating in Operation Crossroads were as follows:

Carriers—carried a black square with a yellow **B** on the vertical stabilizer. The bomb carriers also displayed a pair of wide bands, one black and one yellow, on the fuselage just aft of the national insignia. The last three digits of the serial number were applied in black on the fuselage just behind these bands. Yellow and black bands of the same width as those on the fuselage also were placed on the outer wing surfaces.

Pressure Drop Aircraft — displayed the 509th CG insignia, a **Black Circle** enclosing a **Black Arrow**, on the vertical stabilizer. Bands similar to those on the bomb carriers were place on the fuselage and outer wings except these bands were red. The last three digits of the aircraft serial number were applied aft of the fuselage band.

Weather Reconnaissance Aircraft — these aircraft displayed a **Black Square** with a yellow or white **W** on the vertical stabilizer.

Photographic Aircraft — displayed a **Black Square** with a yellow **F** on the vertical tail. Yellow bands were painted on the fuse-

B-29–96-BW (45 21804) *was named* The Eye *and served as the press photography aircraft during Operation Crossroads. Unlike many of the other aircraft, this B-29 came from the 40th BG. (USAF, courtesy Col. R. Ireland)*

lage and outer wings and the last three digits of the aircraft serial number were placed aft of the fuselage band. These markings also appeared on C-54s assigned to the Air Photographic Unit.[7]

In addition to the markings mentioned above, all Operation Crossroads B-29s and F-13s displayed a large 59th Bombardment Wing insignia on the right side of the aircraft nose. *Dave's Dream* would also display a large shield with crewmember names on the right side of the aircraft nose.

C-54s assigned to the 320th Troop Carrier Squadron carried some of the most colorful markings seen during Operation Crossroads. Their squadron insignia was displayed on both sides of the nose connected to a stylized wing with a long green speed line along the fuselage. Above the speed line was the lettering **320th Troop Carrier Squadron** and on the vertical stabilizer the 58th BW insignia was applied and on the upper tail a stylized plane-in-group number was painted.

There was a very liberal use of aircraft nicknames and nose art, some comical, others more serious minded, during Operation Crossroads with most B-29s and F-13s displaying these unofficial markings. Among the many examples were: *The Belle of Bikini, Over*

This black camouflage B-29 was named The Voice *and as the name indicates was used as the radio broadcast aircraft for the project. Like* The Eye *this aircraft was not part of the 509th CG, which accounts for the lack of 509 numerals on the 58th Bombardment Wing insignia on the forward fuselage. (USAF, courtesy Col. R. Ireland)*

Exposed, Top Secret, Kamode Head, Luke the Spook, Kamra-Kaze, Strange Cargo, Laggin Dragon, Dave's Dream, Enola Gay, Mary Lou, Suella J, Sweet 'n' Lola, The Angellic Pig, and *Warm Front.* Most of the nose art and nicknames would disappear after Operations Crossroads and the return to the United States.[8]

Appendix 1:
SAC Wing Insignia and Squadron Markings Reference Table

GROUP/WING	SQDN ID COLORS	Verified	SQDN INSIGNIA	Verified	WING INSIGNIA	Verified
2nd Bomb Wing			YES		NO	
20th Bomb Sqdn	Yellow — 1948–49	X	Nose-LS B-29			
	Green — 1949–50	X	Nose-BS B-50	X		
	Blue — 1950–53	X				
49th Bomb Sqdn	Blue — 1948–49	X	Nose-LS B-29			
	Yellow — 1949–53	X	Nose-BS B-50	X		
96th Bomb Sqdn	Red	X	Nose-LS B-29	X		
			Nose-BS B-50	X		
2nd Air Refuel Sqdn	Green	X				
5th SRW			YES		YES	X
23rd SRS	Blue	X			Nose-LS B-36	
31st SRS — 1949/50	Green		Tail — BS B-29	X		
31st SRS	Yellow	X			"	
72nd SRS	Red	X	Nose-RS B-36	X	"	
6th Bomb Wing			YES		YES	X
24th Bomb Sqdn	Yellow/Green Striped		Nose-RS B-29/36	X	Nose-LS B-29/36	
39th Bomb Sqdn	Red/Green Striped		"		"	
40th Bomb Sqdn	Blue/Green Striped		"	X	"	
307th Air Refuel Sqdn	Unknown					
7th Bomb Wing			YES		YES	X
9th Bomb Sqdn	Red	X	Nose-RS B-36		Nose-LS B-29/36	
436th Bomb Sqdn	Yellow	X			"	
492nd Bomb Sqdn	Blue	X			"	

GROUP/WING	SQDN ID COLORS	Verified	SQDN INSIGNIA	Verified	WING INSIGNIA	Verified
9th SRW/BW			NO		YES	X
1st Bomb Sqdn	Red	X			Nose-LS B-36/29	
5th Bomb Sqdn	Green	X			"	
99th Bomb Sqdn	Yellow	X			"	
11th Bomb Wing			YES		YES	X
26th Bomb Sqdn	Red	X	Nose-RS B-36	X	Nose-LS B-36	
42nd Bomb Sqdn	Yellow	X	"	X	"	
98th Bomb Sqdn	Blue	X	"	X	"	
22nd Bomb Wing			NO		YES	X
2nd Bomb Sqdn	Red	X			Nose-LS B-29 (Two Versions)	
19th Bomb Sqdn	Blue	X			"	
33rd Bomb Sqdn	Yellow	X			"	
22nd Air Refuel Sqdn	Green	X			Nose-LS KC-97	
28th BW/SRW			YES		YES	X
77th Bomb Sqdn	Blue	X	Tail BS B-29	X	Nose LS B-29/36	
717th Bomb Sqdn	Red	X	Nose BS B-29	X	"	
718th Bomb Sqdn	Yellow	X	Tail BS B-29	X	"	
40th Bomb Wing			YES		NO	
25th Bomb Sqdn	Blue	X	Nose LS B-29 (1946)	X		
44th Bomb Sqdn	Red	X	Nose LS B-29 (1946)	X		
45th Bomb Sqdn	Yellow	X				
43rd Bomb Wing			YES		YES	X
63rd Bomb Sqdn	Yellow/Black Striped	X			Nose-RS B-29/50	
64th Bomb Sqdn	Green	X	Nose-LS B-29/50	X	"	
65th Bomb Sqdn	Red	X	Nose-LS B-50	X	"	
43rd Air Refuel Sqdn	Blue/White Striped	X	Nose-RS KB-29M	X	No	
44th Bomb Wing			YES		YES	X
66th Bomb Sqdn	Blue	X	Nose RS B-29	X	Nose LS B-29	
67th Bomb Sqdn	Orange-Yellow	X	Nose RS B-29	X	"	
68th Bomb Sqdn	Red	X			"	
55th SRW			YES		NO	
38th SRS	Green-Yellow Striped	X			SAC insignia used	
338th SRS	Blue-Yellow Striped	X			beginning March	
343rd SRS	Red-White Striped		Nose LS B-29	X	1952	
55th Air Refuel Sqdn	Blue-White Striped	X				
68th SRW/BW			NO		NO	
24th Bomb Sqdn	Yellow	X				
51st Bomb Sqdn	Green	X				
52nd Bomb Sqdn	Red	X				
72nd SRW Wing			Unknown		Unknown	
60th SRS	Unknown					
73rd SRS	Unknown					
301st SRS	Yellow					

GROUP/WING	SQDN ID COLORS	Verified	SQDN INSIGNIA	Verified	WING INSIGNIA	Verified
90th SRW/BW			Yes		NO	
319th Bomb Sqdn	Red	X	Nose LS B-29	X		
320th Bomb Sqdn	Blue	X				
321st Bomb Sqdn	Yellow	X				
91st SRW			YES		YES	X
91st SRS	Green/Yellow		Nose LS RB-50	X		
322nd SRS	Yellow					
323rd SRS	Red		Mid-Fuselage-LS RB-45C	X	Nose-Front RB-45	
324th SRS	Blue				Nose-Front RB-45	
91st Air Refuel Sqdn	Blue/White		Nose-LS KB-29	X		
92nd Bomb Wing			YES		YES	X
325th Bomb Sqdn	Red	X	Nose-RS B-29/36		Nose-LS B-29/36	
326th Bomb Sqdn	Blue	X	"			
327th Bomb Sqdn	Yellow	X	"			
93rd Bomb Wing			YES		NO	
328th Bomb Sqdn	Blue	X				
329th Bomb Sqdn	Red	X	Nose-LS B-29	X		
330th Bomb Sqdn	Yellow	X	Nose-LS B-29	X		
93rd Air Refuel Sqdn	Green	X				
97th Bomb Wing			YES		YES	X
340th Bomb Sqdn	Red	X			Nose-LS B-50	
341st Bomb Sqdn	Blue	X			"	
342nd Bomb Sqdn	Yellow	X	Nose-RS B-50	X	"	
97th Air Refuel Sqdn	Green	X			Nose-LS KB-29	
98th Bomb Wing			YES		YES	X
343rd Bomb Sqdn	Red	X			Nose-LS B-29	
344th Bomb Sqdn	Green w White Stripes	X	Nose-LS B-29	X	"	
345th Bomb Sqdn	White w Black Stripes	X			"	
106th/320th BW			NO		YES	X
102nd/441st Bomb Sqdn	Red	X			Nose-LS B-29	
114th/442nd Bomb Sqdn	Yellow	X			"	
135th/443rd Bomb Sqdn	Blue	X			"	
106th/320th Air Ref Sqdn	Green	X			Nose-LS KC-97	
111th/99th SRW			NO		YES	X
103rd/346th SRS	Black/White Check				Late 1953 on	
129th/347th SRS	Red/White Check				RB-36s	
130th/348th SRS	Yellow/Black Check					
301st Bomb Wing			NO		YES	X
32nd Bomb Sqdn	Yellow 1948–49	X			Nose-LS	
	Orange 1950–53	X				

GROUP/WING	SQDN ID COLORS	Verified	SQDN INSIGNIA	Verified	WING INSIGNIA	Verified
352nd Bomb Sqdn	Red 1948–49	X			"	
	Green 1950–1953	X				
353rd Bomb Sqdn	Blue	X			"	
301st Air Refuel Sqdn	Red/White	X			"	
303rd Bomb Wing			NO		YES	X
358th Bomb Sqdn	Black	X			Nose-LS B-29	
359th Bomb Sqdn	Blue	X			"	
360th Bomb Sqdn	Red	X			"	
305th Bomb Wing			YES		NO	
364th Bomb Sqdn	Yellow		Nose-LS B-47	X		
365th Bomb Sqdn	Red		"	X		
366th Bomb Sqdn	Blue		"	X		
305th Air Refuel Sqdn	Green					
306th Bomb Wing			YES		YES	X
367th Bomb Sqdn	Yellow		Nose-LS B-47	X	LS on some B-47s	
368th Bomb Sqdn	Blue		Nose-LS B-29/47	X		
369th Bomb Sqdn	Red		Nose-LS B-47	X		
306th Air Refuel Sqdn	Green					
307th Bomb Wing			YES		YES	X
370th Bomb Sqdn	Red	X	Nose-LS B-29	X	Tail B-29 1947–48	
371st Bomb Sqdn	Green 1947–49	X	Nose-LS B-29		Nose-LS B-29 during Korean War	
	Yellow 1949–53	X				
372nd Bomb Sqdn	Blue	X	Nose-LS B-29	X		
308th Bomb Wing			YES		NO	
373rd Bomb Sqdn	Blue	X				
374th Bomb Sqdn	Red	X	Nose-LS B-29	X		
375th Bomb Sqdn	Yellow	X				
310th Bomb Wing			NO		NO	
379th Bomb Sqdn	Red	X				
380th Bomb Sqdn	Blue	X				
381st Bomb Sqdn	Yellow	X				
310th Air Refuel Sqdn	Green					
376th Bomb Wing			NO		NO	
512th Bomb Sqdn	Blue	X				
513th Bomb Sqdn	Yellow	X				
514th Bomb Sqdn	Red	X				
509th Bomb Wing			NO		YES	X
393rd Bomb Sqdn	Yellow	X			Nose-RS 1946–47	
715th Bomb Sqdn	Green; Blue	X			Nose-LS 1953	
830th Bomb Sqdn	Red	X				
509th Air Refuel Sqdn	Green	X				
1st Fighter Wing			YES		YES	X
27th Fighter Sqdn	Yellow	X	Nose-BS	X	Nose-BS	
71st Fighter Sqdn	Red	X	"	X	"	
94th Fighter Sqdn	Blue	X	"	X	"	

GROUP/WING	SQDN ID COLORS	Verified	SQDN INSIGNIA	Verified	WING INSIGNIA	Verified
4th Fighter Wing			YES		NO	
334th Fighter Sqdn	Red	X	Nose-L/RS	X		
335th Fighter Sqdn	White	X	"	X		
336th Fighter Sqdn	Blue	X	"	X		
12th FEW/SFW			NO		YES	X
559th FES/SFS	Red	X			Mid-Fuselage — BS	
560th FES/SFS	Yellow	X	"			
561st FES/SFS	Blue	X	"			
27th FW/FEW /SFW			YES (F-84 only)		YES (Both F-82 and F-84)	X
522nd FS/FES/SFS	Red	X	Mid-Fuselage — RS	X	Mid-Fuselage — LS	
523rd FS/FES/SFS	Yellow (White F-82 era)	X	"	X	"	
524th FS/FES/SFS	Blue	X	"	X	"	
31st FEW/SFW			YES		YES	X
307th FES/SFS	Red	X	Mid-Fuselage — LS	X	Mid-Fuselage — RS	
308th FES/SFS	Yellow	X	"	X	"	
309th FES/SFS	Blue	X	"	X	"	
33rd Fighter Wing			NO		NO	
58th Fighter Sqdn	Red	X				
59th Fighter Sqdn	Yellow	X				
60th Fighter Sqdn	Blue	X				
56th Fighter Wing			YES		YES	X
61st Fighter Sqdn	Red	X	Nose — LS	X	Nose — RS	
62nd Fighter Sqdn	Yellow	X	"	X	"	
63rd Fighter Sqdn	Blue	X	"	X	"	
82nd Fighter Wing			YES (F-51D only)		NO	
95th Fighter Sqdn	Red	X	Nose — LS	X		
96th Fighter Sqdn	White	X	Lower Forward Fuselage — LS	X		
97th Fighter Sqdn	Blue	X	Lower Forward Fuselage — LS	X		
506th SFW			UNK		UNK	
457th SFS	Red	X				
458th SFS	Orange	X				
459th SFS	Blue	X				
508th SFW			NO		YES (1952 only)	X
466th	Red	X			Tail — BS	
467th	Yellow	X	"		"	
468th	Blue	X	"		"	
KEY:	BS = Both Sides					
	LS = Left Side					
	RS = Right Side					

Appendix 2:
Strategic Air Command Order
of Battle, with Tail Markings

February 1948

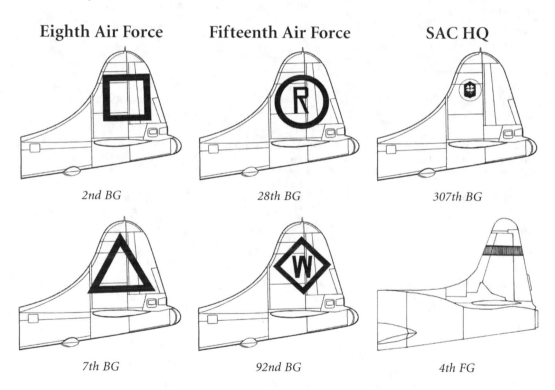

Eighth Air Force	Fifteenth Air Force	SAC HQ
2nd BG	28th BG	307th BG
7th BG	92nd BG	4th FG

Eighth Air Force

Fifteenth Air Force

SAC HQ

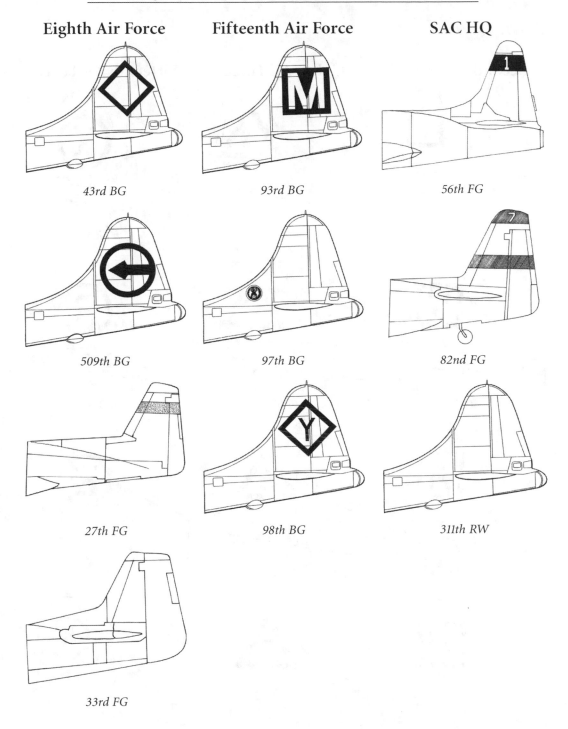

43rd BG

93rd BG

56th FG

509th BG

97th BG

82nd FG

27th FG

98th BG

311th RW

33rd FG

April 1950

Second Air Force	Eighth Air Force	Fifteenth Air Force
2nd BW	*7th BW*	*5th SRW*
91st SRW	*11th BW*	*9th BW*
301st BW	*28th SRW*	*22nd BW*
306th BW	*97th BW*	*43rd BW*

Second Air Force

307th BW

Eighth Air Force

509th BW

27th FEW

Fifteenth Air Force

92nd BW

93rd BW

98th BW (15th AF). Left: Assigned, but not used in 1950. Right: Applied in anticipation of transfer to 2nd AF.

1st FW

July 1952

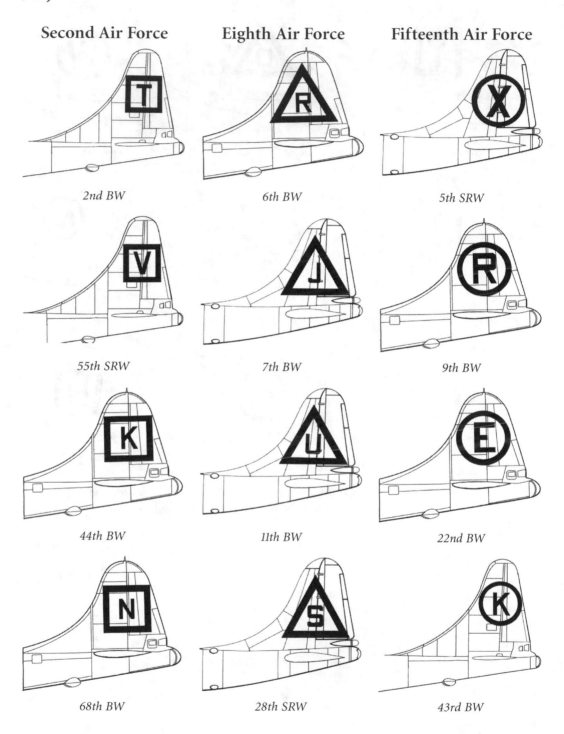

Second Air Force	Eighth Air Force	Fifteenth Air Force
2nd BW	6th BW	5th SRW
55th SRW	7th BW	9th BW
44th BW	11th BW	22nd BW
68th BW	28th SRW	43rd BW

Second Air Force   # Eighth Air Force   # Fifteenth Air Force

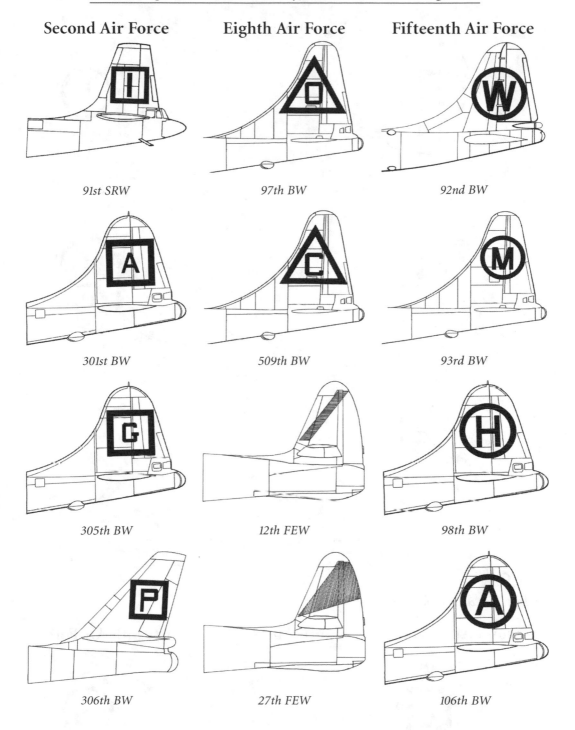

91st SRW   97th BW   92nd BW

301st BW   509th BW   93rd BW

305th BW   12th FEW   98th BW

306th BW   27th FEW   106th BW

Second Air Force

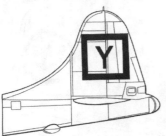

307th BW

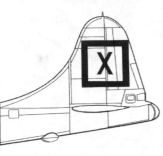

376th BW

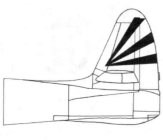

31st FEW

Eighth Air Force

Fifteenth Air Force

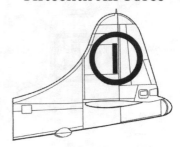

111th SRW

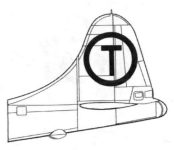

303rd BW

March 1953
(Additions and Changes to July 1952)

Second Air Force

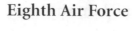

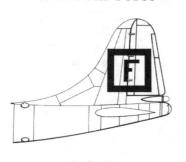

72nd SRW

Eighth Air Force

506th SFW

Fifteenth Air Force

40th BW

Second Air Force

308th BW

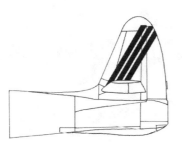

508th SRW

Eighth Air Force

Fifteenth Air Force

55th BW

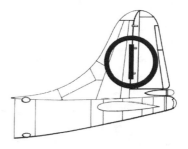

99th SRW (former 111th SRW)

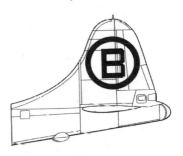

310th BW

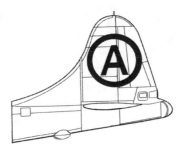

320th BW (former 106th BW)

Chapter Notes

Chapter 1

1. Edward G. Longacre, *Strategic Air Command: The Formative Years, 1944–1949* (Offutt AFB: SAC Office of the Historian, 1990), p. 2.

2. Ibid., pp. 3–4.

3. Ibid., p. 7.

4. Ltr, CG 15th AF to CG AMC, A30 452.1, subj: Schedule of B-29 and P-51 Flyaway Aircraft for Fifteenth Air Force, 13 July 1946, 15th AF File 452.1, NPRC.

5. Strategic Air Command Aircraft Inventory by Station as of 31 December 1946, AFHRA.

6. Longacre, *Strategic Air Command*, p. 11.

7. Ibid., p.12.

8. Ibid., pp. 13–14.

9. Ibid., p.19.

10. Norman Polmar, ed. *Strategic Air Command: People, Aircraft and Missiles* (Annapolis: Nautical and Aviation Publishing Company of America, Inc., 1979), p. 13.

11. *7th BMW Chronology*, TSgt Gregory S. Byard, 7th Bomb Wing History Office, Carswell AFB, n.d.

12. Walton S. Moody, *Building a Strategic Air Force* (Washington, DC: U.S. Government Printing Office, 1995), pp. 208–211.

13. Polmar, pp. 13–16; Robert J. Boyd, *SAC Fighter Planes and Their Operations* (Offutt AFB: SAC Office of the Historian, 1 August 1988), p. 9.

14. Polmar, p. 18.

15. Ibid., pp. 21–22.

16. Ibid., pp. 22–23.

17. Ibid., p. 23.

18. Ibid., pp. 24–25.

19. Ibid., p. 25.

20. Ibid., pp. 26–27.

21. Ibid., p. 28.

22. Ibid., p. 29–30.

23. Ibid., p. 32–34.

Chapter 2

1. Sources for this chapter are Peter M. Bowers, *Boeing Aircraft since 1916* Annapolis: Naval Institute Press, 1989); Dana Bell. *Air Force Colors Volume 3* Carrollton, TX: Squadron/Signal Publications, 1997; HQ AAF Technical Order 07-1-1, General — Aircraft Camouflage, Markings, and Insignia, 7 June 1946; HQ USAF Technical Order 07-1-1, General — Aircraft Camouflage, Markings, and Insignia, 29 September 1947 and 26 July 1948.

Chapter 3

1. Berlin, Earl. *Douglas C-124 Globemaster II*, Steve Ginter, Simi Valley, 2000.

2. Boyd, Robert J. *SAC Fighter Planes and their Operations*, SAC Office of the Historian, Offutt AFB, 1988.

3. Bowers, Peter M. *Boeing Aircraft since 1916*, Naval Institute Press, Annapolis, 1989.

4. Polmar, Norman., ed. *Strategic Air Command: People, Aircraft and Missiles*, Nautical and Aviation Publishing Company of America, Annapolis, 1979.

5. Knaack, Marcelle Size. *Post-World War II Fighters 1945–1973*, Office of Air Force History, Washington, D.C., 1986.

6. USAF Museum Archives Gallery, Late '40s US Bombers, North American RB-45C 'Tornado.' www.wpafb.af.mil/museum/research/bombers/b4/b4-13.htm.

Chapter 4

1. Ltr, HQ SAC, subj: Painting of Aircraft, 26 September 1947, National Personnel Records Center, St. Louis, Missouri (hereafter cited as NPRC).

2. Alwyn T. Lloyd, *B-29 Superfortress in Detail & Scale, Part 2.* (Blue Ridge Summit: Tab Books, Inc., 1987), p. 7.

3. 509th BW History, July 1947, pp. 60–61.

4. Message CG 15th AF to CG SAC, subj: Aircraft Markings as Outlined in 15th Air Force Tactical Doctrine, 29 September 1947, NPRC.

5. Ltr, HQ SAC to CG 8th AF, 15th AF, and 307th BW, subj: Aircraft Identification Markings, 3 November 1947, SAC File 452.1, NPRC.

6. Ltr, HQ 306th BG to Assistant Chief of Air

Staff, Personnel, subj: Organizational Design, 3 December 1948, 15th AF File 452, NPRC.

7. Ltr, HQ SAC to CG 15th AF, subj: Organizational Design, 2 April 1949, 15th AF File 452, 3rd Ind to B/L HQ 306th BG, 14 March 1949, NPRC.

8. Ltr, HQ SAC to CG 15th AF, subj: Aircraft Marking, 15 June 1949, 15th AF File 452, NPRC.

9. Ltr, HQ 15th AF to CG SAC, 1st Ind to B/L HQ SAC dated 15 June 1949, subj: Aircraft Marking, 24 June 1949, 15th AF File 452, NPRC.

10. Ltr, HQ 8th AF to CG SAC, 7th Ind to B/L HQ SAC dated 15 June 1949, subj: Aircraft Marking, 14 September 1949, 8th AF File 452, NPRC.

11. Ltr, HQ 311th Air Division to CG SAC, 1st Ind to B/L HQ SAC dated 15 June 1949, subj: Aircraft Marking, 27 June 1949, 2nd AF File 452, NPRC.

12. Ltr, HQ SAC to CG 15th AF, subj: Tactical Aircraft Markings, 26 October 1949, 15th AF File 452, NPRC.

13. 28th BW History, March 1950, p. 21.

14. Lindsay T. Peacock, *Strategic Air Command* (London: Arms and Armour Press, 1988), p. 18.

15. Ltr, HQ 92nd BW to CG 15th AF, subj: Tactical Aircraft Markings, 20 April 1950, 15th AF File 452, NPRC.

16. Alwyn T. Lloyd, *A Cold War Legacy* (Missoula: Pictorial Histories Publishing Company, Inc., 2000) pp. 150–156.

17. Ltr, HQ SAC to CG 15th AF, subj: Tactical Aircraft Markings, 19 March 1951, 15th AF File 452, NPRC.

18. Historical Outline, 21st Air Division (OTU), DD Form 111 Records Shipment List, 21st AD, 23 November 1954, NPRC.

19. Ltr, HQ 6th AD to CG 2nd AF, subj: Marking of B-47 Aircraft, 4 March 1952, SAC File 452, NPRC.

20. HQ 2nd AF to CG SAC, 1st Ind to B/L HQ 6th AD dated 4 March 1952, subj: Marking of B-47 Aircraft, 19 March 1952, SAC File 452, NPRC.

21. HQ SAC to CG 2nd AF, 6th Ind to B/L HQ 6th AD dated 4 March 1952, subj: Marking of B-47 Aircraft, 21 May 1952, SAC File 452, NPRC.

22. Ltr, HQ SAC to CG 15th AF, subj: Standard SAC Aircraft Markings, 26 November 1952, SAC File 452, NPRC.

23. HQ 15th AF to CG SAC, 1st Ind to B/L HQ SAC dated 26 November 1952, subj: Standard SAC Aircraft Markings, 19 December 1952, SAC File 452, NPRC.

24. Robert J. Boyd, *SAC Fighter Planes and Their Operations* (Offutt AFB: SAC Office of the Historian, 1988), p. 4.

25. History, SAC, 1947, Command Summary, Aircraft Inventory, NPRC.

26. Boyd, p. 9.

27. Ibid. p. 11.

28. Ibid. p. 13.

29. Ibid. p. 15.

30. Ltr, CO 56th FG to CG AAF, subj: Aircraft Markings, 12 July 1946, 15AF File 452.1, NPRC.

31. Ltr, HQ SAC to CG 8th AF, 15th AF and 307th BW, subj: Aircraft Identifications, 3 November 1947, SAC File 452.1, NPRC.

32. Ltr, HQ SAC to CS USAF, subj: Proposed Markings for Strategic Air Command Fighter Type Aircraft, 10 February 1948, SAC File 452, NPRC.

33. Ltr, HQ USAF to CG SAC, 1st Ind to B/L HQ SAC dated 10 February 1948, subj: Proposed Markings for Strategic Air Command Fighter Type Aircraft, 17 February 1948, SAC File 452, NPRC.

34. Ltr, HQ SAC to CG 8th AF, 307th BW, 4th FW and CO 56th FG, subj: Marking Strategic Air Command Fighter Type Aircraft, 20 February 1948, SAC File 452, NPRC.

35. Ltr, HQ 509th BW to CG 8th AF, subj: Marking Strategic Air Command Fighter Type Aircraft, 20 April 1948, 8th AF File 452, NPRC.

Chapter 5

1. HQ SAC, General Orders No. 6, 4 April 1946, pp. 6–7.

2. SAC Aircraft Inventory by Station, 31 December 1946, AFHRA.

3. Robert F. Amos, and others, *Defenders of Liberty: 2nd Bombardment Group/Wing 1918–1993* (Paducah, 1996), pp. 313–314.

4. Ibid., pp. 313–314.

5. Ibid., p. 318.

6. Bowyer, *Force For Freedom: The USAF in the UK since 1948* (Somerset, 1994), p. 38.

7. Amos and others, pp. 315–316.

8. Bowyer, p. 52.

9. Amos and others, pp. 324–327.

10. Ibid., p. 327.

11. Ibid., pp. 327–347.

12. Strategic Air Command General Order 72, dated 25 November 1949, AFHRA.

13. 9th SRG History, December 1949, p. 13.

14. Fred John Wack, *The Secret Explorers: Saga of the 46th/72nd Reconnaissance Squadrons* (Seeger's Printing, Turlock, CA, 1992) pp. 108–110.

15. Ibid., p. 137.

16. Report, SAC Aircraft Status and Projection, 12 September 1952, SAC File 452, NPRC.

17. 6th Bomb Wing History, 1951–1955, n.d., p. 2.

18. Ibid., p. 4.

19. 7th BMW B-36 Chronology, p. 1.

20. Ibid., p. 3.

21. Lloyd, p. 130.

22. 7th BMW B-36 Chronology, p. 8.

23. 9th SRW History, December 1949, p. 4.

24. Ibid, November 1949, 5th SRS Section, p. 7.

25. Ibid, December 1949, 9th SRG Section, p. 13.

26. Ibid, April 1950, 9th SRG Section, p. 23.

27. 7th Bomb Wing—B-36 Association, 11th Bomb Group History, 1949.

28. Ibid., 1951.

29. 22nd BW History, August 1948, p. 6.

30. Bowyers, p. 35.

31. Squadron Leader D. West, "Homebound with the United States Air Force," *Aeronautics* (July, 1950), p. 25.

32. 22nd BW History, March 1952, p. 38.

33. Ibid., pp. 38–39.

34. Ibid., August 1951, p. 24.

35. "Sad Sacks at Home, Life at a U.S. Bomber Base in Britain," *Interavia*, Vol. VI—No. 11, (November, 1951), p. 599.

36. 449th BG History, August 1946, Maintenance Section, p. 2.

37. Bowyer, p. 25, 33.

38. 28th BW History, July 1949, S-4 Section, p. 2.

39. Ibid., December 1949, p. 16.

40. Ibid., March 1950, p. 21.

41. Ibid., April 1950, p. 18.

42. 40th BW History, April 1953, p. 63.

43. Ibid., p. 44.

44. 310th BW History, October 1952, p. 7.

45. Ibid., October 1953, pp. 13–14.

46. *Davis-Monthan and 43rd Bombardment Wing Unit History* (San Angelo: Newsphoto Publishing, 1948), pp. 12–13.

47. Ibid., pp. 71–72.

48. 43rd BW History, October 1948.

49. Lloyd, pp. 107–108.

50. Ibid., p. 136.

51. Bowyer, p. 43.

52. 43rd BW History, July 1949, p. 78.

53. Ltr, HQ 22nd BW to CO 44th BW, subj: Aircraft Markings, 44th BW History, January 1951.

54. 44th BW History, March 1951, p. 4.

55. Ibid., May 1951, p. 5.

56. Ibid., August 1952, Programs and Progress Report, p. 1.

57. Ibid., October 1951, p. 23.

58. Ibid., November 1952, p. 11.

59. *55th Strategic Reconnaissance Wing History: 20 November 1940–1 August 1980* (Offutt AFB: 55th SRW History Office, 1980), p. 7.

60. *History of Ramey AFB, 1950–1951.* (Ramey AFB: Ramey AFB Historical Association, n.d.)

61. 55th SRW History, January 1951, Appendix A.

62. Bruce M. Bailey, *We See All: A History of the 55th Strategic Reconnaissance Wing 1947–1967,* pp. 21–38.

63. 55th SRW History, March 1952, Appendix F.

64. 68th SRW History, May 1952.

65. Ibid.

66. 68th BW History, October 1952, Exhibit No. 19.

67. *History of Ramey AFB, 1952–1953.* (Ramey AFB: Ramey AFB Historical Association, n.d.)

68. Ibid., 1955.

69. HQ, SAC, Programming Plan 22-52, subj: Mission and Assignment of 21st Air Division Units and Bases, 14 June 1952.

70. Message, HQ, 15th AF, ODCO 624, dated 24 January 1951.

71. 90th BW History, May 1952.

72. 91st SRW History, October 1949, pp. 2–3.

73. Ibid., August 1950.

74. Ibid., November 1950, pp. 7–9.

75. Lloyd, p. 161.

76. Message, CG 15th AF to CG SAC, A3B 674 dated 29 September 1947.

77. 92nd BW History, February 1948, p. 31.

78. Ibid., June 1950, Maintenance Section.

79. 93rd BW History, August–October 1947.

80. Ibid., February 1948, p. 27.

81. Ibid., May 1948.

82. Strategic Air Command History, 1948, pp. 191–192.

83. Ibid., p. 193.

84. *History of the 97th Bombardment Wing (Medium)—Biggs Air Force Base* (San Angelo: Newsphoto Publishing, 1948), p. 17.

85. Ltr, CO 97th BW to CG 8th AF, subj: Aircraft Markings, 29 September 1948, 8th AF File A3 452.05, NPRC.

86. Bowyer, p. 35.

87. Richard H. Campbell, *They Were Called Silverplate,* (2003), pp. 145–146.

88. Bowyer, p. 55.

89. Bowyer, p. 95.

90. 98th BG History, September 1947.

91. Bowyer, pp. 41–42.

92. 92nd BW History, December 1949.

93. Ltr, HQ 92nd BW to CG 15th AF subj: Tactical Aircraft Markings, 20 April 1950, 15th AF File 452, NPRC.

94. *Air Force Magazine,* "An Air Force Goes From Brooklyn," October 1951, pp. 45–48.

95. 106th BW History, June 1951, p. 4.

96. Ibid., August 1951, p. 22.

97. Ibid., January 1952.

98. Ibid., May 1953.

99. Ibid., July 1953, p. 12.

100. 111th BW History, April 1951, p. 3.

101. Ibid., June 1951, Materiel Section.

102. Ltr, HQ 15th AF ODCOT 452 dated 11 June 1951.

103. Ltr, HQ 111th BW (L) to CG 15th AF, subj: Tail Insignia, 26 June 1951.

104. 1st Ind. dated 7 July 1951 to Ltr, HQ 111th BW(L) to CG 15th AF, subj: Tail Insignia, 26 June 1951.

105. 111th SRW History, August 1951, Operations and Training, p. 2.

106. *Commemorating the Tour of Duty of the 301st Bombardment Wing in the United Kingdom, May–December 1950,* 301st BW Public Information Office. Printed in the United Kingdom by West

Suffolk Newspapers Ltd., Bury St. Edmunds, England

107. Walton S. Moody, *Building a Strategic Air Force* (Washington, DC, 1995) pp. 209, 214, 222.

108. Bowyer, p. 35.

109. *301st Bomb Wing — Barksdale AFB History 1950* (Baton Rouge: Army and Navy Publishing Company, 1950), p. 16.

110. Ibid.

111. Bowyer, p. 61.

112. Ibid., p. 96.

113. 303rd BW History, October 1951, p. 9.

114. General Orders Number 1, Hqd. 36th Air Division, 9 January 1952.

115. 303rd BW History, October 1952, pp. 6–10; November 1952, pp. 9–10.

116. Ibid., January 1953, pp. 7–9.

117. 305th BW History, March 1951, pp. 19–20.

118. 305th BW Staff Minutes, 7 March 1951.

119. 305th BW History, March 1951, pp. 19–20.

120. 305th BW Staff Minutes, 4 April 1951.

121. Bowyer, p. 97.

122. 305th BW History, July 1952, Exhibit: D-1, D-1a.

123. Ltr, HQ 306th BG to CS, USAF, subj: Organizational Design, 3 December 1948, 15th AF File 452, NPRC.

124. 3rd Ind. dated 11 January 1949 to B/L from HQ 306th BG, subj: Organizational Design, dated 3 December 1948, 15th AF File 452, NPRC.

125. 3rd Ind. dated 2 April 1949 to B/L from HQ 306th BG, subj: Organizational Design, dated 14 March 1949, 15th AF File 452, NPRC.

126. Lloyd, p. 165.

127. Ltr, HQ 36th AD to CG 2nd AF, subj: Marking of B-47 Aircraft, 4 March 1952; 1st Ind. to B/L 19 March 1952; 2nd Ind. to B/L dated 9 April 1952; 3rd Ind. to B/L dated 15 April 1952; 4th Ind. to B/L dated 6 May 1952; 5th Ind. to B/L dated 13 May 1952; and 6th Ind. to B/L dated 21 May 1952.

128. 307th BG History, January 1947, Chapter I, p 1.

129. Ibid., May 1947, p. 33.

130. Bowyer, pp. 26, 38.

131. Bowyer, p. 38.

132. Bowyer, p. 51.

133. 307th BG History, December 1949, Section IV, Supply and Maintenance, p. 6.

134. 308th BW History, May 1952.

135. Ibid., September 1952.

136. Ibid., July 1952, p. 27.

137. Ibid.

138. 310th BW History, August 1952, p. 5.

139. Ibid., pp. 4–5.

140. Ibid., January 1953.

141. 40th BW History, April 1953, pp. 62–63.

142. Untitled Report, History of the 376th Bombardment Wing, n.d., p. 9.

143. Ibid., pp. 10–11.

144. HQ Strategic Air Command, General Orders No 6, 4 April 1946, p. 7.

145. *RAAF Roswell — New Mexico.* 509th Bombardment Group (VH) History (San Angelo: Newsphoto Publishing, 1947), p. 9.

146. Ibid., pp. 101, 137, 155.

147. Ibid., pp. 17, 109, 141, 161.

148. 509th BG History, July 1947, Chapter XII, Special Projects, pp. 60–61.

149. Bowyer, p. 41.

150. Ibid., p. 76.

Chapter 6

1. Robert J. Boyd, *SAC Fighter Planes and their Operations* (Offutt AFB: SAC Office of the Historian, 1988) p. 9.

2. Boyd, p. 7.

3. Report, Strategic Air Command Aircraft Inventory by Station, 31 December 1947, AFHRA.

4. 4th FG History, November 1947, 335th Fighter Squadron Section, pp. 4–6.

5. Ibid., March 1948, 335th Fighter Squadron Section, p. 4.

6. Ltr, HQ SAC to CS USAF, subj: Proposed Markings for Strategic Air Command Fighter Type Aircraft, 10 February 1948, SAC File 452, NPRC.

7. Boyd, p. 41.

8. Bowyer, p. 77.

9. Report, Strategic Air Command Aircraft Inventory by Station and Unit, August 1947, December 1947. AFHRA.

10. Boyd, p. 8.

11. *North American Magazine, Ridin' Herd on the Heavies,* March 1949, p. 20.

12. Ltr, HQ SAC to CS USAF, subj: Proposed Markings for Strategic Air Command Fighter Type Aircraft, 10 February 1948, SAC File 452, NPRC.

13. Ltr, HQ 27th FW thru CG 8th AF to CG SAC, subj: Approved Color Schemes and Markings of Aircraft 27th Fighter Wing, 24 February 1949, SAC File 452.

14. Boyd, p. 37.

15. *27th Fighter-Escort Wing "Just Famous,"* (Dallas: Taylor Publishing Company) 1951.

16. Boyd, p. 37.

17. Ibid., p. 46.

18. *Boeing Magazine, Fighters Can Be Global, Too,* August 1952, p. 10.

19. Boyd, pp. 41–43.

20. Strategic Air Command Aircraft Inventory by Station and Unit, November, December 1947, AFHRA.

21. Ltr, 509th BW to CG 8th AF, subj: Marking Strategic Air Command Fighter Type Aircraft, 20 April 1948, 8th AF File 452, NPRC.

22. Ltr, HQ SAC to CS USAF, subj: Proposed Markings for Strategic Air Command Fighter Type Aircraft, 10 February 1948, SAC File 452, NPRC.

23. Report, Location of Fifteenth Air Force Aircraft, May 1946, AFHRA.

24. David R. McLaren, *Beware The Thunderbolt: The 56th Fighter Group in World War II* (Atglen: Schiffer Publishing Ltd., 1994) p. 166.

25. Report, Aircraft Inventory By Station, 31 December 1946, SAC History, Jun–Dec 1946, AFHRA.

26. Ltr, CO 56th FG to CG AAF, subj: Aircraft Markings, 12 July 1946, SAC File 452, NPRC.

27. 56th FG History, October 1946, p. 3.

28. McLaren, pp. 186–87.

29. Boyd, p. 69.

30. Report, SAC Aircraft Inventory by Station and Unit, May 1947, AFHRA.

31. Ibid. December 1947.

32. *82nd Fighter Group History,* (New York: Robert W. Kelly Publishing Corp., 1949) p. 7.

33. 82nd FG History, June 1948.

34. Ibid. March 1948, pp. 6–7.

35. Ibid. May 1949.

36. *82nd Fighter Group Unit History*, 1949

37. 506th SFW History, March 1953.

38. Ibid., April 1953.

39. Ibid., May 1953.

40. Boyd, p. 49.

41. 2 AF Regulation 24–25 dated 14 August 1952.

42. "Longstride Nectar Alpha One," *Combat Crew Magazine*, Vol. IV, No. 6, (December, 1953), pp. 8–11.

43. 508th FEW History, December 1952, Mobility Memo #3 dated 8 December 1952.

Chapter 7

1. Ken White, *The World in Peril*, p. 11.

2. Fred John Wack, *The Secret Explorers*, p. 59.

3. 91st SRW History, October 1949, 91st SRG Section, pp. 2–3.

4. Ibid. November 1950, pp. 7–9.

5. *RAAF Roswell — New Mexico*, pp. 71–90.

6. 1st Strategic Support Unit History, September 1948, p. 26.

7. Gordon S. Williams, "Green Hornet," *Boeing Magazine*, (March, 1950), pp. 10–11.

8. 2nd Strategic Support Squadron History, July 1950, p. 3.

9. 3rd Strategic Support Squadron History, April 1952, p. 14.

10. Capt. George Cully and E. Richard Staszak, "C-124 Globemaster II Part 5: In Operational Service," *IPMS Space Park*, Vol. 8 No. 3, (September, 1980), p. 11.

Chapter 8

1. Army Air Forces Operations Crossroads, *FOTOMICS ... a complete Pictorial Record of Task Unit 1.52*, 1946, p. 2.

2. Ibid.

3. Polmar, p. 9.

4. Lloyd, *B-29 Superfortress in detail & scale—part 2*, p. 4.

5. 509th BG History, June 1946, p. 1.

6. Polmar, p. 9.

7. Lloyd, pp. 4–8.

8. Ibid.

Bibliography

The collection of official USAF unit histories at the Air Force Historical Research Agency, Maxwell AFB, Alabama, served as a major source of information for this book. The histories for Strategic Air Command, the numbered air forces, and the specific wings and groups mentioned in this book were consulted numerous times.

Many of the older noncurrent SAC organizational records were stored at the National Personnel Records Center in St. Louis, Missouri. Much of the primary source documentation of SAC aircraft markings was gleaned from these records over a 15-year period. However, many of these records have been moved to the National Archives at College Park, Maryland.

Books

Amos, Robert F., and others. *Defenders of Liberty: 2nd Bombardment Group/Wing 1918–1993.* Paducah, KY: Turner Publishing Company, 1996.

Archer, Robert D., and Victor G. *USAAF Aircraft Markings and Camouflage 1941–1947.* Atglen, PA: Schiffer Military/Aviation History, 1997.

Bailey, Bruce M. *We See All: A History of the 55th Strategic Reconnaissance Wing, 1947–1967.* 55th ELINT Association, 1982.

Bell, Dana. *Air Force Colors, Pacific and Home Front 1942–47.* Vol. 3. Carrollton, TX: Squadron/Signal Publications, 1997.

Berlin, Earl. *Douglas C-124 Globemaster II.* Simi Valley, CA: Steve Ginter, 2000.

Bowers, Peter M. *Boeing Aircraft Since 1916.* London/Annapolis: Putnam/Naval Institute Press. 1989.

_____. *Boeing B-29 Superfortress.* North Branch, MN. Specialty Press, 1999.

Bowyer, Michael J.F. *Force for Freedom: The USAF in the UK Since 1948.* Somerset, England: Patrick Stephens Limited, 1994.

Boyd, Robert J. *SAC Fighter Planes and Their Operations.* Offutt AFB, NE: Office of the Historian, Strategic Air Command, 1988.

Byard, TSgt Gregory S. *7th BMW B-36 Chronology.* Carswell AFB: 7th BW History Office, n.d.

Campbell, Richard H. *They Were Called Silverplate: A History of Silverplate B-29 Deliveries and Operations from 1943–1960.* Tucson: Becam Press, 2003.

Commemorating the Tour of Duty of the 301st Bombardment Wing in the United Kingdom May–Dec 1950. UK: Printed by West Suffolk Newspapers, Ltd.

Davis, Larry. *Air War Over Korea: A Pictorial Record.* Carrollton, TX: Squadron/Signal Publications, 1982.

_____. *The 4th Fighter Wing in the Korean War.* Atglen, PA: Schiffer Military History, 2001.

D-M AFB 43rd Bombardment Wing. San Angelo, Texas: Newsphoto Publishing, 1948.

Door, Robert F. *B-29 Superfortress Units of the Korean War.* Osceola, WI: Osprey, 2003.

82nd Fighter Group 1949. New York: Robert W. Kelly Publishing Co., 1949.

Ellis, Paul. *Aircraft of the U.S.A.F. Sixty Years in Pictures.* New York, NY: Jane's, 1980.

Fahey, James C. *USAF Aircraft 1947–1956.* Wright-Patterson AFB, OH: Air Force Museum Foundation, Inc, 1978.

_____. *U.S. Army Aircraft 1908–1946.* New York, NY: Ships and Aircraft, 1946.

Far East Air Forces (FEAF) Bomber Command. Steadfast and Courageous: B-29s Over Korea 1950–1953. Washington, DC: Air Force History Office and Museum Program, 2000.

55th Strategic Reconnaissance Wing History. 20 November 1940 to 1 April 1983. Pursuit to Defend... Offutt AFB: 55th SRW Historian's Office, 1983.

Fotomics ... a Complete Pictorial Record of Task Unit 1.52. Army Air Forces Operation Crossroads, 1946.

History of Ramey AFB, 1950–1953. Ramey AFB: Ramey AFB Historical Association, n.d.

History of the 97th Bombardment Wing (Medium)—Biggs Air Force Base. San Angelo: Newsphoto Publishing, 1948.

Jacobson, Meyers K. *Convair B-36: A Comprehensive History of America's "Big Stick."* Atglen, PA: Schiffer Military History, 1997.

Jenkins, Dennis R. *Magnesium Overcast.* North Branch, MN: Specialty Press, 2001.

Kinzey, Bert. *F-84 Thunderjet.* Vol. 59. Carrollton, TX: Squadron/Signal Publications, 1999.

Knaack, Marcelle Size. *Post–World War II Fighters 1945–1973.* Washington, DC: Office of Air Force History, 1986.

Lloyd, Alwyn T. *B-29 Superfortress in Detail and Scale.* Part 2. Fallbrook, CA: Aero Publishers, 1983.

_____. *B-47 Stratojet.* Blue Ridge Summit, PA: Tab Books, 1986.

_____. *A Cold War Legacy, A Tribute to Strategic Air Command—1946–1992.* Missoula, MT: Pictorial Histories Publishing Company, 2000.

Longacre, Edward G. *Strategic Air Command: The Formative Years (1944–1949).* Offutt AFB, NE: Office of the Historian, Strategic Air Command, 1990.

Maurer, Maurer. *Air Force Combat Units of World War II.* Washington, DC: Office of Air Force History, 1983.

_____. *Combat Squadrons of the Air Force—World War II.* Maxwell AFB, AL: USAF Historical Division, Air University, 1969.

McLaren, David R. *Beware the Thunderbolt! The 56th Fighter Group in World War II.* Atglen, PA: Schiffer Military/Aviation History, 1994.

_____. *Lockheed P-80/F-80 Shooting Star.* Atglen, PA: Schiffer Publishing Ltd., 1996.

_____. *Republic F-84 Thunderjet, Thunderstreak and Thunderflash: A Photo Chronicle.* Atglen, PA: Schiffer Military/Aviation History, 1998.

Menard, David W. *Before Centuries: USAF Fighters 1948–1959.* Charlottesville, VA: Howell Press, 1998.

_____. *USAF Plus Fifteen: A Photo History 1947–1962.* Atglen, PA: Schiffer Military/Aviation History, 1993.

Moody, Walton S. *Building a Strategic Air Force.* Washington, DC: Air Force History Office and Museum Program, 1995.

91st Strategic Reconnaissance Wing, 1950. Barksdale Air Force Base, Strategic Air Command. Baton Rouge: Army Navy Publishing Co., 1950.

Peacock, Lindsay. *Boeing B-47 Stratojet.* London: Osprey Air Combat, 1987.

Peacock, Lindsay T. *Strategic Air Command.* London: Arms and Armour Press, C. 1988.

Polmar, Norman, ed. *Strategic Air Command: People, Aircraft and Missiles.* Annapolis: Nautical and Aviation Publishing Company of America, Inc., 1979.

RAAF Roswell—New Mexico: 509th Bomb Group (VH) History. San Angelo: Newsphoto Publishing, 1947.

Technical Order No. 07-1-1, *General—Aircraft Camouflage, Markings and Insignia,* 7 June 1946, 28 September 1947, and 26 July 1948.

Thompson, Warren. *F-84 Thunderjet Units Over Korea.* Lonodon: Osprey Aviation, 2000.

301st Bombardment Wing, Barksdale AFB, 1950. Strategic Air Command. Baton Rouge: Army Navy Publishing Co., 1950.

27th Fighter Escort Wing, First to Fly Republic's F-84 Thunderjet in Combat, Korea. Dallas, TX: Taylor Publishing Co., 1951.

USAF Museum Archives Gallery, Late '40s US Bombers, North American RB-45C 'Tornado.' www.wpafb.af.mil/museum/research/bombers/b4/b4-13.htm.

Wack, Fred John. *The Secret Explorers: Saga of the 46th/72nd Reconnaissance Squadrons.* Turlock, CA: Seeger's Printing, 1992.

White, Ken. *World in Peril—The Origin, Mission and Scientific Findings of the 46th/72nd Reconnaissance Squadron.* Elkhart, IN: K.W. White & Associates, C. 1992.

Magazines

"An Air Force Goes from Brooklyn." *Air Force Magazine,* October 1951.

Cully, George, and E. Richard Staszak. "C-124 Globemaster II, Part 5: In Operational Service." *IPMS Space Park,* Vol. 8, No. 3, September 1980.

"Fighters Can Be Global, Too." *Boeing Magazine,* August 1952.

"Ridin' Herd on the Heavies." *North American Magazine,* March 1949.

Rodrigues, Richard A. "Strategic Air Command Tail Markings, 1946–1953." *AAHS Journal*, Spring 1996.

"Sad Sacks at Home, Life at a U.S. Bomber Base in Britain." *Interavia*, Vol. 6, No. 11, November 1951.

Schilling, Col. David C. "Longstride — Coca Alpha One, Nectar Alpha One." *Combat Crew Magazine*, Vol. 14, No. 6, December 1953.

West, D. "Homebound with the United States Air Force." *Aeronautics*, July 1950.

Williams, Gordon S. "Green Hornet." *Boeing Magazine*, March 1950.

Index